Typographic Design:

3 3 0
/ 5

Form and Communication

"The whole duty of typography,
 as of calligraphy,
 is to communicate with the imagination,
 without loss by the way,
 the thought or image
 intended to be communicated
 by the Author."

Thomas James Cobden-Sanderson

St. Barbara. Polychromed
walnut sculpture, Fifteenth-
century German or French,
The Virginia Museum of
Fine Arts

Typographic Design:

Form and Communication

Rob Carter

Ben Day

Philip Meggs

VNR

Van Nostrand Reinhold Company
New York

Printed in the United States of America

Van Nostrand Reinhold Company Inc.
115 Fifth Avenue
New York, New York 10003

Van Nostrand Reinhold Company Limited
Molly Millars Lane
Wokingham, Berkshire RG11 2PY, England

Van Nostrand Reinhold
480 La Trobe Street
Melbourne, Victoria 3000, Australia

Macmillan of Canada
Division of Canada Publishing Corporation
164 Commander Boulevard
Agincourt, Ontario M1S 3C7, Canada

16 15 14 13 12 11 10 9 8 7 6 5 4 3 2

Library of Congress Cataloging in Publication Data
Carter, Rob.
   Typographic design.
   Bibliography: p.
   Includes index.
   1. Printing, Practical — Style manuals. 2. Printing,
Practical — Layout. 3. Graphic arts. I. Day, Ben.
II. Meggs, Philip B. III. Title.
Z253.C32 1985 686.2'24 85-667
ISBN 0-442-26166-7 (pbk.)

For Sally, Melanie, and Libby

While typography has changed and expanded during the past two decades, the resource materials available today do not reflect the nature and scope of typographic design in our times. It is the authors' intention to provide a concise, yet comprehensive, overview of the fundamental information necessary for effective typographic-design practice. A knowledge of form and communication encompasses a range of subjects, including our typographic heritage, letterform anatomy, visual organization, and the interface between form and meaning.

In addition to these fundamentals, this volume presents other topics critical to informed design practice. Recent research provides the designer with an expanded awareness of legibility factors, enabling increased communicative clarity. Technological complexity requires comprehension of earlier and current typesetting processes, for both affect the language of typography. Theoretical and structural problem-solving approaches, evolved by design educators, reveal underlying concepts. Case studies in applied problem solving demonstrate a knowledge of typographic form and communication. An understanding of typographic classification and form subtlety is gained from the study of type specimens.

Throughout this book, the authors share a compilation of information and examples with practitioners and students. It yields both insights and inspiration, bringing order to the complex and diversified subject of typographic design.

Contents

Typography is an intensely visual form of communication. Because this visible language communicates thoughts and information through human sight, its history is presented here in chronological visual form on four timelines. This evolution is shown in the context of world events, architectural development, and art history.

The first timeline predates typography. It begins with the invention of writing over five thousand years ago and ends with the invention of movable type in Europe during the middle of the fifteenth century. The second timeline covers the long era of the handpress and handset metal types. This period, from Gutenberg's invention of movable type to the end of the eighteenth century, lasted about three hundred and fifty years. In the third timeline, the industrial revolution and nineteenth century are revealed as an era of technological innovation accompanied by an outpouring of new typographic forms. The fourth timeline begins with the year 1900 and continues until the present. The aesthetic concerns of modernism, the need for functional communication, and technical progress have shaped twentieth-century typographic design.

**From the origins
of writing
to Gutenberg's
invention of
movable type:
3150 B.C.–A.D.1450**

Note: Picture credits and further descriptive information start on page 255.

1.
c. 3150 B.C.: The earliest written documents are impressed clay tablets from Sumer. The signs represent clay tokens, which were used for record keeping before the invention of writing.

2.
c. 3000 B.C.: Cuneiform, the earliest writing system, consisting of wedge-shaped marks on clay tablets, was invented by the Sumerians.

2500 B.C.: Egyptians begin to make papyrus, a new writing material derived from the stems of the papyrus plant.

3.
c. 2600 B.C.: Completion of the pyramids at Giza, Egypt.

4.
c. 2400 B.C.: False-door stele inscribed with hieroglyphic writing, from Old Kingdom Egypt.

5.
c. 2100 B.C.: Cuneiform tablet listing expenditures of grain and animals.

6.
c. 1800–1400 B.C.: Stonehenge, a megalithic monument of thirty-foot-tall stones set into circular patterns.

7.
c. 1570–1349 B.C.: Polychromed wood sculpture from New Kingdom Egypt, with hieroglyphic inscriptions.

8.
c. 1450 B.C.: Detail, *The Book of the Dead* of Tuthmosis III, hieroglyphic writing on papyrus.

c. 3150 B.C.

1.

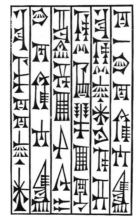

2.

5.

7.

3.

4.

6.

9.
c. 1500 B.C.: The twenty-two characters of the Phoenician alphabet.

c. 800 B.C.: Homer writes the *Iliad* and *Odyssey*.

540 B.C.: The first public library is established in Athens, Greece.

10.
389 B.C.: Inscription in the Phoenician alphabet on a fragment of a marble bowl.

11.
Fourth Century B.C.: Greek manuscript writing.

12.
448–432 B.C.: The Parthenon, temple of the goddess Athena, on the Acropolis in Athens, Greece.

13.
414–413 B.C.: Fragment of a Greek record of sale, carved on stone.

c. 160 B.C.: Parchment, a new writing material made from animal skins, is developed in the Greek state of Pergamum.

44 B.C.: Julius Caesar is murdered.

14.
c. 50 B.C.–A.D. 500: Roman square capitals *(capitalis quadrata)* were carefully written with a flat pen.

c. A.D. 33: Crucifixion of Christ.

15.
c. 79: Brush writing from a wall at Pompeii, preserved by the volcanic eruption of Vesuvius.

105: Ts'ai Lun invents paper in China.

150: The Roman codex, with folded pages, begins to be used alongside the rolled scroll.

16.
c. 100–600: Roman rustic writing *(capitalis rustica)* conserved space by using more condensed letters written with a flat pen held in an almost vertical position.

c. 1500 B.C.

8.

9.

11.

13.

MARTISQ·DOLO

14.

15.

CONNERIANTIRIA
SINMANIBUSUESTRI
VLTROASIAMMACNO

16.

10.

17.
118–25: The Pantheon, Rome.
18.
Undated: The fluid gestural quality, harmonious proportions, and beautiful forms of Roman writing are effectively translated into the permanent stone carving of monumental capitals *(capitalis monumentalis).*

19.
312–315: Arch of Constantine, Rome. Carved into marble, monumental Roman capitals survived the thousand-year Dark Ages.

325: Emperor Constantine adopts Christianity as the state religion of the Roman Empire.

c. 400–1400: During the thousand-year medieval era, knowledge and learning are kept alive in the Christian monastery, where manuscript books are lettered in the scriptoria.

452: Attila the Hun invades and ravages northern Italy.

476: Emperor Romulus Augustulus, last ruler of the western Roman Empire, is deposed by the Ostrogoths.
20.
533–49: Church of Sant' Apollinare in Classe, Ravenna.
21.
Third–Sixth Centuries: Uncials are rounded, freely drawn majuscule letters, first used by the Greeks as early as the third century B.C.

22.
Third–Ninth Centuries: Half-uncials, a lettering style of the Christian Church, introduces pronounced ascenders and descenders.
23.
Sixth–Ninth Centuries: Insular majuscules, a formal style with exaggerated serifs, was developed by Irish monks from the half-uncials.

A.D. 118

17.

19.

18.

20.

musadquequamuisconsci mitatisnostraetrepidatio murtamenfideinestuincit
21.

monzuautscm
22.

magnum quod erit
23.

eft quiautemsuperp
27.

4

732: The Battle of Tours ends the Muslim advance into Europe.

800: Charlemagne is crowned emperor of the Holy Roman Empire by Pope Leo III.
24.
c. 800: Portrait of Christ from *The Book of Kells,* a Celtic manuscript.

868: The earliest extant printed manuscript, the *Diamond Sutra,* is printed in China.
25.
Tenth Century: High Cross at Kells, Meath County, Ireland.
26.
c. Eleventh Century: Round tower on the Rock of Cashel, Tipperary County, Ireland, a lookout and refuge against Viking invaders.

27.
Eighth–Twelfth Centuries: Caroline minuscules became the standard throughout Europe after Charlemagne issued his reform decree of 796, calling for a uniform writing style.

1034: Pi Sheng invents movable type in the Orient.

1096–1099: The First Crusade.
28.
1163–1250: Construction of Notre Dame Cathedral, Paris.

29.
Eleventh–Twelfth Centuries: Early Gothic lettering, a transitional style between Caroline minuscules and Textur, has an increased vertical emphasis.
30.
Twelfth Century: Bronze and copper crucifix from northern Italy.

1215: The Magna Carta grants constitutional liberties in England.

31.
Thirteenth–Fifteenth Centuries: Gothic Textura Quadrata, or Textur, the late Gothic style with rigorous verticality and compressed forms.

1347–1351: First wave of the Black Death, a plague that decimates the European population.
32.
Thirteenth Century: Byzantine School, *Madonna and Child on a Curved Throne.*

A.D. 732

32.

25.

26.

nosto qui seder super thronum et agno. Et omnes angli stabant in circuitu throni z cciderunt z adora uerunt deum dicentes. amen. Bñ dictio z claritas z sapientia z gra rum actio. honor z uirtus z fortitu do deo nro in scla sclorum. amen

31.

early gothic

29.

24.

28.

30.

5

33.
Thirteenth–Fifteenth Centuries: Rotunda, a more rounded Gothic letter, flourished in southern Europe.
34.
Fourteenth Century: Lippo Memmi, *Saint John the Baptist.*
35.
1420–36: Filippo Brunelleschi, Dome of Florence Cathedral.

1431: Jeanne d'Arc is burned at the stake.
36.
Fifteenth Century: First page of a block-book *Apocalypse.* Woodblock printing probably appeared in Europe before 1400.
37.
1440–45: Fra Filippo Lippi, *Madonna and Child.*

c. 1450: Johann Gutenberg invents movable type in Mainz, Germany.
38.
c. 1450–55: Page from Gutenberg's forty-two-line Bible, the first European typographic book.

39.
Woodblock print of the hand-printing press, with compositors setting type from a type case in the background.
40.
The cathedral in the medieval city of Mainz, Germany.

c. 1200

34.

37.

35.

38.

Rotunda
33.

36.

39.

40.

Typography from Gutenberg to the nineteenth century: A.D. 1450–1800

The humanist philosophy that flowered during the Renaissance embraced the study of classical literature, a belief in human dignity and worth, a spirit of individualism, and a shift from religious to secular concerns.

1450–1500: The first half century of typographic printing is called the Incunabula.
41.
1465: Sweynheym and Pannartz, the first type designed in Italy. It had some Roman features.

42.
1467: Sweynheym and Pannartz, the first roman-style type, influenced by Roman inscriptional capitals and manuscripts written in Caroline minuscules.
43.
1470: Nicolas Jenson, early Venetian roman typeface.
44.
1475: William Caxton, typography from the first book printed in the English language.

45.
c. 1485: Filippino Lippi, *Portrait of a Youth.*
46.
1486: Erhard Ratdolt, the earliest known specimen sheet of printing types.

1492: Christopher Columbus discovers America.

47.
c. 1494: Scholar and printer Aldus Manutius established the Aldine Press in Venice to publish works by the great Greek and Roman thinkers.
48.
1495: Francesco Griffo (punch cutter for Aldus Manutius), roman type first used in *De aetna* by Pietro Bembo.

1450

bat ille ihefus:q quom p̄mū aufes uocareꞇ moifes figurā p̄fentiens iuffit eū ihefum uocari: uꞇ dux miliꞇiꞇ delectus effet aduerfus amalech qui oppugnabant filios iſrahel: eꞇ aduerfariū debellaret p noıs figuram: eꞇ populū m̄
41.

effe fenfum femitaſ querıtur. tanꝗ illi ad cogitandum rheda & quadrıgıſ opuſ eēt. Democrıtuſ quaſi ın puteo quodam ſic alto uꞇ funduſſıt nulluſ: uerıtatem ıacere demerſam nımırum ſtulte
42.

ab omnipotenti dëo miſſus deus uerbum quaſi lucis iſi cunctis annūciat. Non hinc aut alrunde: ſed undiꝗ cun ad deum uerum: græcos ſimul et barbaros omnem ſexū
43.

In the tyme of p̄ troublous worldꝛ/ and of the fions beyng andꝛ reygnyng as well m the top englondꝛ andꝛ fraunce as m all other placeſ vn
44.

45.

47.

46.

lud admirari ,quod uulgus folet:magnu effe fcilicet tantas flammas ,tam immen fos ignes poſt hominum memoriam ſem
48.

7

49.
1501: Francesco Griffo, the first italic typeface, based on chancery script handwriting.

50.
Home of Albrecht Dürer, Nuremberg, Germany.

51.
Woodblock initial by Geoffroy Tory, who returned to France from study in Italy in 1505, inspired by roman letterforms and Renaissance design ideals.

52.
1523: Lodovico Arrighi, an Italian writing master, introduces his formal chancery italic type.

53.
1517: Martin Luther posts his ninety-five theses on the door of Wittenberg Palace Church, launching the Reformation.

53.
1525: Albrecht Dürer, construction of the letter *B*.

54.
1529: Geoffroy Tory, construction of the letter *B*.

55.
1519–47: Pierre Nepveu, Château of Chambord, France.

56.
c. 1480–1561: Claude Garamond, outstanding designer of Old Style typefaces during the French Renaissance.

1501

50.

51.

53.

54.

55.

56.

49.

52.

57.
c. 1540: Titian, *Portrait of Cardinal Pietro Bembo.*

1543: Copernicus publishes his theory of the heliocentric solar system.
58.
1544: Simone de Colines, title page with woodcut border.

59.
1546: Jacques Kerver, typography, illustration, and decorative initials which were combined into a rare elegance during the French Renaissance.
60.
after 1577: El Greco, *Saint Martin and the Beggar.*

1582: Pope Gregory XIII initiates the Gregorian Calendar, which is still in use.

1584: Sir Walter Raleigh discovers and annexes Virginia.
61.
1595: Johann Theodor de Bry, illustrative initial *E.*

1603: Shakespeare writes *Hamlet.*
62.
1607: Carlo Maderna, façade of St. Peter's, the Vatican.

1609: Regular weekly newspapers appear in Strasbourg, Germany.

63.
1621: Jean Jannon, typefaces upon which twentieth-century Garamonds are based.
64.
1628: The Vatican Press, specimen of roman capitals.

c. 1540

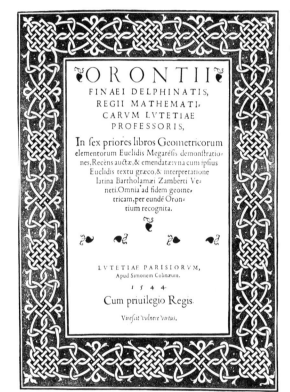

58.

57.

60.

FRANCISCVS

64.

61.

59.

62.

63.

65.
1632–43: The Taj Mahal, India.
66.
c. 1630: Sir Anthony van Dyck, portrait of *Henri II de Lorraine*.

1639: The first printing press in the British Colonies is established in Massachusetts.

1657: First fountain pen is manufactured in Paris.
67.
c. 1664: Jan Vermeer, *Woman Holding a Balance*.

1666: The great fire of London.

1667: Milton writes *Paradise Lost*.

68.
c. 1670: Christoffel van Dyck, Dutch Old Style type.

1686: Sir Isaac Newton sets forth his law of gravity.
69.
1675–1710: Sir Christopher Wren, St. Paul's Cathedral, London.

During the eighteenth century, type design went through a gradual transition from Old Style to Modern Style fonts designed late in the century.

1700: The emergence of the Rococo Style.
70.
1702: Philippe Grandjean (punch cutter), Romain du Roi, the first transitional face.

71.
1709: Matthaus Poppelmann, Zwinger Palace, Dresden.

1709: England adopts the first modern copyright law.
72.
1720: William Caslon, Caslon Old Style types which from this date were used throughout the British Empire.

1632

65.

66.

Ad me profectam esse aiebant. D. quid Quæso, igitur commorabare, ubi id
68.

67.

69.

73.

sa doctrine et de ses lois. Après, il nous fait voir tous les hommes renfermés en un seul homme, et sa femme même tirée de lui ; la concorde des mariages et la
70.

lumes in-4° sur papier-vélin de la fabrique de messieurs Matthieu Johannot pere et fils, d'Annonai, premiers fabricants de cette sorte de papiers en
81.

ABCDEFGHIKLMN
OPQRSTUVWXYZJ
Quousque tandem abutere, Catilina, patientia nostra ? qu
Quousque tandem abutere, Catilina, patientia nostra? quam-

This new Foundery was begun in the Year 1720, and finish'd 1763; and will (with God's leave) be carried on, improved, and inlarged, by WILLIAM CASLON and Son, Letter-Founders in LONDON.

72.

71.

73.
1722: Castletown, near Dublin, Ireland.

1738: First spinning machines are patented in England.
74.
1744: Benjamin Franklin, title page using Caslon type.
75.
1750: François Boucher, *The Love Letter* (detail).

76.
1750s: John Baskerville creates extraordinary transitional typefaces.
77.
1765: Thomas Cotterell introduces display types two inches tall (shown actual size).
78.
1768: Pierre Simon Fournier le Jeune, ornamented types.

79.
1773: Johann David Steingruber, letter *A* from *Architectonishes Alphabet.*
80.
1774: John Holt, broadside of the American revolutionary era, using Caslon type.

1775: James Watt constructs the first efficient steam engine.

1776: The American Declaration of Independence is signed.

81.
1784: François Ambroise Didot, the first true Modern Style typeface.

1789: The fall of the Bastille launches the French Revolution.
82.
1791: Giambattista Bodoni, Modern Style typefaces of geometric construction, with hairline serifs.

1791: The American Bill of Rights guarantees freedoms of religion, speech, and the press.

1793: French King Louis XVI and Marie Antoinette are sent to the guillotine.

1796: Aloys Senefelder invents lithography.

1799: Nicolas-Louis Robert invents the papermaking machine.

1722

M. T. CICERO's
CATO MAJOR,
OR HIS
DISCOURSE
OF
OLD-AGE:
With Explanatory NOTES.

PHILADELPHIA:
Printed and Sold by B. FRANKLIN,
MDCCXLIV.

74.

LA
DIVINA
COMMEDIA
DI
DANTE ALIGHIERI
CON
ILLUSTRAZIONI

TOMO I.

PISA
DALLA TIPOGRAFIA
DELLA SOCIETÀ LETTERARIA
MDCCCIV.

82.

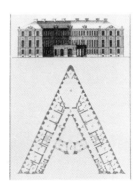

76.

75.

C

77.

To the PUBLICK.

80.

HISTOIRE
DE
LOUIS DE BOURBON,
SECOND DU NOM,
PRINCE
DE CONDÉ,
PREMIER PRINCE DU SANG,
Surnommé *LE GRAND,*

LIVRE PREMIER.
1621-1643.

78.

79.

The nineteenth century and the Industrial Revolution: A.D. 1800–1899

The Industrial Revolution had a dramatic impact upon typography and the graphic arts. New technology radically altered printing, and designers responded with an outpouring of new forms and images.
83.
c. 1803: Robert Thorne designs the first Fat Face.

1804: Napoleon Bonaparte crowned Emperor of France.

1808: Beethoven composes his Fifth Symphony.
84.
1812: Jacques-Louis David, *Napoleon in his Study.*

1814: Friedrich Koenig invents the steam-powered printing press.

85.
1815: Vincent Figgins shows the first Egyptian (slab-serif) typefaces.
86.
1815: Vincent Figgins shows the earliest shaded type.

87.
1816: William Caslon IV introduces the first sans serif type.
88.
1818: Page from *Manuale Tipographico,* which presented the lifework of Giambattista Bodoni.
89.
1821: Robert Thorne, Tuscan styles with splayed serifs.

1800

83. 84.

85.
ABCDEFGHIJK

86.
ABCDEFGHIKM

87.
LETTERFOUNDER

89.
Manchester

✳✦❧ PARANGONE ❧✦✳

Quousque tandem abutêre, Catilina, patientiâ nostrâ? quamdiu etiam furor iste tuus nos eludet? quem ad finem sese effrenata jactabit audacia? nihilne te nocturnum præsidium Palatii, nihil urbis vigiliæ, nihil timor populi, nihil concursus bonorum omnium, nihil hic munitissimus habendi se-

MARCUS TULL. CICERO

ORATOR ATQUE PHILOSOPHUS.

CHERASCO

88.

90.

12

90.
1822: Thomas Jefferson, rotunda of the University of Virginia in the neoclassical style based on Greek and Roman architecture.

1822: Joseph Niepce produces the first photographic printing plate.

91.
c. 1826: Bower, Bacon and Bower, early reversed type entitled White.

1826: Joseph Niepce takes the first photograph from nature.

92.
1827: Darius Wells invents the mechanical router, making the manufacture of large display wood types possible.
93.
1833: Vincent Figgins introduces outline types.

94.
1836: Davy and Berry, poster printed with wood type.

1830s–80s: Wood-type posters and broadsides flourished in America and Europe.
95.
1836: Vincent Figgins, perspective type.

96.
1837: Handbill set in Fat Face.

1837: Victoria crowned Queen of England.

1822

91.

DARIUS WELLS.
92.

95.

96.

94.

HOUSEHOLD FURNITURE, PLATE, CHINA-WARE, JEWELS, WATCHES

93.

Working Men, Attention!!

Globe Office
Saturday, November 20, 1837

It is your imperious duty to drop your *Hammers and Sledges!* one and all, to your post repair, *THIS AFTERNOON,* at *FIVE* o'clock P. M. and attend the

GREAT MEETING

called by the papers of this morning, to be held at the **CITY HALL,** then and there to co-operate with such as have the **GREAT GOOD OF ALL THEIR** *FELLOW CITIZENS* at Heart. Your liberty! yea, your *LABOUR!!* is the subject of the call: who that values the services of **HEROES** of the *Revolution* whose blood achieved our Independence as a Nation, will for a moment doubt he owes a few hours this afternoon to his wife and children?

HANCOCK.

97.
c. 1840–52: Sir Charles Barry and A. W. N. Pugin, Houses of Parliament, inspiration for the Gothic Revival.

98.
c. 1841: Wood and Sharwoods, ornamental type.

During the 1840s, ornamented type becomes increasingly important.

99.
1845: Robert Besley, the first Clarendon style.

1848: The California gold rush begins.

1851: Joseph Paxton designs the Crystal Palace.

100.
1853: Handbill combining Egyptian, outline, and decorative types.

101.
1854: Broadside using elongated Fat Face fonts.

1854: The United States makes its first treaty with Japan.

1856: Sir Henry Bessemer develops process for converting iron to steel.

102.
1859: William H. Page and Company, Ornamented Clarendons.

1859: Charles Darwin publishes *Origin of Species by Means of Natural Selection.*

103.
1860: *Charleston Mercury,* broadsheet announcing the dissolution of the Union.

c. 1840

97.

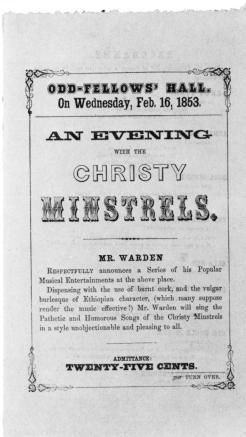

100.

AT Orange Court House Virginia, on Tuesday the 27th day of June, prox., being the day after the County Court of Orange in that month; I shall sell at public auction, to the highest bidder, that part of the Library of the late James Madison, which, in a recent division of his books with the University of Virginia, fell to the share of my testator; and at the same time I will sell other books, the property of my said testator. In all there are some

SEVEN OR EIGHT HUNDRED VOLUMES,

among which are many very rare and desirable works, some in Greek, some in Latin, numerous others in French, and yet more in English, in almost all the departments of Literature; not a few of them being in this manner exposed to sale only because the University possessed already copies of the same editions. The sale beginning on the day above mentioned, will be continued from day to day till all the books shall have been sold, on the following terms:

Cash will be required of each purchaser whose aggregate purchases shall amount to no more than Five dollars; those whose purchases shall exceed that amount, will have the privilege either to pay the cash or to give bond with approved security, bearing interest from the date, and payable six months thereafter.
ELHANON ROW, Administrator,
with the will annexed of John P. Todd, dec'd.

May 30, 1854.

101.

108.

audacia tua? nihilne te nocturnum præsidium palatii, nihil urbis vigiliæ, nihil timor

99.

1861–65: American Civil War.

1863: Abraham Lincoln signs the Emancipation Proclamation.
104.

c. 1865: Honoré Daumier: *The Third-Class Carriage.*

1866: The first successful transatlantic cable is laid.

1867: Alfred Nobel invents dynamite.

1867: Christopher Sholes constructs the first practical typewriter.
105.

1869: Currier and Ives, *American Homestead Winter.*

106.
c. 1875: J. Ottmann, chromolithographic card for Mrs. Winslow's Soothing Syrup.

1876: Alexander Graham Bell invents the telephone.

1877: Thomas Edison invents the phonograph.

1879: Thomas Edison invents the electric lightbulb.
107.

1883: The Brooklyn Bridge is opened to traffic.

1883: William Jenney designs the first skyscraper, a ten-story metal frame building in Chicago.

108.
c. 1885: Maverick and Wissinger, engraved business card.
109.
c. 1880s: Lettering printed by chromolithography.
110.
1886: Ottmar Mergenthaler invents the Linotype, the first keyboard typesetting machine.

1861

104.

105.

106.

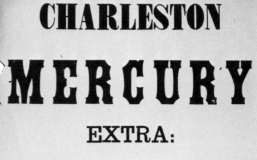

103.

110.

102.

109.

107.

15

111.
1887: Advertisement for
Estey Organs.

1887: Tolbert Lanston invents
the monotype.

112.
1889: Alexandre Gustave
Eiffel, the Eiffel Tower.
113.
c. 1890s: Coca-Cola syrup jug.
114.
1892: Paul Gauguin,
By the Sea.

115.
William Morris' typeface de-
signs: 1890, Golden; 1892,
Troy; 1893, Chaucer.

116.
1891–98: William Morris'
Kelmscott Press launches a
revival of printing and
typography.
117.
1892: William Morris, page
from *News from Nowhere.*

1887

111.

112.

113.

115.

116.

Afloat again

CHAPTER XXIV. UP THE THAMES.
THE SECOND DAY.

HEY were not slow to take my hint; & indeed, as to the mere time of day, it was best for us to be off, as it was past seven o'clock, & the day promised to be very hot. So we got up and went down to our boat; Ellen thoughtful and abstract-ed; the old man very kind and courteous, as if to make up for his crabbedness of opinion. Clara was cheerful & natural, but a little subdued, I thought; and she at least was not sorry to be gone, and often looked shyly and timidly at Ellen and her strange wild beauty. So we got into the boat, Dick saying as he took his place, "Well, it is a fine day!" and the old man answering "What! you like that, do you?" once more; and presently Dick was sending the bows swiftly through the slow weed-checked stream. I turned round as we got into mid-stream, and waving my hand to our hosts, saw Ellen lean-ing on the old man's shoulder, and caressing his healthy apple-red cheek, and quite a keen pang smote me as I thought how I should never see the beautiful girl again. Presently I insisted on taking the sculls, and I rowed a good deal that day; which no doubt accounts for the fact that we got very late

230

117.

118.
1893: Henri van de Velde, title page for *Van Nu en Straks*.

1895: The Lumière brothers give the first motion-picture presentation.

119.
1897: Edmond Deman, title page in the curvilinear Art Nouveau style.
120.
1890s–1940s: Inspired by Kelmscott, Americans Frederic Goudy and Bruce Rogers bring renewed excellence to book and typeface design.

121.
1897: Will Bradley, title page in his "Chap Book" style, reviving Caslon type and colonial woodcut techniques.

1898: Zeppelin invents his airship.

122.
1899: Josef Hoffmann, catalog cover for a Vienna Secession exhibition.
123.
1898–1902: Hector Guimard, entrance to Paris Metro Station.

1893

118.

119.

122.

120.

121.

123.

124.
1900: Peter Behrens, dedication page from *Feste des Lebens und der Künst.*

1903: The Wright brothers succeed in the first powered flight.

1905: Einstein proposes his theory of relativity.

125.
1909: Filippo Marinetti founds Futurism, experimentation with typographic form and syntax.
126.
c. 1910: German sans serif "block style."
127.
1913: Wassily Kandinsky, *Improvisation 31 (Sea Battle).*

1914–18: World War I.

1915: Kasimir Malevich, Suprematist paintings shown at the *0.10* group exhibition.
128.
c. 1916: Bert Thomas, British war bonds poster.

1917–22: The Dada movement protests the war and conventional art.

129.
1917: John Heartfield, Dadaist advertisement.
130.
1917: Vilmos Huszar, *De Stijl* magazine cover.

1918: Czar Nicholas II and his family are executed.
131.
1919: Raoul Hausmann, Dada poem.

1900

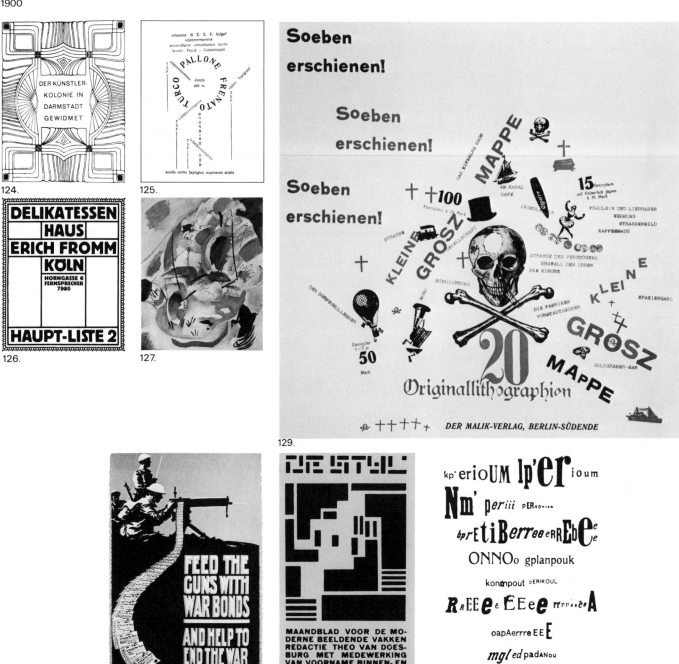

124.

125.

126.

127.

129.

128.

130.

131.

1920: Women's suffrage is granted in the United States.

1920: Bolsheviks triumph in the Russian Revolution.
132.
1921–25: Piet Mondrian, *Diamond Painting in Red, Yellow, and Blue.*

133.
c. 1923: Alexander Rodchenko, Russian Constructivist poster.

1924: Surrealist manifesto.

134.
1924: Gerrit Rietveld, Schroeder house.
135.
1925: El Lissitzky, title page.
136.
1925: Herbert Bayer, universal alphabet.

137.
1925: Constantin Brancusi, *Bird in Space.*
138.
1925: Jan Tschichold, title page for his article, "Elementary Typography."

139.
1926: Piet Zwart, advertisement.

1927: Charles Lindbergh makes the first solo Atlantic flight.
140.
1928: Piet Zwart, advertisement.

1920

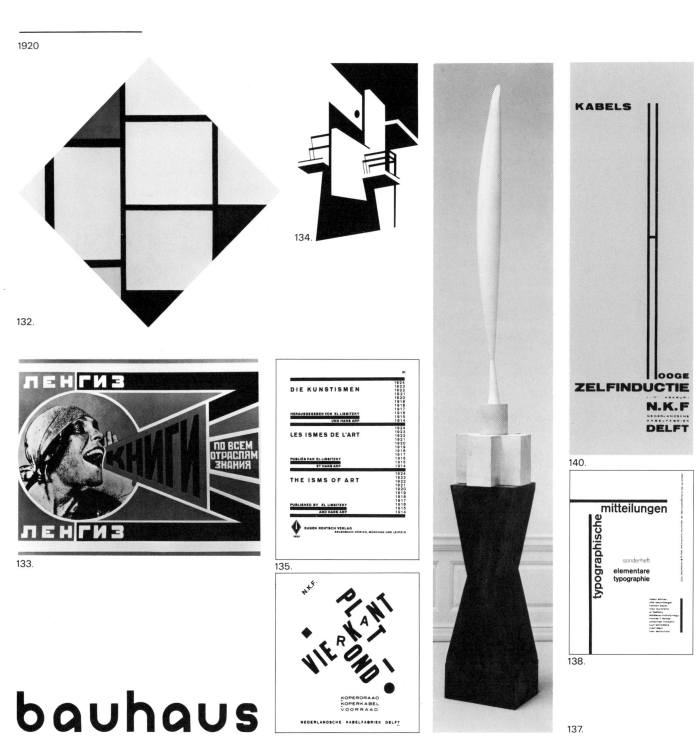

132.

133.

135.

136.

139.

140.

138.

137.

19

1929: The New York Stock Market collapses, and the Great Depression begins.
141.
1930: Paul Renner, prospectus for Futura.

142.
1930: Chrysler Building, an example of the Art Deco decorative geometric style.
143.
1931: Max Bill, exhibition poster.
144.
c. 1932: Alexey Brodovitch, exhibition poster.

1933: Adolf Hitler becomes chancellor of Germany.
145.
1936: Walker Evans, family of sharecroppers.

1939: Germany invades Poland; World War II begins.
146.
1942: Jean Carlu, advertisement.
147.
1944: Max Bill, exhibition poster.

1945: Atomic bombs destroy Hiroshima and Nagasaki, ending World War II.
148.
1948: Paul Rand, title page.

1929

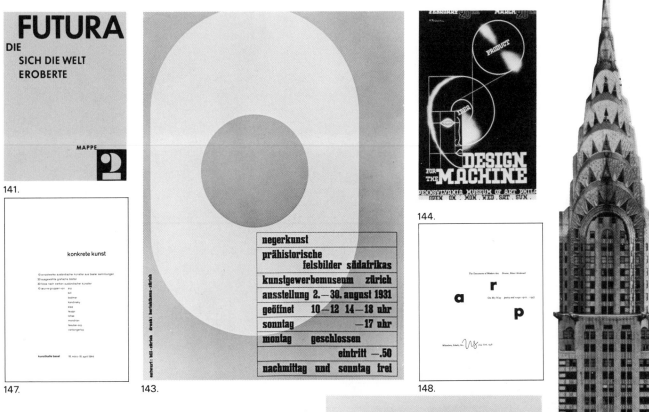

141.

147.

143.

144.

148.

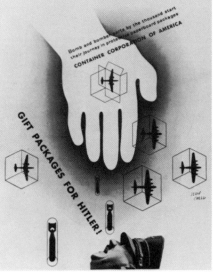

142.

145.

146.

20

149.
1948: Willem de Kooning: *Painting*.
150.
1950: Ladislav Sutnar, book cover.

1950: North Korea invades South Korea.

151.
1950–55: Le Corbusier, Notre Dame de Haut.

1952: School segregation is declared unconstitutional by the U.S. Supreme Court.

152.
1952: Henri Matisse, *Woman with Amphora and Pomegranates*.
153.
1955: Josef Müller-Brockmann, concert poster.
154.
1956: Saul Bass, advertisement.

155.
1956: Willem Sandberg, book cover.

1957: Russia launches Sputnik I, the first earth satellite.

156.
1959: Saul Bass, film title.
157.
1959: Frank Lloyd Wright, the Guggenheim Museum, New York.
158.
1959: Carlo L. Vivarelli, magazine cover.

1948

149.

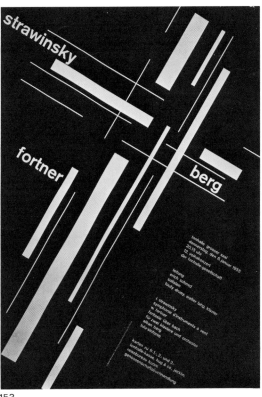

Neue Grafik
New Graphic Design
Graphisme actuel

158.

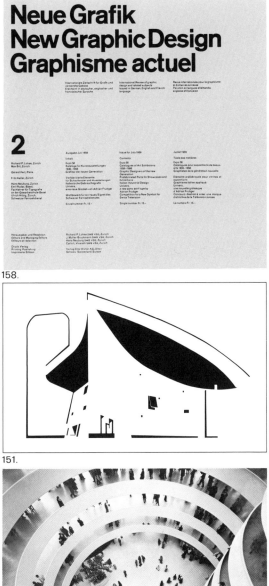

151.

152.

155.

153.

154.

150.

157.

156.

21

1959

159.

160.

161.

162.

163.

164.

165.

166.

167.

168.
c. 1968: Seymour Chwast and
Milton Glaser, poster.
169.
1968: R. Buckminster Fuller,
American Pavilion, Montreal
World's Fair.

170.
c. 1967: Symbol for the environmental movement.
171.
1969: First moon walk.

172.
1972: Wolfgang Weingart,
typographic interpretation of
a poem.
173.
1974: Herb Lubalin, news-
paper cover.

174.
1974: Cook and Shanosky,
standard symbol signs.

175.
1976: American Bicentennial.
Symbol design by Bruce
Blackburn.

1968

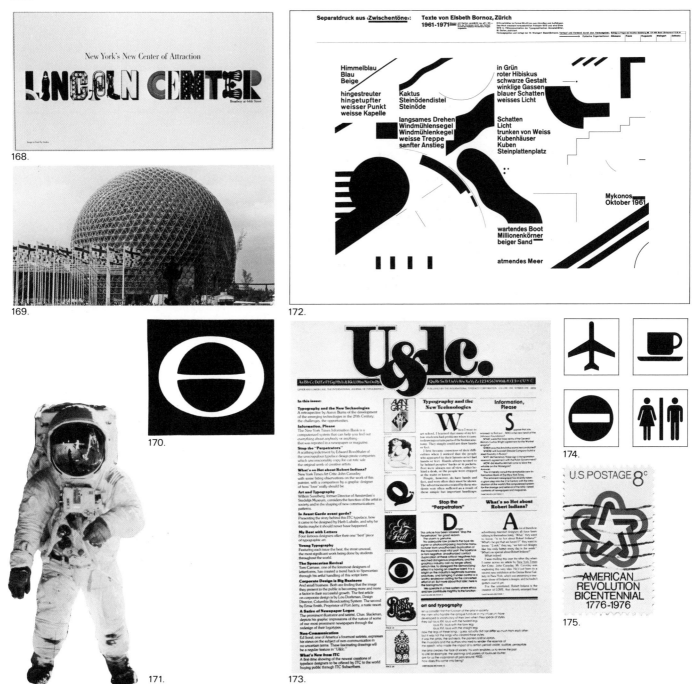

168.

169.

170.

171.

172.

173.

174.

175.

176.
1977: Pompidou National
Center of Arts and Culture,
Paris.
177.
1977: Bill Bonnell, RyderTypes
trademark.

178.
1978: Willi Kunz, poster
design.
179.
1979: Richard Greenberg,
film titles.
180.
1982: Tim Priddy,
advertisement.

181.
1983: Michael Graves, Portland, Oregon, city hall.
182.
1980s: Digital typography and
computer technology impact
typographic design.

1977

178.

176.

177.

179.

180.

181.

182.

Typographic design is a complex area of human activity, requiring a broad background for informed practice. This chapter explores the basic language of typography. Letterforms, the fundamental components of all typographic communications, are carefully examined. Nomenclature, measurement, and the nature of the typographic font and family are presented.

The alphabet is a series of elemental visual signs in a fixed sequence, representing spoken sounds. Each letter signifies only one thing: its elementary sound or name. The twenty-six characters of the alphabet can be combined into thousands of words, creating a visual record of the spoken language. This is the magic of writing and typography, which have been called "thoughts-made-visible" and "frozen sounds."

The four timelines in chapter one graphically present the evolution of letterforms and typographic design from the beginning of writing to the present. Our contemporary typographic forms have been forged by this historical evolution. Typography evolved from handwriting, which is created by making a series of marks by hand; therefore, the fundamental element constructing a letterform is the linear stroke. Each letter of our alphabet developed as a simple mark whose visual characteristics clearly separated it from all the others.

The marking properties of brush, reed pen, and stone engraver's chisel influenced the early form of the alphabet (Fig. 183). The reed pen, used in ancient Rome and the medieval monastery, was held at an angle, called a cant, to the page. This produced a pattern of thick-and-thin strokes. Since the time of the ancient Greeks, capital letterforms have consisted of simple, geometric forms based on the square, circle, and triangle. The basic shape of each capital letter can be extracted from the structure in Figure 184, which is composed of a bisected square, a circle, a triangle, an inverted triangle, and two smaller circles.

The resulting vocabulary of forms, however, lacks several important attributes: optically adjusted proportions, expressive design properties, and maximum legibility and readability. The transition from rudimentary marks to letterforms with graphic clarity and precision is a matter of design.

Because early capital letters were cut into stone, these letters developed with a minimum number of curved lines, for curved strokes were difficult to cut (Fig. 185). Lowercase letters evolved as reed-pen writing. Curved strokes could be quickly written and were used to reduce the number of strokes needed to write many characters.

The parts of letterforms
Over the centuries, a nomenclature has evolved that identifies the various components of individual letterforms. By learning this vocabulary, designers and typographers can develop a greater understanding and sensitivity to the visual harmony and complexity of the alphabet. The following list (Fig.

186) identifies the major components of letterform construction. In medieval times, horizontal guidelines were drawn to contain and align each line of lettering. Today, letterforms and their parts are drawn on imaginary guidelines to bring uniformity to typography.

Baseline: An imaginary line upon which the base of each capital letter rests.

Capline: An imaginary line that runs along the tops of the capital letters.

Meanline: An imaginary line that establishes the height of the body of lowercase letters.

x-height: The distance from the baseline to the meanline. Typically, this is the height of lowercase letters and is most easily measured on the lowercase *x*.

All characters align *optically* on the baseline. The body heights of lowercase characters align optically at the x-height, and the tops of capitals align optically along the capline. To achieve precise alignments, the typeface designer makes optical adjustments.

Apex: The peak of the triangle of an uppercase *A*.

Arm: A projecting horizontal stroke that is unattached on one or both ends, as in the letters *T* and *E*.

Ascender: A stroke on a lowercase letter that rises above the meanline.

Bowl: A curved stroke enclosing the counterform of a letter. An exception is the bottom form of the lowercase roman *g*, which is called a loop.

Counter: The negative space that is fully or partially enclosed by a letterform.

Crossbar: The horizontal stroke connecting two sides of the letterform (as in *e*, *A*, and *H*) or bisecting the main stroke (as in *f* and *t*).

183.
Strokes written with the reed pen (top), and brush (middle), and carved with a chisel (bottom).

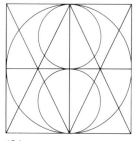

184.

185.
Capital and lowercase letterform construction.

Capline

Meanline

x-height

Baseline

Descender: A stroke on a lowercase letterform that falls below the baseline.

Ear: A small stroke that projects from the upper right side of the bowl of the lowercase roman *g*.

Eye: The enclosed part of the lowercase *e*.

Fillet: The contoured edge that connects the serif and stem in bracketed serifs. (Bracketed serifs are connected to the main stroke by this curved edge; unbracketed serifs connect to the main stroke with an abrupt angle without this contoured transition.)

Hairline: The thinnest strokes within a typeface that has strokes of varying weights.

Leg: The lower diagonal stroke on the letter *k*.

Link: The stroke that connects the bowl and the loop of a lowercase roman *g*.

Loop: See *Bowl*.

Serifs: Short strokes that extend from and at an angle to the upper and lower ends of the major strokes of a letterform.

Shoulder: A curved stroke projecting from a stem.

Spine: The central curved stroke of the letter *S*.

Spur: A projection—smaller than a serif—that reinforces the point at the end of a curved stroke, as in the letter *G*.

Stem: A major vertical or diagonal stroke in a letterform.

Stroke: Any of the linear elements within a letterform; originally, any mark or dash made by the movement of a pen or brush in writing.

Tail: A diagonal stroke or loop at the end of a letter, as in *R* or *j*.

Terminal: The end of any stroke that does not terminate with a serif.

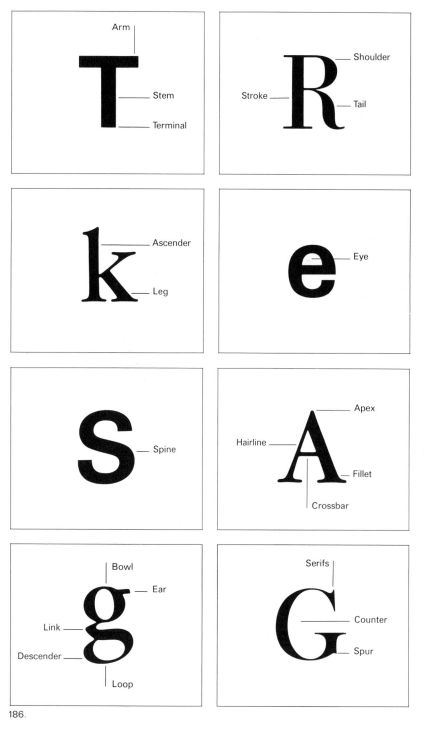

186.

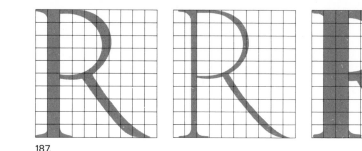

187.

1499 Old Style

1757 Baskerville

1793 Bodoni

1816 First sans serif

c. 1928 Ultra Bodoni

1957 Univers 55

188.

Proportions of the letterform

The proportions of the individual letterform are an important consideration in typography. Four major variables control letterform proportion and have considerable impact upon the visual appearance of a typeface: the ratio of letterform height to stroke width; the variation between the thickest and thinnest strokes of the letterform; the width of the strokes; and the relationship of the x-height to the height of capitals, ascenders, and descenders.

The stroke-to-height ratio. The roman letterform has the stroke-width-to-capital-height proportion found on Roman inscriptions (Fig. 187). Superimposition on a grid demonstrates that the height of the letter is ten times the stroke width. In the adjacent rectangles, the center letter is reduced to one-half the normal stroke width, and the letter on the right has its stroke width expanded to twice the normal width. In both cases, pronounced change in the weight and appearance of the letterform occurs.

Contrast in stroke weight. A change in the contrast between thick and thin strokes can alter the optical qualities of letterforms. The series of *O*s in Figure 188, shown with the date of each specimen, demonstrates how the development of technology and printing has enabled typeface designers to make thinner strokes.

In the Old Style typography of the Renaissance, designers attempted to capture some of the visual properties of pen writing. Since the writing pens of the period had a flat edge, they created thick and thin strokes. *Stress* is the term to define this thick-

ening of the strokes, which is particularly pronounced on curves. Note how the placement of weight within the Old Style *O* creates a diagonal axis. As time has passed, type designers have been less influenced by writing.

By the late 1700s, the impact of writing declined, and this diagonal axis became completely vertical in many typefaces of that period. In many of the earliest sans serif typefaces, stress disappeared completely. Some of these typefaces have a monoline stroke that is completely even in weight.

Expanded and condensed styles. The design qualities of the typographic font change dramatically when the widths of the letterforms are expanded or condensed. The word *proportion*, set in two sans serif typefaces, demonstrates extreme expansion and condensation (Fig. 189). In the top example, set in Aurora Condensed, the stroke-to-height ratio is one to nine. In the bottom example, set in Information, the stroke-to-height ratio is one to two. Although both words are exactly the same height, the condensed typeface takes up far less area on the page.

X-height and proportion. The proportional relationship between the x-height and capital, ascender, and descender lengths influences the optical qualities of typography in a significant way. The same characters are set in seventy-two-point type using three typefaces with widely varying x-heights (Fig. 190). This example demonstrates how these proportional relationships change the appearance of type. The impact of x-height upon legibility will be discussed in chapter four.

190.
On the same size body (72 point), the x-height variation among three typefaces— Garamond Old Style, Bodoni, and Helvetica— are shown. The proportion of the x-height to the point size significantly affects the appearance of type.

72 Points

PROPORTION PROPORTION

A font is a set of characters of the same size and style containing all the letters, numbers, and marks needed for typesetting. A typographic font exhibits structural unity when all the characters relate to one another visually. The weights of thick and thin strokes must be consistent, and the optical alignment of letterforms must appear even. The distribution of lights and darks within each character and in the spaces between characters must be carefully controlled to achieve an evenness of tone within the font.

In some display faces, the font might include only the twenty-six capital letters. In a complete font for complex typesetting, such as for textbooks, it is possible to have nearly 200 characters. The font for ITC Garamond Book (Fig. 191) includes most of the following types of characters.

Capitals: The set of large letters that is used in the initial position.

Lowercase: The set of smaller letters, so named because in metal typesetting these were stored in the lower type case.

Small caps: A complete set of capital letters that are the same height as the x-height of the lowercase letters. These are often used for abbreviations, cross references, and emphasis.

Ranging figures: Numbers that are the same height as the capital letters and sit on the baseline.

Old Style figures: A set of numbers that are compatible with lowercase letters; *1*, *2*, and *0* align with the x-height; *6* and *8* have ascenders; and *3*, *4*, *5*, *7*, and *9* have descenders.

Superior and inferior figures: Small numbers, usually slightly smaller than the x-height, used for footnotes and fractions. Superior figures hang from the capline, and inferior figures sit on the baseline.

Fractions: Common mathematical expressions made up of a superior figure, an inferior figure, and a slash mark. These are set as a single type character.

Ligatures: Two or more characters linked together as one unit, such as *ff*. The ampersand is a ligature originating as a letter combination for the French word *et* ("and") in medieval manuscripts.

Digraphs: A ligature composed of two vowels which are used to represent a diphthong (a monosyllabic speech sound composed of two vowels).

Mathematical signs: Characters used to notate basic mathematical processes.

Punctuation: A system of standard signs used in written and printed matter to structure and separate units and to clarify meaning.

Accented characters: Characters with accents for foreign language typesetting or for indicating pronunciation.

Dingbats: Assorted signs, symbols, reference marks, and ornaments designed for use with a type font.

Monetary symbols: Logograms used to signify monetary systems (U.S. dollar and cent marks, British pound mark, and so on).

189.

abcdefghijklmnopqrstuvwxyz
ABCDEFGHIJKLMNOPQRSTUVWXYZ
ABCDEFGHIJKLMNOPQRSTUVWXYZ
1234567890 $ˢ£¢&

1234567890/1234567890
fffiffififlfflÇØÆŒßßçøæœ
(:;,.!¡?¿""'*#«»)[]₀%°○'''•
§‡†@™®+=÷--

191.

Optical relationships within a font

Mechanical and mathematical letterform construction can result in serious spatial problems caused by the diversity of form within the alphabet. These letterform combinations (Fig. 192) show the optical adjustment necessary to achieve visual harmony within the font. The apexes extend beyond the guidelines. Otherwise, they would appear too short. Curved letterforms are slightly larger than letters that terminate squarely with the guidelines. This prevents them from appearing too small.

In two-storied capitals and figures, the top half appears too large if the form is divided in the mathematical center. To balance these letters optically, their top halves are drawn slightly narrower than the bottom. Horizontal strokes in both curved and straight letterforms are drawn slightly thinner than vertical strokes. Otherwise, the horizontals would appear too thick.

Tight junctions where strokes meet are often opened slightly to prevent the appearance of thickening at the joint. Letters combining diagonal and vertical strokes must be designed to achieve a balance between the top and bottom counterforms. Strokes can be tapered slightly to open up the spaces, and adjustments in the amount of stroke overlap can achieve a harmony of parts.

Letters whose vertical strokes determine their height are drawn slightly taller than letters whose height is determined by a horizontal stroke. Optically, they will appear the same height. The stroke weight of compact letterforms, such as those with closed counterforms, are drawn slightly smaller than the stroke weight of letterforms having open counterforms. This optically balances the weight. Curved strokes are usually thicker at their midsection than the vertical strokes, to achieve an even appearance.

These adjustments are very subtle and are often imperceptible to the reader. However, their overall effect is a more ordered and harmonious appearance.

AEV OEC

HRESKXB

EOR

Wrap

MKV

HE

BHM

mij

192.

Unity of design in the type font

Tremendous diversity of form exists in the typographic font. Twenty-six capitals, twenty-six lowercase letters, ten numerals, punctuation, and other graphic elements in a font must be integrated into a system that can be successfully combined into innumerable words.

Letterform combinations from the Times Roman Bold font (Fig. 193) demonstrate several design principles that bring wholeness to typography. Letterforms share similar parts. We see this in the repetition of diagonals in *A V W M*. Likewise, the letters *b d p q* and *m n h u* share parts.

A repetition of curves, verticals, horizontals, and serifs combined bring variety and unity to typesetting using this typeface. The designer has created many subtle relationships. For example, the bottom strokes of the capital *Z* and *L* have longer serifs than the bottom stroke of the *E*. This change in detail compensates for the larger counterform on the right side of the first two letters. All well-designed fonts of type display this principle of repetition with the variety that is found in Times Roman Bold.

DCGOQ

AVWM jiru

FEB mnhut

bdpq SCGH

BRKPR atfr

ZLE MYX

bq bhlk ceo

193.

31

An infinite variety of typestyles are available today. Phototypography, with its simple and economical introduction of new typefaces, has made the entire history of typography accessible. Numerous efforts have been made to classify typefaces, with most falling into the following major categories. Some classification systems add a decorative or novelty category for the wide range of fanciful typestyles that defy categorization.

Old Style

Old Style type began with designs of the punchcutter Francesco Griffo, who worked for the famous Venetian scholar-printer Aldus Manutius during the 1490s. Griffo's designs evolved from earlier Italian type designs. His Old Style capitals were influenced by carved Roman capitals; lowercase letters were inspired by fifteenth-century humanistic writing styles, based on the earlier Carolingian minuscules. Old Style letterforms have the weight stress of rounded forms at an angle, as in handwriting. The serifs are bracketed (that is, unified with the stroke by a tapered, curved line). Also, the top serifs on the lowercase letters are at an angle.

Italic

Italic letterforms slant to the right. Today, we use them primarily for emphasis and differentiation. When the first italic appeared in the earliest "pocket book," printed by Aldus Manutius in 1501, it was used as an independent typestyle. The first italic characters were close-set and condensed; therefore, Manutius was able to get more words on each line. Some italic styles are based on handwriting with connected strokes and are called scripts.

Transitional

During the 1700s, typestyles gradually evolved from Old Style to Modern. Typefaces from the middle of the eighteenth century, including those by John Baskerville, are called Transitional. The contrast between thick and thin strokes is greater than in Old Style faces. Lowercase serifs are more horizontal, and the stress within the rounded forms shifts to a less diagonal axis. Transitional characters are usually wider than Old Style characters.

Modern

Late in the 1700s, typefaces termed Modern evolved from Transitional styles. These typefaces have extreme contrasts between thick and thin strokes. Thin strokes are reduced to hairlines. The weight stress of rounded characters is vertical. Serifs are horizontal hairlines that join the stems at a right angle without bracketing. The uppercase width is regularized; wide letters such as *M* and *W* are condensed and other letters, including *P* and *T*, are expanded. Modern-style typefaces have a strong geometric quality projected by rigorous horizontal, vertical, and circular forms.

&

Egyptian

In 1815, the English typefounder Vincent Figgins introduced slab-serif typestyles under the name Antique. At the time, there was a mania for ancient Egyptian artifacts, and other typefounders adopted the name Egyptian for their slab-serif designs. These typestyles have heavy square or rectangular serifs that are usually unbracketed. The stress of curved strokes is often minimal. In some slab-serif typefaces, all strokes are the same weight.

&

Sans Serif

The first sans serif typestyle appeared in an 1816 specimen book of the English typefounder William Caslon IV. The most obvious characteristic of these styles is, as the name implies, the absence of serifs. In many sans serif typefaces, strokes are uniform, with little or no contrast between thick and thin strokes. Stress is almost always vertical. Many sans serif typefaces are geometric in their construction; others combine both organic and geometric qualities.

Typographic measurement

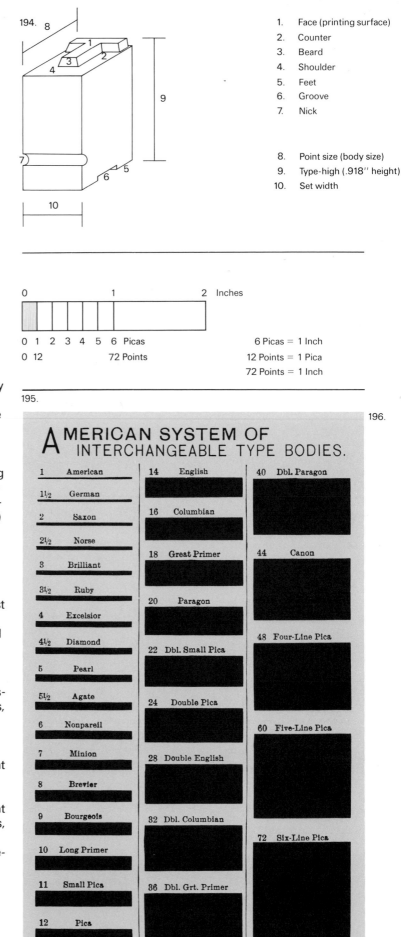

194.

1. Face (printing surface)
2. Counter
3. Beard
4. Shoulder
5. Feet
6. Groove
7. Nick

8. Point size (body size)
9. Type-high (.918″ height)
10. Set width

Our measurement system for typography was originally developed for the handset metal type invented by Johann Gutenberg around A.D. 1450. The rectangular, metal block of type (Fig. 194) has a raised letterform on top, which was inked to print the image.

Metal type measurement

The small sizes of text type necessitated the development of a measuring system with extremely fine increments. There were no standards for typographic measurements until the French type designer and founder Pierre Simon Fournier le Jeune introduced his point system of measurement in 1737. The contemporary American measurement system, which was adopted during the 1870s, has two basic units: the point and the pica (Fig. 195). There are approximately seventy-two points in an inch (each point is 0.138 inches) and twelve points in a pica. There are about six picas in an inch.

Metal type exists in three dimensions, and an understanding of typographic measurement begins with this early technology. All metal type must be the exact same height, which is called type-high (0.918 inch). This uniform height enabled all types to print a uniform impression upon the paper. The depth of the type, which is called the point size or body size, is measured in points. Before the development of the point and pica system, various sizes of type were identified by names, such as brevier, long primer, and pica; these became 8-point, 10-point, and 12-point type. The chart (Fig. 196), reproduced from a nineteenth-century printers' magazine, shows the major point sizes of type with their old names. Types that are 12-point and under are called text type and are primarily used for body copy. Sizes above 12-point are called display type, and they are used for titles, headlines, signage, and the like. Traditional metal type had a range of text and display sizes in increments from 5-point to 72-point (Fig. 197).

0   1   2   Inches

0 1 2 3 4 5 6   Picas   6 Picas = 1 Inch
0 12   72 Points   12 Points = 1 Pica
                                     72 Points = 1 Inch

195.

196.

AMERICAN SYSTEM OF INTERCHANGEABLE TYPE BODIES.

1 American	14 English	40 Dbl. Paragon
1½ German		
2 Saxon	16 Columbian	
2½ Norse		
3 Brilliant	18 Great Primer	44 Canon
3½ Ruby		
4 Excelsior	20 Paragon	
4½ Diamond		48 Four-Line Pica
5 Pearl	22 Dbl. Small Pica	
5½ Agate		
6 Nonpareil	24 Double Pica	
7 Minion		60 Five-Line Pica
8 Brevier	28 Double English	
9 Bourgeois		
10 Long Primer	32 Dbl. Columbian	
11 Small Pica		72 Six-Line Pica
	36 Dbl. Grt. Primer	
12 Pica		

196.
Reproduced actual size from
The Inland Printer, April 1885.

34

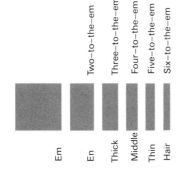

Two-to-the-em
Three-to-the-em
Four-to-the-em
Five-to-the-em
Six-to-the-em

Em
En
Thick
Middle
Thin
Hair

This line has word spacing with em quads.

This line has word spacing with en quads.

This line has word spacing with thick quads.

This line has word spacing with middle quads.

This line has word spacing with thin quads.

This line has word spacing with hair quads.

As shown in Figure 194, the width of type is called the set width and varies with the design of each individual letter. The letters *M* and *W* have the widest set width; *i* has the narrowest. The length of a line of type is the sum of the set width of all the characters and spaces in the line. It is measured in picas.

Spatial measurement
The designer measures and specifies the spatial intervals between typographic elements. These intervals are: interletter spacing, traditionally called letterspacing, which is the interval between letters; interword spacing, also called wordspacing, which is the interval between words; and interline spacing, traditionally called leading (because thin strips of lead are placed between lines of metal type to increase the spatial interval between them), which is the interval between two lines of type.

In traditional metal typography, interline and interword spacings are achieved by inserting metal blocks called quads between the pieces of type. Because these are not as tall as the type itself, they do not print. A quad that is a square of the point size is called an *em*; one-half an em quad is called an *en*. In metal type, other smaller divisions of space are fractions of the em (Fig. 198). These metal spacers are used for letter- and wordspacing, paragraph indentations, and centering or justifying lines of type.

For design considerations, the em of a condensed typestyle can be narrower than a square, and the em of an expanded typestyle can be wider than a square. This is demonstrated by the em quads from four styles in the Univers family of typefaces (Fig. 199).

5	Point
6	Point
7	Point
8	Point
9	Point
10	Point
11	Point
12	Point
14	Point
18	Point
24	Point
30	Point
36	Point
42	Point
48	Point
54	Point
60	Point
72	Point

197.

Univers   53 em   55 em   57 em   59 em

199.

This line is set with plus one unit of interletter spacing.
This line is set with normal, unaltered interletter spacing.
This line is set with minus one unit of interletter spacing.
This line is set with minus two units of interletter spacing.
This line is set with minus three units of interletter spacing.
201.

While em and en are still used as typographic terms, spacing in keyboard phototypesetting and digital typesetting is controlled by a computer, using a unit system. The *unit* is a relative measurement determined by dividing the em (that is, the square of the type size) into equal vertical divisions. Different typesetting systems use different numbers of units; sixteen, thirty-two, and sixty-four are common. The width of each character (Fig. 200) is assigned a unit value or width. During typesetting, the character is exposed, then the typesetting machine advances the number of units assigned to that character before exposing the next character. The unit value includes space on each side of the letter for normal interletter spacing. Adding or subtracting units can expand or contract the space between letters, changing the tone of the typography (Fig. 201). As will be discussed later, spacing influences the aesthetics and legibility of typesetting.

Some letter combinations, such as *TA*, have awkward spatial relationships. Such interletter space can be adjusted, making the interval more consistent with other letter combinations. This is called kerning. In metal type, kerning was achieved by sawing notches in the types. Computer-controlled typesetters can be programmed to make an automatic adjustment when these awkward combinations appear.

| 13 Units | 10 Units | 9 Units | 5 Units | 10 Units | 11 Units |

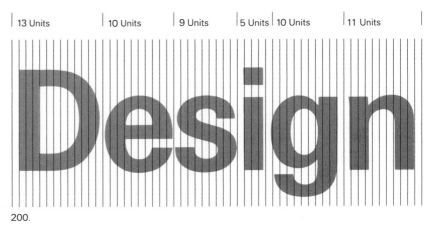

200.
The unit value of each letter in
the word *Design* is shown.

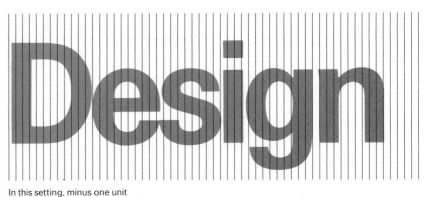

In this setting, minus one unit
is used for tighter interletter
spacing.

In this setting, minus two units
is used. The letters touch.

A type family consists of a group of related typefaces, unified by a set of similar design characteristics. Each face in the family is an individual one that has been created by changing visual aspects of the parent font. Early type families consisted of three fonts: the regular roman face, a bolder version, and an italic. The roman, bold, and italic fonts of the Baskerville family (Fig. 202) demonstrate that a change in stroke weight produces the bold version, and a change in stroke angle creates the italic. The bold font expands typographic possibilities by bringing impact to titles, headings, and display settings. In addition to weight and angle changes, members of a type family are created by changing proportions or by design elaboration.

Weight changes. By simply changing the stroke width relative to the height of the letters, a whole series of alphabets, ranging from extremely light to very bold, can be produced. In England, a classification standard has been developed that contains eight weights: extralight, light, semilight, medium, semibold, bold, extrabold, and ultrabold. Most type families do not, however, consist of eight weights. Four weights—light, regular or book, medium, and bold—are often sufficient for most design purposes. In the Avant Garde family (Fig. 203) stroke weight is the only aspect that changes in these five fonts.

Proportion. Changing the proportions of a typestyle by making letterforms wider (expanded) or narrower (condensed), as discussed earlier, is another method for adding typefaces to a type family. Terms used to express changes in proportion include: ultra-expanded, extra-expanded, expanded, regular, condensed, extra-condensed, and ultra-condensed.

Sometimes confusion results because there is no standardized terminology for discussing the variations in type families. For example, the regular face is sometimes called normal, roman, or book. Terms used to name light weights include lightline, slim, and hairline. Black, elephant, massive, heavy, and thick have been used to designate bold weights in some type families. Names given to condensed variations include narrow, contracted, elongated, and compressed. Expanded faces have been called extended, wide, and stretched.

202.

Baskerville

Baskerville

Baskerville

AVANT GARDE

AVANT GARDE

AVANT GARDE

AVANT GARDE

AVANT GARDE

203.

Futura Italic
Baskerville Italic
Bodoni Italic

204.

Angle. In our discussion about the basic classification of typefaces, italics were presented as a major independent category. They were first introduced four hundred years ago as a new style. Now italics serve as a member of type families, and they are used for contrast or emphasis. Italic fonts that retain curvilinear strokes inspired by handwriting are called cursives or scripts. In geometric typefaces constructed with drafting instruments, the italic fonts created by slanting the stroke angle are called obliques. Baskerville Italic (Fig. 204) is a cursive, demonstrating a handwriting influence; Futura Italic is an oblique face; and Bodoni Italic has both cursive and oblique qualities. Although the Bodoni family was constructed with the aid of drafting instruments, details in the italic font (such as some lower serifs) have a cursive quality.

Elaboration. In design an elaboration is an added complexity, fullness of detail, or ornamentation. Design elaboration can be used to add new typefaces to a type family. These might include outline fonts, three-dimensional effects, and the application of ornaments to letterforms. Some of the variations of Helvetica (Fig. 205) that are available from the German firm of Dr. Boger Photosatz GmbH include outlines, inlines, perspectives, rounded terminals, and even an antique effect.

While many elaborations are gaudy and interfere with the integrity and legibility of the letterforms, others can be used successfully. Goudy Hand-tooled (Fig. 206) is based on Goudy Bold. A white linear element is placed on each major stroke. Dimensionality is suggested, and the face alludes to incised inscriptional lettering.

Decorative and novelty typestyles should be used with great care by the graphic designer. At best, these express a feeling appropriate to the content and allow for unique design solutions. Unfortunately, the use of design elaboration is often a mere straining for effect.

The Cheltenham family

One of the earliest and most extensive type families is the Cheltenham series of typefaces (Fig. 207). The first version, Cheltenham Old Style, was initially designed around the turn of the century by architect Bertram G. Goodhue in collaboration with Ingalls Kimball of the Cheltenham Press in New York City. When this typeface went into commercial production at the American Type Founders Company, designer Morris F. Benton supervised its development. Benton designed about eighteen additional typefaces for the Cheltenham family. Variations developed by other typefounders and manufacturers of typesetting equipment expanded this family to more than thirty styles. The design properties linking the Cheltenham family are short slab serifs with rounded brackets, tall ascenders and long descenders, and a moderate weight differential between thick and thin strokes.

Cheltenham
Cheltenham
Cheltenham
Cheltenham
Cheltenham
Cheltenham
Cheltenham
Cheltenham
Cheltenham
Cheltenham
Cheltenham
Cheltenham
Cheltenham
Cheltenham
Cheltenham
Cheltenham
Cheltenham
Cheltenham
Cheltenham
Cheltenham
Cheltenham

207.

Goudy Handtooled

206.

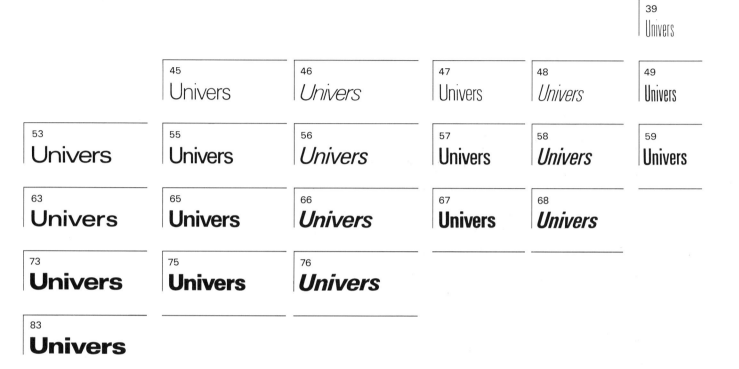

205.
Elaborations of Helvetica
Medium.

39
Univers

45
Univers

46
Univers

47
Univers

48
Univers

49
Univers

53
Univers

55
Univers

56
Univers

57
Univers

58
Univers

59
Univers

63
Univers

65
Univers

66
Univers

67
Univers

68
Univers

73
Univers

75
Univers

76
Univers

83
Univers

208.

The Univers family

A full range of typographic expression and visual contrast becomes possible when all the major characteristics—weight, proportion, and angle—are orchestrated into a unified family. An outstanding example is the Univers family (Fig. 208). This family of twenty-one typestyles was designed by Adrian Frutiger. Instead of the usual terminology, Frutiger used numerals to designate the typefaces. Univers 55 is the "parent" face; its stroke weight and proportions are the norm from which all the other designs were developed. The black-and-white relationships and proportions of Univers 55 are ideal for text settings. Careful study of Figure 208 reveals that the first digit in each font's number indicates the stroke weight, three being the lightest and eight the heaviest. The second digit indicates expansion and contraction of the spaces within and between the letters, which results in expanded and condensed styles. Roman fonts are designated with an odd number, and oblique fonts are designated with an even number.

In the design of Univers, Frutiger sparked a trend in type design toward a larger x-height. The lower-case letters are larger relative to ascenders, descenders, and capitals. The size and weight of capitals are closer to the size and weight of lower-case letters, creating increased harmony on the page of text. Because the twenty-one members of the Univers family share the same x-height, capital height, and ascender and descender length and are produced as a system, they can be intermixed and used together without limitation. This gives the designer extraordinary flexibility (Fig. 209).

209.
Typographic interpretation of
The Bells by Edgar Allan Poe
using the Univers family.

Hear the

sledges with the **Bells**

SILVER **Bells**- -

What a world of **merriment** their *melody* foretells!

How they *tinkle,*

tinkle,

tinkle, in the icy air of night!

While the stars that

o v e r s p r i n k l e

All the heavens seem to t w i n k l e

With a *crystalline* delight:

Keeping *time, time,* **time,**

In a sort of **R**unic rhyme,

To the **tin**tin*nabu***la**tion that so *musically* wells

From the *bells,*   bells,   Bells,

Bells,

BELLS,   **Bells**- -

From the *jingling* and the *tingling* of the bells.

Like the anatomy of typography, typographic syntax and communication have a language that must be learned to understand typographic design. Syntax is the connecting of typographic signs to form words and sentences on the page. The elements of design — letter, word, line, column, and margin — are made into a cohesive whole through the use of visual hierarchy, typographic space, ABA form, and grid systems. In this chapter, the relationship between form and meaning is also addressed. The imaginative designer can expand and clarify content through the communicative use of visual form.

Typographic syntax

In grammar, syntax is the manner in which words are combined to form phrases, clauses, or sentences. We define *typographic syntax* as the process of arranging typographic elements into a cohesive whole. The study of typographic syntax begins with its basic unit, the letter, and progresses to word, line, column, and margin.

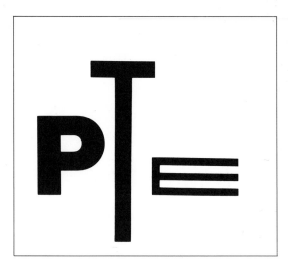

210.
This composition demonstrates contrasting visual characteristics of three letterforms. (Designer: Robert Boyle)
211.
Through precise letterform drawing and carefully considered form-to-counterform interaction, two dissimilar letters form a cohesive sign. (Designer: Gail Collins)
212.
Two letterforms are each broken into two geometric shapes of varying size and density, and the four resulting forms are combined into a delicate, asymmetrically balanced symbol. (Designer: Frank Armstrong)

211.

The letter

Our initial discussion of typographic syntax addresses the intrinsic character of the individual letter. This well-drawn form, exhibiting subtlety and precision, is the unit that distinguishes one family of type from another. It exists in various weights, sizes, and shapes (Fig. 210).

Although the letter typically functions as part of a word, individual letters are frequently combined into new configurations. As shown in Figures 211 and 212, combinations of letters *A* and *g* and *P* and *Q* reveal a stable gestalt. In the illustrated examples, there is an expressiveness and boldness to the individual letters. The syntax displayed here is an example of letter combinations acting as signs, extracted from a larger system of signs.

A typographic sign is visually dynamic because of its interaction with the surrounding white space or void — the white of the paper. This form-to-void relationship is inherent in the totality of typographic expression. The repetition of the letter *T* in Figure 213 is balanced and complemented by its white space. On the title page for Hans Arp's book *On My Way,* the visual interplay between the three letterforms animates the page (Fig. 214). This equilibrium and spatial interaction, and the manner in which it is achieved will be discussed further in our study of typographic space.

Contemplating this ability of space to define form, Amos Chang observed, "...it is the existence of intangible elements, the negative, in architectonic forms which makes them come alive, become human, naturally harmonize with one another, and enable us to experience them with human sensibility."

213.
It is the figure/ground reversal in the repetition of the letter *T* that creates a balanced and expressive poster. (Designer: Willi Kunz)

214.
A dynamic composition is formed by the precise spatial location of the letterforms *a, r,* and *p,* which also spell the author's name. (Designer: Paul Rand)

213.

212.

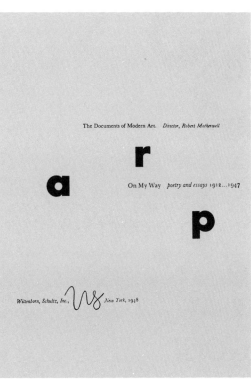

214.

A star, a glass, and a word
contribute to form a sign for
joy. The word's meaning is expressed visually and poetically.
(Designer: Frank Armstrong)

217.
This dissection of the word
Camerata displays the letterform combinations and the
relationships between con-
sonants and their connecting
vowels. Contrast and repetition create lateral movement
within a word, and the overall
arrangement relates to the
word's meaning. (Designer:
Sergio de Jesus)

215.

217.

216.
Word-to-word interaction
exhibits rhythmic recurrences
of form and counterform. Individual letterforms are paired
and their corresponding interi-
or counters are related here.
(Designer: John Rodgers)

olivetti olivetti

The word

By definition, a word has the potential to express an idea (Fig. 215), object, or event. Word signs are independent of the things they represent, yet by design they can be made to signify and reveal their meaning.

Form and counterform relationships, found within individual letterforms, also exist within individual words. Speaking on the structural consideration of form and counterform and the designing of typefaces, Adrian Frutiger stated: "The material of typography is the black, and it is the designer's task with the help of this black to capture space, to create harmonious whites inside the letters as well as between them."

By observing this principle and by combining form and counterform into word units, the designer discovers subtle typographic connections and rhythms (Fig. 216). The word unit is a constellation of individual letterforms, suggesting a union and forming a cohesive whole. Optically adjusted spaces and consistent counterform relationships assure the overall clarity of this union.

Discussing interletter spacing, the painter and graphic artist Ben Shahn tells about his training as an apprentice who lettered on lithographic stones in 1913. The shop foreman explained, "Imagine you have in your hand a glass that will hold only so much water. Now you must provide space between your letters—whatever their slants and curves may be—to hold just that much water, no more or less." The universal principle for spacing letters is this: the typographer, calligrapher, or designer attempts to make the interletter space

between each pair of letters appear equal to the space between every other pair of letters. Because these counterform spaces have such different configurations, this spacing must be achieved through optical balance, rather than through measurement.

Figure 217 shows a dissection of the word *Camerata*, displaying various interletter relationships, including both geometric and organic features. In this example, the word's internal pattern is created by the visual properties of the individual letterforms and their various juxtapositions. This arrangement displays the nature of the internal pattern. *Camerata* is an Italian word meaning "a room full of people"; this meaning supplies yet another interpretation of the overall pattern. Such form-to-content relationships will be discussed later in this chapter.

A concern for form and counterform is evident in the equilibrium that is established among the letterforms comprising the word *Camerata.* It is extremely important to see the interior rhythms of a single word. In the example shown, the letters *C, m, r,* and *t* function as elements of contrast, while the three *as* and the *e* act as the unifying elements. A similar use of contrast and repetition is demonstrated by the progression of letterforms within the corporate logotype for Olivetti (Fig. 218).

Obviously, not all words offer the potential for such a rich typographic internal pattern. The complex and lively forms reproduced here clearly show the variety and fullness of form that exists in some deceptively simple word units.

218.
In the Olivetti logo, the x-height establishes continuity, and the five ascending vertical forms create a horizontal rhythm. The repetition of rounded forms (*o* and *e*) and the "echo effect" of a rounded form followed by vertical strokes create a lively unity; the angled strokes of the letter *v* introduce an element of contrast (Designer: Walter Ballmer)

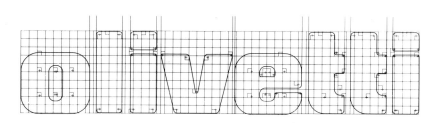

*Of all the achievements
of the human mind, the birth of the alphabet
is the most momentous.*

220.

222.

The line

Words are joined to form verbal sentences and typographic lines. The configuration and placement of lines of type are significant structural concerns. In its most basic form, a line of type consists of a single point size and a single weight extended horizontally over a specific line width.

Lines of type can be arranged symmetrically (Fig. 219), or asymmetrically (Fig. 220). The viewer/reader must sense a clearly established relationship between individual lines of type and the surrounding space (Fig. 221).

The smallest change in point size, weight, or line length controls the overall emphasis given to a line of type. The designer or typographer must determine when the overall effect is balanced and fully integrated. All design considerations—typeface selection, alignments, and spacing—should display connections that are apparent and distinct (Fig. 222). Jan Tschichold states, "The relationship of the sizes must in any case be clearly visible, its effect must be lively, and it must always follow the sense of the text exactly."

The length of a group of lines of type can be equal (justified) or unequal (flush left/ragged right, ragged left/flush right, or centered). The examples in this section illustrate various typographic alignments. Typographic form becomes lively and harmonious through these alignments, which enhance individual lines of type and activate the surrounding space (Figs. 223 and 224).

The placement of punctuation marks is of special significance to these alignments. In Figure 225 punctuation marks extend into the margin. Slight adjustments and subtle refinements heighten the degree of unity.

Typographic rules are used in conjunction with type and separate one line of type from another or one group of typographic lines from another as in Figure 221, or in footnotes. Rules are found in a variety of forms (Fig. 226) and in numerous sizes and weights. (The use of visual punctuation, including typographic rules, is detailed in *Visual hierarchy.*)

Earlier, we discussed kerning and the optical spacing of letterforms. Control of these factors make possible a judicious use of letterspacing in a line of type. The orientation of lines raises a multiplicity of other spacing concerns; for example, interword spacing, interline spacing, and line-to-page relationships, as well as the establishment of columns and margins.

219.
Symmetrical placement produces a quiet, balanced configuration.
220.
Asymmetrical placement achieves a dynamic division of space on the page. (Designer: Ivy Li)

221.
Type and rules combine to bring a sense of unity to the page. Note the recurrence of similar space intervals and the attention given to individual line breaks (the rhythmic pattern of line endings). (Designer: Cheryl Van Arnam)

222.
This multiple-line composition contains varying line weights, yet expresses wholeness through the careful placement of all elements. It displays the diversity possible in the spacing of lines of type. (Designer: Wolfgang Weingart)

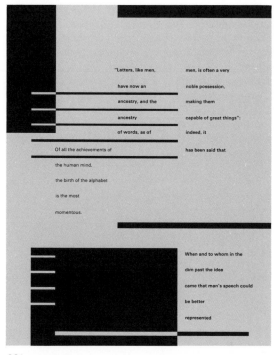

221.

"Bauhaus Masters"
Marcel Breuer
Paul Klee
Herbert Bayer

"Bauhaus Masters"
Marcel Breuer
Paul Klee
Herbert Bayer

225.

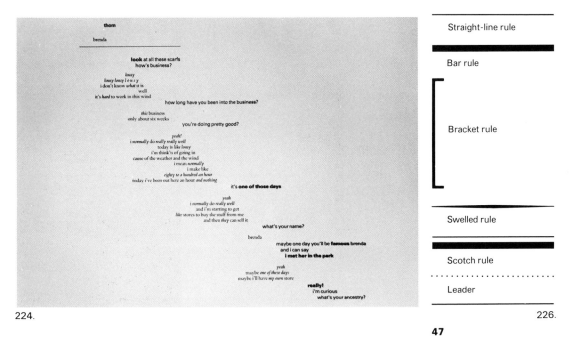

223.

Elements are organized
within the aural field
according to the principles of
r h y t h m

m e l o d y

and **h a r m o n y**
which determine spatial orientation
in the visual field.

Activation of pitch as an effective variable transforms
a rhythmic sequence into melody.
A vertical displacement of visual elements results
from differentiation of pitch values
generating another level of spatial complexity.
As the magnitude of displacement
from a horizontal axis
increases
spatial orientation
becomes ambiguous.

Harmonic relationships

Aural rhythm in its fundamental state is a succession of positive elements, subject to variable duration and volume at constant pitch, separated by variable durations of silence.
are primarily defined

Translation of rhythm produces a sequence of visual elements in horizontal orientation to the field.
by the intervals

A vertical orientation

Although these elements have a common horizontal axis, volume modifications cause a limited degree of vertical extension.
between pitch values
Curvilinear and oblique variations are developed
of visual elements

as visual representations of certain expressive techniques
Increasingly complex spatial relationships are developed from the variation of positive and negative duration values.
in the articulation of sounds.
in complete opposition
is achieved

In the visual field

a smooth transition between successive sounds
to rhythmic sequences.
through the translation

is represented as a curvilinear form

while a horizontal succession of oblique forms
of an harmonic sequence
is equivalent to a rapid alternation of sounds.

which is based

on a simultaneous occurrence

of sounds.

223.
Complex and subtle relationships in interline spacing are achieved here by varying type size, weight, and spatial interval which separate the statements for the reader. The overall effect is rhythmic and expressive. (Designer: Frank Armstrong)

224.
In this conversation, the placement of lines and intervals reflects the dialogue. (Designer: Warren Lehrer)

225.
In the *top* setting the lines are flush left, but the edge appears uneven because of the punctuation. In the bottom version, "hanging" the punctuation into the margin is an adjustment resulting in an optically aligned edge.

224.

Straight-line rule

Bar rule

Bracket rule

Swelled rule

Scotch rule

Leader

226.

227.
Six columns of type are arranged horizontally, allowing
ample breathing space for the
photographic image. Varying
column depths make possible
a clear integration of typographic and pictorial form.
(Art Director: Bart Crosby;
Designer: Carl Wohlt)

228.
Three columns of type create
a vertical movement. Their uneven depths serve to balance
other elements. The use of
rules and bold headings breaks
the overall grayness of the
text. (Art Directors: Bart
Crosby and Carl Wohlt)

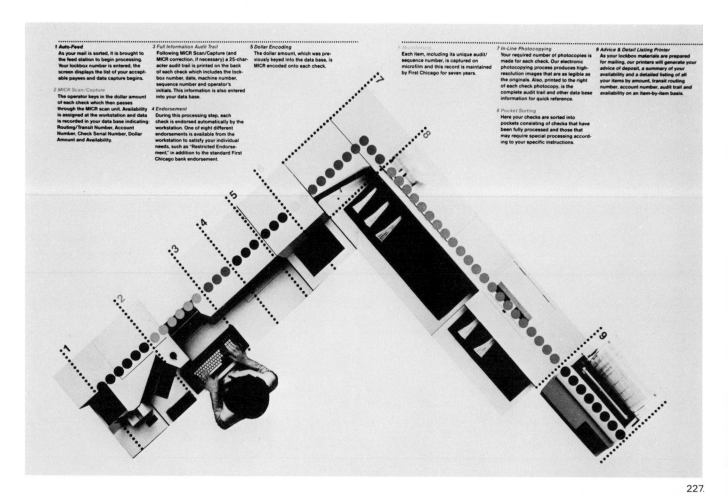

227.

228.

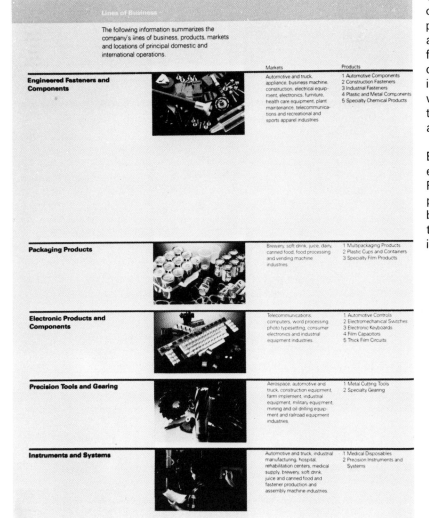

Column and margin

The visual qualities of a column of text are based on contrast, ratio (depth-to-width), and texture, properties that determine an optically balanced arrangement and affect the form and counter-form relationships of columns and margins. The depth and width of all columns (and their adjoining space intervals) should be carefully examined, with attention given to typographic texture and tone. Texture is the tactile appearance of the type, and tone is its lightness or darkness.

Either horizontal or vertical movements may be emphasized. One will often dominate, as shown in Figures 227 and 228. Eye movement across the page (side to side and top to bottom) is controlled by column rhythms and rules. By their manipulation, the designer can group information according to its role in a given layout (Fig. 229).

229.
Columns and margins are carefully balanced through the use of contrasting type sizes and weights and of two rule weights. (Art Director: Bart Crosby; Designer: Carl Wohlt)

230.
In this annual report there are
subtle spatial relationships.
These include the form/
counterform of the column to
the margin; the placement of
heading and subheading,
which extend into the margin
for emphasis; and the column
mass to rules, photograph,
and caption.
(Designer: Frank Armstrong)

231.
This magazine page exhibits
the needed contrast between
text and caption elements. The
column width of the text is
double the column width of
the caption. (Art Director: Ben
Day; Designer: Anne Stewart)

The one- and two-column arrangements shown in Figures 230 and 231 display some of the possibilities for text-column placement. In the two-column arrangement, the column depth is equal. Vitality and contrast are achieved by the placement of the adjacent photograph, its caption, and the bar rule containing the title. In both examples, the caption-column width and the text-column width are of different lengths. This change in column measure must be sufficient to bring about definite contrast, indicating that the caption is not part of the text.

Other possibilities for column contrast are shown in Figure 232. Variations between the columns are produced by a change in interline spacing and changes in type size and weight. Relative to one another, the columns can be seen as open or closed, light or dark. The resulting change in density becomes a design consideration. These transitions make possible a stepped progression into the white of the page. The critically placed spatial intervals create a pronounced movement and tension.

Type size may vary from column to column (Fig. 233) or within a column from top to bottom (Fig. 234). This variation emphasizes the copy presented in the larger type size. (For further discussion, see *Visual hierarchy.*) This change in visual weight contributes to a variation in page density, a form of contrast which makes it possible to balance various type elements, adding rhythmic qualities to the page through a deliberate arrangement of light to dark relationships.

The typographic properties of a given column of text are partly defined by the surrounding white space on the page. The selection of appropriate margins for clarity and balance depends on the information contained within the page. For example, in an open arrangement the type explains components of an automated workstation (see Figure 227). In the more compact arrangement illustrated in Figure 228, a large amount of running copy must be presented. Other requirements might include the need to place folios (page numbers) or running heads in the margins.

The scale and proportion of columns and margins and their relationship to one another must be carefully adjusted. The column proportion (two units wide to three units high) is the same as the page proportion in the diagram in Figure 235. The margin ratio is two margin units to three to four to six, as indicated. In other words, the bottom margin is twice as high as the top margin. Jan Tschichold has pointed out that this complex series of column-to-margin ratios, based on the golden section, is found in numerous medieval manuscripts.

Paragraph breaks within a column greatly influence the relationship between a column of text and its surrounding margins. A break may be introduced as an indentation, as a space interval, or as a combination of both. Designers have also developed their own ways to indicate paragraphs (Fig. 236). The overall page organization will determine the most suitable method.

When columns, margins, and their interrelationships are clear and appropriate to content, the result is a printed page of distinction. Every problem demands a fresh approach, yet the underlying principle of an ordered unity that is responsive to the meaningful blend of form and counterform is always the goal.

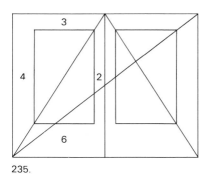

235.

232.
This experimental text composition reveals various combinations of typographic texture and tone.

236.
Placement of a bullet (a typographic dot used for emphasis) upon intercolumn rules designates new paragraphs in this booklet design. (Designer: Jeff Barnes)

234.

· · · · · · · · · · · · · · · · ·
· · · · · · · · · · · · · · ·
· · · · · · · · · · · · ·
· · · · · · · · · · · · · · · · · ·
· · · · · · · · · · · · · ·

independence in the student. "Accordingly, handicraft in the workshops was right from the start, not an end in itself, but laboratory experiment preparatory to industrial production. If the initial products of the Bauhaus looked like individual craft products, this was a necessary detour for the groping student whom we avoided to prod with a foregone conclusion."
• We salvaged the best of experimental education and added to it a carefully constructed program of information-based design that produced noncommercial products that worked. It was a different school with different people with different goals in a different time. Our aim was to produce designers who had the will, the ability, and the ethical base to change American production for the better.
• I was somewhat concerned that this might be a middle-of-the-road

236.

1982: Highlights

The Bridgeport Hospital family, 4,367 members strong, is a special and meaningful community. Our goals blend the values of fine health care and human compassion with a balanced regard for technology and the demands of cost containment. Our mission is health care; the time clock of our Hospital community is idiosyncratic and without regard for "appropriate hours of rest." Every person in this community values, and is valued for, his and her role in the complex process of healing. The photographs and essay on these pages bring to your attention some of the highlights of fiscal year 1982.

The state Commission on Hospitals and Health Care (CHHC) approved three certificate of need applications from Bridgeport Hospital in 1982: *a linear accelerator*, whose high energy X-ray and electron beams destroy cancer cells in the treatment of patients with cancer; *a full body CAT-Scanner*, a computerized diagnostic tool that produces X-ray pictures of thin sections of the entire human body; and *a new, state-of-the-art, cardiovascular laboratory*, and *a special radiologic procedures lab* for the diagnoses of cardiovascular disease and peripheral vascular diseases.

Historically, patients undergoing surgery spend a fair amount of time in the hospital for pre-operative testing and post-operative recuperation. In an attempt to realistically assess and better meet the needs of patients as well as to improve operating room utilization, Dr. Claude Duval, chairman of the department of Anesthesiology, in conjunction with assistant administrator Erica Pifer, began work on modifying our existing one-day surgery center project. On April 20, the facility expanded its operation with a dedicated team of nurses in a new area constructed by plant operations.

New Faces Highlight the Year.

Dennis Wasson, M.D., an attending surgeon, served as president of the Bridgeport Hospital attending staff in 1981 and was re-elected in 1982 to serve as president of the 478 active and courtesy physicians. At the annual meeting of the medical staff in 1983, Anthony Musto, M.D., an attending physician in Ophthalmology, was named president of the Bridgeport Hospital attending staff for 1983 and Dr. Wasson was named Chief of Staff and chairman of the attending staff executive committee. Howard L. Taubin, M.D., an attending physician in the section of Gastroenterology, was chairman of the executive committee and Chief of Staff in 1982. Some of the other personnel changes during the year include the naming of Robert M. Daly, M.D., as chairman of the newly created department of Psychiatry; and the appointment of Wesley D. Simmons to the newly created post, vice president of finance.

Two new sections of the department of Surgery were established during 1982. Glenn W. Sandberg, M.D., was named chief of the new section of Cardiothoracic Surgery and Stuart A. Levinson, M.D., was named chief of the new section of Vascular Surgery.

Wilbur Stratton
pharmacist
Department of Pharmacy

230.

---

by Joseph Dyer

For centuries the mainstay of music and art in the Western world was a system of patronage sustained by the twin pillars of court and church. Musicians, if not entirely comfortable with the arrangement, adjusted to the demands of their princely or ecclesiastical employers. Haydn's international fame eventually freed him from the constraints of court service. Mozart chafed under the yoke of subordination forced upon him at Salzburg, until in desperation he threw it off for a freelance career. Beethoven broke completely with the old system. His genius was such that, despite the coarseness of his manners and sometimes insolent behavior, patrons and would-be recipients of dedications paid court to him.

With a change in the social climate and the development of a large middle-class audience founded on the new mercantile and industrial wealth, composers became less dependent on direct subsidy. Profits from publication further strengthened their independence. Patronage, however, continues to be an important factor even in its modern form, institutionalized by governments and foundations.

The works on Handel & Haydn's February program represent different facets of this historical phenomenon. For Mozart the delightful "Epistle" Sonata, K. 244, constituted little more than the fulfillment of an obligation connected with his duties as a cathedral musician. Haydn's *Theresienmesse* and the Poulenc Organ Concerto owe their existence to special relationships between their composers and two princess-patrons.

When Haydn returned from his second trip to England in 1795, he had a new master. Nicolaus II Esterházy, grandson of the prince for whom he had created so many masterpieces between 1762 and 1790. Haydn was no longer willing to accept the servant-master relationship which had prevailed in the past. Princess Marie

took a series of lovers, and poured out her dismay in lacrymose poetry. Notwithstanding his divided loyalties, her husband saw to it that her name day in September was celebrated in a manner befitting the concert of a Hungarian potentate. The festivities–concerts, theatrical events, fireworks, hunting parties–occupied several weeks. Yearly, between 1796 and 1802 (with the exception of 1802) a new Mass by Haydn was sung in the Bergkirche at Eisenstadt as the centerpiece of the religious observances.

The prince was not a man of cultivated musical tastes, and his favorite church music tended to the conservative side. According to one of Haydn's pupils, Johann Nepomuk Hummel, the six late Masses of his teacher reflect the taste of the princess, "for whom a Mass in an attractive elegant style would have more value than a learned or more serious work." (Due to a misunderstanding, the Mass in B flat of 1799 was assumed to have been written for Marie Therese, wife of Emperor Francis II, hence the name *Theresienmesse*.)

Marie Hermenegild expressed her affection for Haydn's devoted service in many touching ways. She commiserated with the sufferings caused by the agonizing decline in his physical condition. With accustomed thoughtfulness she sought to soften the blow of his brother Johann's death in 1805 by bringing the news to him personally. A year later, learning that Haydn's pension was insufficient for his living expenses, she appealed to her husband. Prince Nicolaus wrote to Haydn immediately, expressing his "esteem and friendship" for him and increasing his retirement income by a generous amount.

The princess paid Haydn many visits at his house in Gumpendorf, where he lived as a semi-invalid. Her solicitude also assured a steady supply of special wine from the princely cellars. The famous depiction of a performance of

A seventeenth-century engraving of the Bergkirche (mountain-church) at Eisenstadt, where the last six Masses of Haydn were performed in honor of Princess Esterházy's name day (September 8). Prince Nicholas II was accustomed to ride up the steps into the church on horseback.

Haydn, Poulenc and the Princesses

Hermenegild helped to smooth over the dissimilar expectations of her haughty husband and his famous *Kapellmeister*. Haydn knew how to place the diplomat as well, and the two men soon established an understanding based on mutual respect.

Prince Nicolaus II had a particular interest in church music, an unusual passion for one of Vienna's most notorious débauchés. He established his paramours in houses of their own, where (in the words of an English observer) "they share his favours and diminish his faculties." The princess resigned herself to these indignities.

Haydn's *Creation* in the great hall of the old University of Vienna shows her presenting her shawl to Haydn as protection against the chill–a beautiful expression of her tender concern for the genius who honored her with so many masterpieces.

The Princess Edmond de Polignac (1865-1943), led a nearly legendary existence, immersed in all the leading literary, artistic and musical currents which had Paris as their center. She was born Winnaretta Singer, eighteenth child of Isaac Merritt Singer (of sewing machine fame). When she was two years of age, the family moved to

231.

---

the thought or image intended to be communicated by the Author. And the whole duty of beautiful typography is not to substitute for the beauty or interest of the thing thought and intended to be conveyed by the symbol, a beauty or interest of its own, but, on the one hand, to win access for that communication by the clearness and beauty of the vehicle, and on the other hand, to take advantage of every pause or stage in that communication to interpose some characteristic & restful beauty in its own art.

• Typography
achievements
design

• Letters
communication
alphabet

• words
invention
writing
expression

· · · · · · · · · · · · · · ·
· · · · · · · · · · · · · · · · · · ·
· · · · · · · · · · · · · · ·   · · · · · · · · · · · · · · · ·
· · · · · · · · · · · · · · · ·   · · · · · · · · · · · · · · · · ·
· · · · · · · · · · · · · ·   · · · · · · · · · · · · · · · ·
· · · · · · · · · · · · · · · ·   · · · · · · · · · · · · · · · ·

233.

232.

237.
Ancient Egyptian hieroglyphics
from *The Book of the Dead* of
Tuthmosis III.

By definition, visual hierarchy means a group of visual elements arranged according to emphasis. This emphasis is achieved through contrasts which stress the relative importance and separation or connection of typographic elements. A careful study of visual hierarchy makes possible a greater understanding of the order of typographic communications.

Ancient Egyptian hieroglyphics (Fig. 237) and a Dada collage (Fig. 238) have very different visual hierarchies. The hieroglyphic writing displays a precise visual pattern. These signs, of even texture and size, are arranged systematically according to their role in the language system to which they belong. By contrast, the Dada collage reveals a kinetic and lively hierarchy of typographic form. The Dada composition projects a random order and a casual posture.

The study of visual hierarchy is the study of the relationships of each part to the other parts and to the whole. It emphasizes the relationship of each typographic element to the expressed content of the page. Two notable terms significant to this investigation are counterpart and counterpoint. A typographic counterpart is one of two elements that fits and completes another (Figs. 239 and 240). A typographic counterpoint is a contrasting but parallel element. Unlike counterpart relationships, counterpoint relationships do not complete the whole; rather, they function as a rhythmic support, bringing unity and integration between parts (Fig. 241).

238.
Dada collage poem by Raoul Hausmann.

239.

240.

241.

240.
In this diagram, similar visual properties are found in the photographic image and the letter *s*. The principle of typographic counterpart—the integration and visual flow between parts—is demonstrated. (Designer: Ivy Li)

241.
In these arrangements, the dominant elements (addition and multiplication signs) influence the shape and structure of the other forms, creating counterpoint relationships within the imposed hierarchy. The addition sign establishes horizontal and vertical alignments. The diagonal configuration of the multiplication sign is reflected in the text. (Designer: Lark Pfleegor)

Through the process of elaboration (Fig. 242), typographic hierarchies proceed from single units to complex structures. In the organization of a publication format, graphic elements (Fig. 243) join together to form larger structures. These structures are integrated consistently from the smallest details to the totality of the double-page spreads.

Similar to the attention given to verb tense in written language, visual hierarchy is achieved through parallel construction. This is the typographic indication of likeness or analogy between linked parts. Typographic design makes use of parallel structures, maintaining contrast, vitality, and structural integration (Figs. 244 and 245).

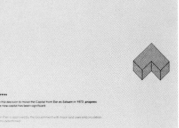

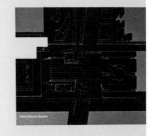

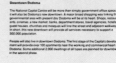

243.

242.
The designer began with a digit and a period and created new configurations through additive and subtractive processes. (Designer: Amy Ruark)

243.
Elements from architectural plans—as single forms and repeated patterns—are used to give movement, unity, and a sense of hierarchy to the page compositions. (Designers: Rob Carter, Meredith Davis, and Robert Meganck)

244.
Parallel construction is
achieved through the repetition of form and pattern. A
hierarchy of sizes becomes
rhythmic through the modular
construction of letterforms.
(Designer: Wolfgang Weingart)
245.
The repetition of the letter *A*
in two different point sizes
creates a hierarchical structure
in this provocative concept.
(Designer: Paul Rand)

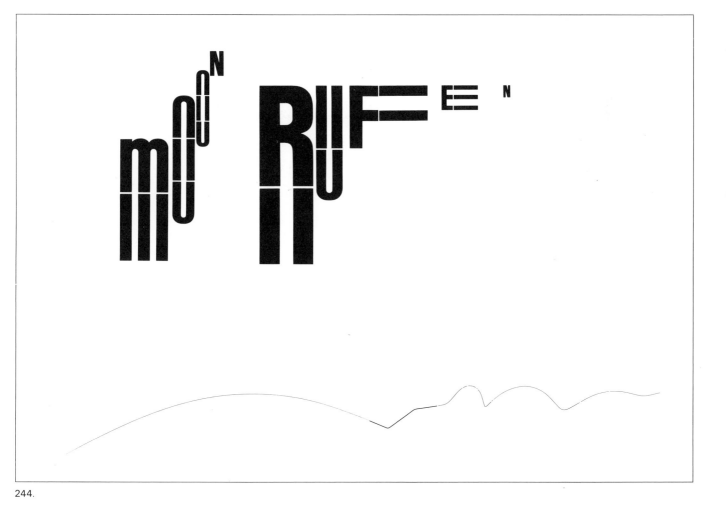

244.

245.

Often, hierarchy in a typographic arrangement is based on the relationships of those typographic units that can be designated as questioning forms and those designated as answering forms (Fig. 246). Visual hierarchy is more clearly understood with this juxtaposition of opposites in mind. The typographic unit assigned the questioning role invites or calls for an answer.

The most prominent visual element of a typographic hierarchy is often a questioning form. Consider the role of both typographic form and pictorial form: do individual components of a composition suggest a question or an answer? The questioning component expresses dissonance (unrelieved tension), while the answering component expresses consonance (relieved tension).

A visual hierarchy of typographic elements is partly governed by visual punctuation. As a writer uses standard punctuation marks to separate words and clarify meaning, a designer introduces visual punctuation (space intervals, rules, or pictorial elements) to separate, connect, and emphasize words or lines. Visual punctuation stresses a rhythmic organization (Figs. 247 and 248) that clarifies the reader/viewer's understanding of the content and structure of a typographic arrangement. If visual punctuation helps to clarify the meaning of the typographic message, visual accentuation is the stressing of particular qualities important to the typographic structure of that message. Here the concern is with relative emphasis: the properties of a typographic arrangement or sign that make it dominant or subordinate in a visual hierarchy.

The expression of the visual properties (round and straight, thick and thin, geometric and organic) of typographic signs becomes manifest through visual accentuation. The bold and compelling mark combining the letter *A* and the scroll of a violin (Fig. 249) is an example of visual accentuation through the use of contrast. The geometric properties of the letter *A* are revealed in opposition to the organic properties of the musical instrument. In this example, selective details in both the letter

and pictorial form are accentuated visually, yet the integrity of the original letter and object is retained. The letter *A* and the violin are incomplete, yet each retains its essence.

Another factor, typographic joinery, enhances this essence. Typographic joinery is the visual linking and connecting of elements in a typographic composition through structural relationships and form repetition. The assembly of separate typographic elements to form a precisely connected sign is seen in the logotype for the American Broadcasting Corporation (Fig. 250). The pronounced geometry and emphasis given to the circular forms exemplify visual accentuation through the use of repetition. The shape of the circle is common to every part of this mark. The three letterforms and their circular container are blended to become one sign.

A visual configuration is seen at different distances (far, middle, close). Its hierarchical order is influenced greatly by this shift in the viewing experience. Attention to visual hierarchy and its perceptual framework is central to those graphic media (signage, posters, and exhibitions) where the viewing experience is in constant flux (Fig. 251).

Typography's hierarchical order of elaboration and joinery derives from the basic process of pattern forming found in nature, in verbal and written language, the arts, and computer technology. This is aptly described by György Doczi, speaking of his research on proportional harmonies in art and design: "The rhythms of writing are created by the same pattern-forming process of sharing that creates rhythms of dance, music, and speech. Movements shared make dance; patterns shared make music and speech."

In summary, the shared patterns of typography find expression through visual dynamics, which enable it to function as both a message carrier and a rhythmic, visual structure. The typographic message, with all its limitless thought and diversity of form, is shaped by this subtle and meaningful hierarchical language.

246.
The word *sassafras* calls for a response and the phrase *a flavoring agent* provides the reply. (Designer: Ivy Li)
247.
In these typographic exercises, rules and space intervals are used as visual punctuation. (Designers: Bryan Leister and Rebecca Lantz)

ABC abc *abc* abc

250.
As typographic joinery becomes more developed, the
unity of a mark is enhanced
dramatically. (ABC logo,
Designer: Paul Rand)

248.

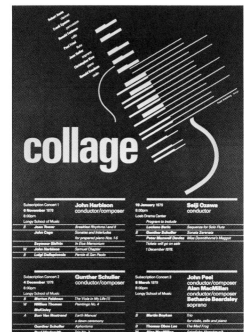

249.

248.
In this poster, a complex system of rules separate, connect,
and emphasize the names of
composers and conductors,
and other information about
numerous events. In the top
area of the poster, rules perform a different function; they
combine to create a rhythmic
visual sign for music.
(Designer: Frank Armstrong)

249.
Visual accentuation is demonstrated by this symbol. Striking
visual contrast is achieved
through the opposition of geometric and organic form.
(Designer: Nick Schrenk)

251.
In this signage for NASA, viewing context determines the
visual hierarchy. For example,
the size and position of the
arrow in the interior direction-
al signage is quite different
from its size and position on
the roadside signage. (Designer: Danne and Blackburn)

Typographic space

252.
Spatial elements are balanced in relationship to one another through the principle of compensation. Each element corresponds to one or more additional elements suggesting a balanced tension. Smaller elements are attracted to larger ones. Tension also exists between the edge of the composition and adjacent elements. These basic forces affect typographic organization and are a means to dynamic asymmetrical composition. (Designer: Jean Brueggenjohann)

"Speech proceeds in time and writing proceeds in space." Applying Karl Gerstner's statement to typographic design, typographic space is the rhythmic and dimensional field in which typographic communication exists. This space consists of positive form and void (the spatial ground); it establishes a cohesive typographic arrangement. Unity is achieved through the principle of visual compensation; that is, the spatial balance and integration of typographic elements. For Amos Chang, discussing the relationship between compensation and visual dynamics, "this process of growth from deficiency to compensation brings inherent movement to physical form... we may borrow an important rule of balance from the anatomy of a zoological being, man in particular ...man's body is in a state of balance when his arms and legs are in a position to be moved effectively to compensate for position changes of the body."

Visual compensation is expressed through implied movement and a pronounced equilibrium. A fully integrated typographic space is one in which all contrasting elements compensate each other (Figs. 252–54). In Figure 255, typographic dissonance and consonance are compensated by the contrast of visual dynamics. The letterform construction *gv* suggests expansion and dissonance, while *fj* suggests contraction and consonance. This is another example of the question-and-answer relationships discussed earlier. In Figure 256, movement is perceived as dynamic, yet the duality of consonance and dissonance is in a state of visual balance and unity.

253.
Pictorial and typographic forms combine to produce a balanced equilibrium. The placement of the two pointed arches balances the three rounded arches, and the ruled line moving into the margin corresponds to the letter-spaced word, *Messiah*.

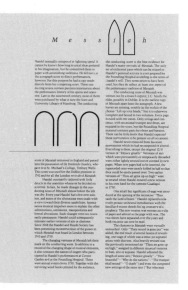

This dynamic poster combines both large three-dimensional letterforms and a complex arrangement of two-dimensional elements. From the arrangement emerges a spatial wholeness: the overlapping of elements is precise and expressive. Compensation is achieved through the articulate placement of all elements, with particular attention given to the surrounding void. (Designer: Frank Armstrong)

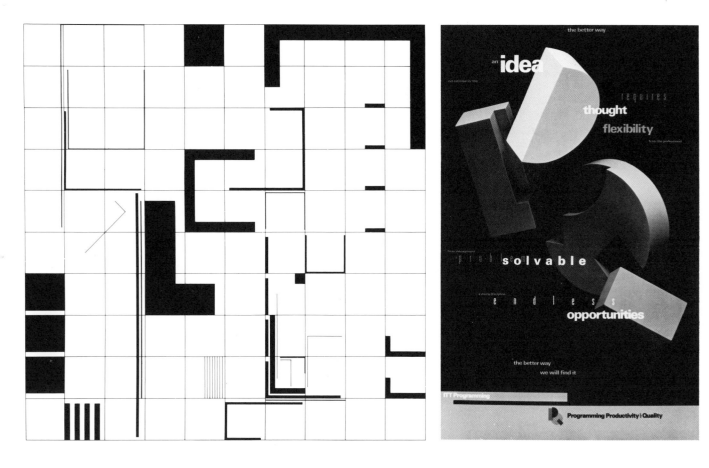

256.

The contrast between geometric and gestural letterforms is dissonant. Unity is achieved by the carefully planned shape correspondences and form-to-void relationships.

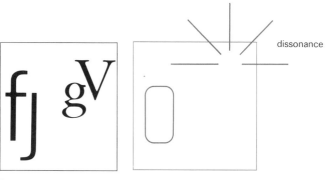

255.
(Designer: Lark Pfleegor)

257.
(Designer: Jennifer Mugford Wieland)

258.
In this asymmetrically balanced composition, the edge of the type column corresponds to the central axis of the circle.
(Designer: Sergio de Jesus)

Structurally, typographic space is defined by form and void relationships that determine a composition's underlying spatial order. This substructure is developed and enhanced through optical adjustment (Figures 257–61). Often inconspicuous, optical adjustment is the precise visual alignment of typographic elements in space. The designer's understanding and use of optical adjustment is necessary for visual clarity.

Visual compensation and optical adjustment within the typographic space link printed elements and the spatial ground. This structural integration is not an end in itself; its order, simple or elaborate, acts as a stimulus, controlling the visual dynamics of message transmission and response.

Nathan Knobler's observation in *The Visual Dialogue* that "psychologists tell us the need to understand, to find meaning in the world about us, is coupled with a need for stimulation and involvement" applies to design. To communicate with clarity and exactitude, the designer must be aware of the need to stimulate and involve the viewer. In typographic problem solving, the designer creates complex, highly interactive spatial environments that establish coherence between the viewing experience and typographic form, between the verbal statement and written language.

259.
Typographic elements are aligned with the horizontal and vertical edges of the geometric configuration.

260.
In this contents page, alignments—including an optical adjustment of the left point of the photograph—bring unity to the space. (Designer: Debra Thompson)

261.
In this catalog cover, richly textured elements are precisely adjusted to each other, combining both symmetrical and asymmetrical alignments. (Designer: Wolfgang Weingart)

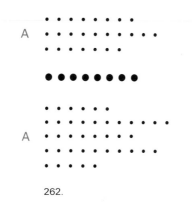

262.

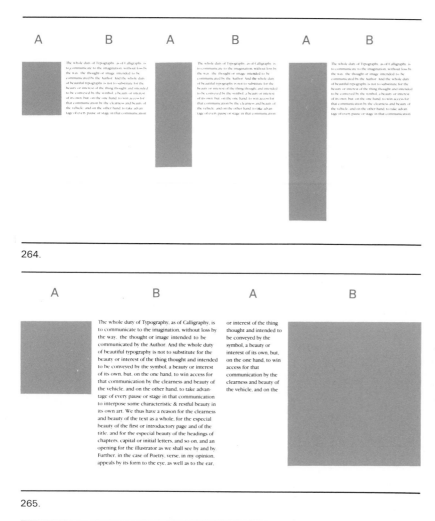

264.

265.

Visual relationships exist within an observable framework of repetition and contrast. In typographic communication, this framework provides a method for interpreting visual form. It is through the principles of repetition and contrast that the typographic designer creates visual order.

Musical structure follows the same pattern of repetition and contrast, defined as the three-part form of statement-departure-return (ABA). The unifying components (the two *A*s) function as repetition, while the middle component (the *B*) functions as contrast. Arnold Schoenberg observed that "the principal function of form is to advance our understanding. It is the organization of a piece which helps the listener to keep the idea in mind, to follow its development, its growth, its elaboration, its fate." The same is true in typographic communication, where the ABA form, a visual relationship expressing the connection of typographic elements, is clearly apparent in principles of elaboration, compensation, and joinery. ABA form provides a working plan for the typographic designer; it defines both the large-scale structures and the details. Speaking on this organization in music, Joseph Machlis stated, "the forms…are not fixed molds into which the composer pours his material. What gives a piece of music its aliveness is the fact that it adapts a general plan to its own requirements." Similarly, typographic design must be an organic unity in which a given visual order (ABA form) is sensitively manipulated to enhance content.

A	B	A
The whole duty of Typography, as of Calligraphy, is to communicate to the imagination, without loss by the way, the thought or image intended to be	Old Style Of all the achievements of the human mind, the birth of the alphabet is the most momentous. "Letters, like men, have now an ancestry, and the ancestry of words, as of men, is often a very noble possession, making them capable of great things": indeed, it has been said that the invention of writing is more important that all the victories ever won or constitutions devised by man. The history of writing is, in a way, the history of the human race, since in it are bound up, severally and together, the development of thought, of expression, of art, of intercommunication, and of mechanical invention. When and to whom in the dim past the idea came	Garamond selected from the confused mass of picture ideographs, phonograms, and their like, which constituted the first methods of representing human speech, we have no certain means of knowing. But whatever the source, the development did come; and we must deal with it. To present briefly the early history of the alphabet requires that much

266.

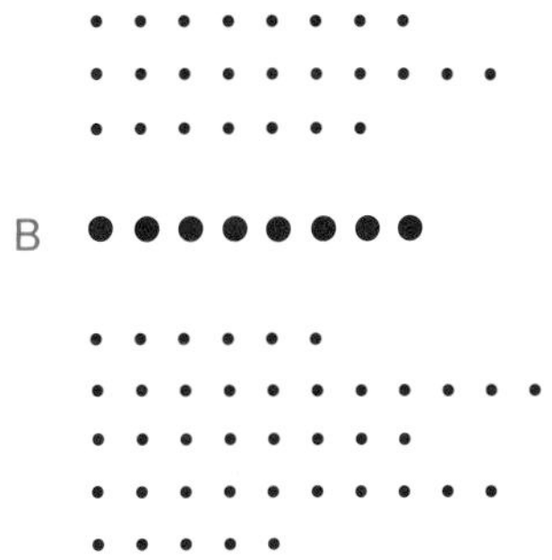

263.

ABA form	the reassuring visual accent achieved by repetition (A + A) and contrast (B)
	Repetition the process of repeating a typographic element (Fig. 262)
	Contrast to set a typographic element in opposition (Fig. 263)
ABA variations	can be conjunctive and stress connections and associations (Fig. 264)
ABA variations	can be disjunctive and stress variety and change (Fig. 265)
ABA form	a structural order governed by principles of proportion and rhythm
	Proportion the relation in magnitude, quantity, or degree of one typographic element to another (A A B A A B A A)
	Rhythm the movement marked by recurrence of strong and weak pulsations (Fig. 266)
ABA form	the functional linking between individual typographic elements and the whole through positioning and demands of the message (Fig. 267)

Bass

Thomas Coleman
Anthony Beadle

Flute

Elinor Preble

Oboe

Peggy Pearson
Raymond Toubman

Clarinet

William Wrzesien
Andre Lizotte

A

S Y M P H O N Y

H A L L

B

Bassoon

Francis Nizzari
Ronald Haroutunian

French Horn

Oaneka Oaujub
Jean Rife

A

267.

A   B   a

268.

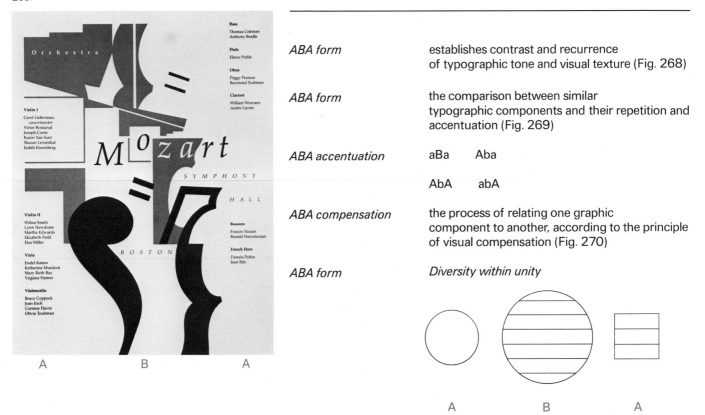

A   B   A

ABA form — establishes contrast and recurrence of typographic tone and visual texture (Fig. 268)

ABA form — the comparison between similar typographic components and their repetition and accentuation (Fig. 269)

ABA accentuation — aBa   Aba

AbA   abA

ABA compensation — the process of relating one graphic component to another, according to the principle of visual compensation (Fig. 270)

ABA form — *Diversity within unity*

A   B   A

A   B   A

ABA elaboration   a b a   a b a c

(Fig. 271)

ABA joinery   A

B

A

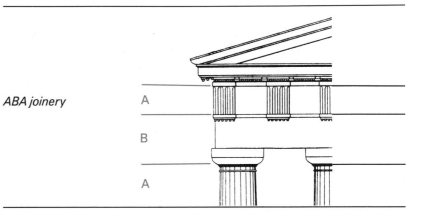

**Of all the achievements of the human mind,
the birth of the alphabet is the most momentous.**

B

Aa Bb Cc Dd Ee Ff Gg Hh Ii Jj Kk Ll Mm
Nn Oo Pp Qq Rr Ss Tt Uu Vv Ww Xx Yy Zz

A

"**Letters,** like men, have now an ancestry, and the
ancestry of words, as of men, is often a very noble possession,
making them capable of great things."

270.

269.

The viewer of typographic communication perceives form relationships as being either in opposition or correspondence. This principle suggests
that a fully integrated typographic composition
depends upon the successful blending of elements
of contrast and repetition. The viewer seeks a
variety that stimulates both eye and mind, while
structuring the communications experience. This
is the dual basis of ABA form.

As we stated earlier, the viewer responds not only
to elements of contrast and repetition, but also to
the particular way in which they are combined
through principles of compensation, elaboration,
and joinery. This organic unity can enhance typographic form, expand its meaning, and help clarify
its purpose.

ABA form is comprised of both simple and complex patterns that give order and emphasis to the
visual linking of typographic elements. These are
not fixed systems but are a way of understanding
the interrelationships of typographic form.

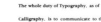

271.

65

The typographic grid

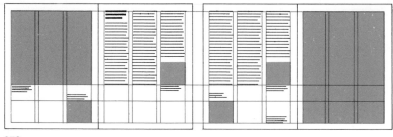

273.

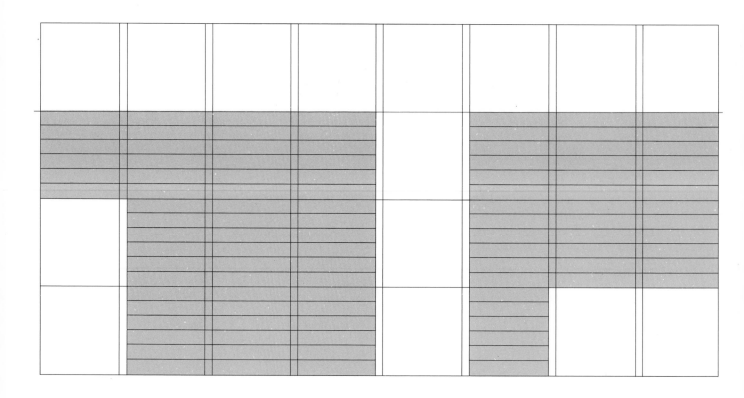

272.
A diagram of a thirty-two-unit grid, including a flow line, placed one unit from the top edge. The alignment of columns along this flow line is constant, in contrast to the column depths, which vary. The variation from left- to right-hand page results in an accentuated rhythm. The unoccupied units function not simply as leftover space, but as part of the geometry of the page.

274.
In this booklet format, typographic form and pictorial images are juxtaposed according to a predetermined grid. (Designer: Danne and Blackburn, for NASA)

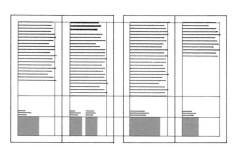

274.

273.
A three-column grid enables the designer to combine one-, two-, and three-column elements into a balanced arrangement. Note the horizontal flow line. (Designer: Danne and Blackburn, for NASA)

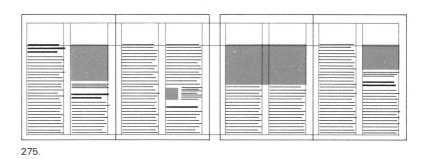

275.

While ABA form is characterized by the repetition and contrast of typographic elements, in the typographic grid there is a purposeful regularity in the division of space. ABA structures govern the relationship of parts one to another; the grid determines their ordered locations on the printed page.

A clear example of spatial division based on a grid is found in the repetition of columns and their intervals (Fig. 272). The column width is dominant, the spatial interval subordinate. The depth, clustering, and number of columns also create a desirable tension between form and void. A grid makes it possible for a system of relationships to be established among many visual components: typography, pictorial images, and spatial intervals (Fig. 273). Grids describe horizontal, vertical, and diagonal divisions of space which, whether dominant or subordinate, should be carefully planned.

Typographic grids control the visual organization of the page through grid modulation, the development of spatial divisions determined by a grid unit or module (Fig. 274). This organization is achieved through an orderly combination of related parts that support and enclose printed matter. Establishing primary and secondary divisions of space defines limits and boundaries.

Grids allow for the distribution of typographic elements into a clearly intelligible order. Within the internal structure created, headlines, text, and captions are integrated (Fig. 275). The area occupied by each element corresponds to a specific area within the grid. Figure 275 shows the flexibility that is possible when the basic module is transformed into others of larger or smaller size.

A grid ratio is a mathematical relationship between two or more grid measurements. These ratios are perceived visually. The ratio X:2X (one unit to two units) indicates the relative size of grid dimensions (Fig. 276). This stepped progression of X:2X establishes an underlying modular system among the parts.

The layout in Figure 277 displays various typographic configurations within a grid organization. These grid relationships are deliberately arranged so as to be neither static nor unstable. A wide range of dynamic and subtle possibilities are demonstrated. Grid constraints are not restrictions; rather, they are stimuli for an organic spatial unity.

Typographic grids act as a common denominator into which any detailed scheme or program can be placed. They are composed of coordinates that determine the proportional relationships of elements to the page, bringing order to the distribution of printed information.

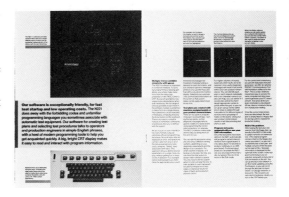

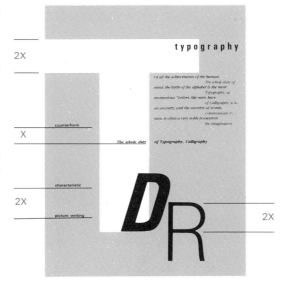

275.
The grid can be subdivided, as for the one-third-column-wide photograph, or extended, as for the two-column-wide photograph. (Designer: Danne and Blackburn, for NASA)

277.
Typographic and photographic components are characterized by a rhythmic tension. The division of space achieves balance and visual impact but never at the expense of the functional clarity of the text. (Designer: John Kane)

276.
This exploratory composition exhibits the modular relationships among elements. (Designer: Debra Thompson)

ping pong
ping pong ping
pong ping pong
ping pong

The typographic message is verbal, visual, and vocal. While typography is read and interpreted verbally, it may also be viewed and interpreted visually, heard and interpreted audibly. It is a dynamic communication medium. In this sense, early twentieth-century typography became a revolutionary form of communication, bringing new expressive power to the written word.
Consider the concrete poem "ping pong" (Fig. 278). The geometric structure of this poem is composed of a repetition of the words *ping* and *pong*. As these words are repeated, they signify the sound of a bouncing ping-pong ball, and the circular letters *p, o,* and *g* reflect the shape of the ball. The full impact of this poem is achieved when it is read aloud. By hearing the sounds and viewing the typographic forms, the typographic message is strengthened.

Significant departures from the use of conventional typographic forms occurred in Europe at the beginning of the twentieth century. During this activist period, experimentation in all the visual and performing arts was affected by potent social and philosophical changes, industrial and technological developments, and new attitudes about aesthetics and modern civilization. Typographic design was pulled into this artistic revolution as poets and visual artists realized that both meaning and form could be intensified in typographic communications.

The Futurist manifesto, written by the Italian poet Filippo Marinetti in 1909, profoundly influenced thinking in Europe and Russia. Futurism praised technology, violence, danger, movement, and speed. Futurist typography, known as "free typography," demonstrated these ideas in a highly expressive manner (Fig. 279 and see Figure 125). The chill of a scream was expressed in bold type, and quick impressions were intensified through italics. Letters and words raced across the page in dynamic motion.

Among the movements affected by Futurism were Dadaism in France, Switzerland, and Germany; de Stijl in Holland; and Constructivism in Russia. Each of these historical movements has had a penetrating effect upon typography. Artists and designers associated with these movements saw typography as a powerful means of conveying information relating to the realities of industrialized society (Figs. 280–82; also see Figures 129–35). They disdained what typography had become: a decorative art form far removed from the realities of the time. The architect Otto Wagner further emphasized that "all modern forms must be in harmony with the new requirements of our time. Nothing that is not practical can be beautiful." Written in 1920, the second de Stijl manifesto clearly demonstrated the concern for a new, expressive typography (Fig. 283). With dramatic changes taking place in the form and content of typography, the typographic message became a multifaceted and expressive form of communication. Typography needs to be read, seen, heard, felt, and experienced.

278.
"ping pong" (Poet: Eugen Gomringer)
281.
Title lettering for *De Stijl.* (Designer: Theo van Doesburg)

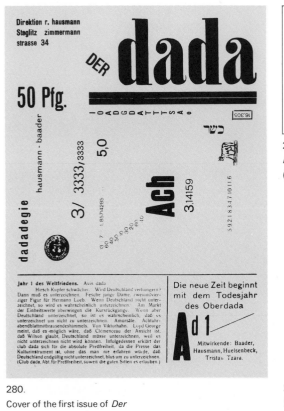

280.
Cover of the first issue of *Der Dada.* (Editor: Raoul Hausmann)

279.
Les mots en liberte futuristes. (Designer: Filippo Marinetti)

282.
Constructivist cover design for *Veshch, Gegenstand, Objet.* (Designer: El Lissitzky)

THE WORD IS DEAD...
THE WORD IS IMPOTENT
asthmatic and sentimental poetry
the "me" and "it"
       which is still in common use
       everywhere...
is influenced by an individualism fearful of space
       the dregs of an exhausted era...

psychological analysis
and clumsy rhetoric
have KILLED THE MEANING OF THE WORD...

the word must be reconstructed
       to follow the SOUND as well as
       the IDEA
if in the old poetry
       by the dominance of relative and
       subjective feelings
the intrinsic meaning of the word is destroyed
we want by all possible means
       syntax
       prosody
       typography
       arithmetic
       orthography
to give new meaning to the word and new force
to expression

the duality between prose and poetry can no longer
be maintained
the duality between form and content can no longer
be maintained
Thus for the modern writer form will have a directly
spiritual meaning
it will not describe events
it will not *describe* at all
but ENSCRIBE
it will recreate in the word the common meaning of
events
a constructive unity of form and content...

Leiden, Holland, April 1920.

     Theo van Doesburg
     Piet Mondrian
     Anthony Kok

As a dynamic representation of verbal language, typography must communicate. This functional role is fulfilled when the receiver of a typographic message clearly and accurately understands what is in the mind of the transmitter. This objective, however, is not always accomplished. With a proliferation of typographic messages littering the environment, most are missed or ignored. The messages that are noted, possessing effective qualities relating to form and content, are appropriate to the needs of both message transmitter and message receiver.

The impact of an effective typographic message cannot be easily measured. Some may assume that since printed and broadcast messages are ephemeral, they have little impact upon their audience. This assumption is false. Because typographic ephemera are rhetorical, they often have a long-range effect upon a message receiver, influencing change within the context of social, political, and economic events. The symbol of solidarity expressed by Polish workers (Fig. 284), the social statements made with graffiti in urban environments, and the typography on billboards aimed at passing motorists all operate as purposeful messages directed toward a predetermined audience within a specific context.

Effective typographic messages result from the combination of logic and intuitive judgment. Only the neophyte approaches this process in a strictly intuitive manner; a purely logical or mechanical procedure undermines human expression. Keeping these two extremes in balance requires the use of a functional verbal-visual vocabulary capable of addressing a broad spectrum of typographic communication.

283.
De Stijl manifesto of 1917.

to scrape   to crease   to peel   to melt   to splinter

Verbal/visual equations

Language, in any of its many forms, is a self-contained system of interactive signs that communicate ideas. Just as elocution and diction enhance and clarify the meaning of our spoken words, typographic signs can be manipulated by a designer to achieve more lucid and expressive typographic communication.

Signs operate in two dimensions: syntactic and semantic. When the mind is concerned with the form of a sign, it is involved with typographic syntax. When it associates a particular meaning with a sign, it is operating in the semantic dimension.

All objects in the environment can potentially function as signs, representing any number of concepts. A smog-filled city signifying pollution, a beached whale representing extinction, and confetti implying celebration (see Figure 181), each functions as a sign relating a specific concept.

Signs may exist at various levels of abstraction. A simple example will illustrate this point. Let us consider something as elemental as a red dot. It is a sign only if it carries a particular meaning. It can represent any number of things: balloon, ball, or Japanese flag. The red dot becomes a cherry, for example, as the mind is cued by forms more familiar to its experience (Fig. 285).

The particular syntactic qualities associated with typographic signs determine a specific meaning. A series of repeated letters, for example, may signify motion or speed, while a small letter in a large void may signify isolation. These qualities, derived from the operating principles of visual hierarchy and ABA form, function as cues, permitting the mind to form concepts. Simple syntactic manipulations, such as the repetition of letters, or the weight change of certain letters, enable words visually to mimic verbal meaning (Fig. 286). In another example, the letter *E* has been visually altered, relating it to the meaning of specific descriptive words (Fig. 287).

285.
Signs exist at various levels of abstraction. A form is a sign, however, only when it carries a message. As the mind is cued by forms familiar to experience, information is conveyed.
286.
Simple syntactic manipulations are controlled by such factors as repetition, size change, position change, or weight change. These enable words to mimic verbal meaning visually.
287.
These elaborations of the letter *E* express a variety of concepts. (Designers: Carol Anthony, Linda Dronenburg, and Rebecca Sponga.)

leav e

in ter val

diet

ststutter

dro p

286.

285.

288.
Typographic signs combine to form a more complex sign, suggesting a decorated Christmas tree. (Designer: Donna Funk)

In language, signs are joined together to create messages. Words as verbal signs, grouped together in a linear fashion, attain their value vis-à-vis other words through opposition and contrast. Words can also evoke meaning through mental association. These associative relations are semantically derived. Since typography is both visual and verbal, it operates in a linear fashion, with words following each other in a specific sequence, or in a nonlinear manner, with elements existing in many syntactic combinations. For example, in the visual poem "O Christmas Tree," the choice of the typeface, Futura Light, is very important. The capital letter *O* is a perfect circle, signifying ornaments; the linear strokes of other letterforms suggest the texture of evergreen needles (Fig. 288). This typographic message is derived from the mental associations formed by contrasting typographic signs.

Two terms important to the understanding of signs are denotation and connotation. When considering the meaning of typographic signs, denotation refers to objective meaning, the factual world of collective awareness and experience. For example, a denotative interpretation of a yellow *O* would be: "This is a yellow letter *O*" or "This is a yellow circle." Connotative interpretations of the yellow *O* might be: "This is the sun, a slice of lemon, or a golden ring." Connotative observations are often conditioned, for they relate to overtones and are drawn from prior personal experience.

Typographic signs are both verbal and visual. The associations formed between the verbal and visual attributes are verbal/visual equivalencies, which are found in a variety of configurations. These reveal the associative nature of signs composing the typographic message and help us to further understand its multifaceted attributes. Figures 289–301 illustrate the nature of some of these verbal/visual equations.

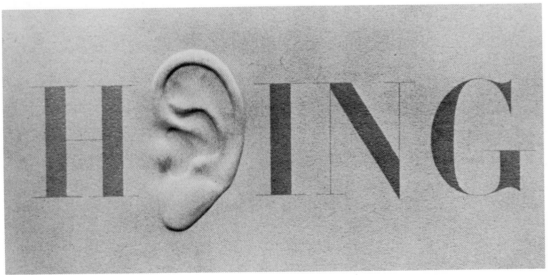

289.
Visual substitution: The visual sign of an ear is substituted for the letters *E*, *A*, and *R*. (Designer: Lou Dorfsman)

291.
Simultaneity: The numeral *8* functions as the letter *g* in this logotype used for a group exhibition of paintings by the early twentieth-century American art group, The Eight.

Eight

292.
Visual transformation: A mother, father, and child are suggested through the visual transformation of the letters *I* and *i*. (Designer: Herb Lubalin)

Families

Taking
Things
Apart
and
Putting
Things
Together

what chemistry is
what chemists do
and what the results
have been

sponsored by the
American Chemical
Society
on the occasion
of its 100th
anniversary

Union Carbide
270 Park Ave.
New York, N.Y. 10017

April 5-May 28, 1976
9:30-4:30 weekdays
Closed April 16,17
and Sundays
Admission: free

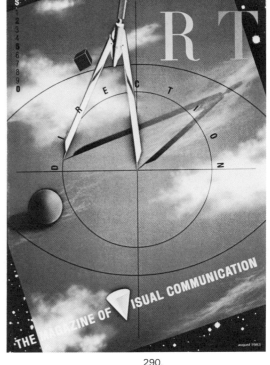

290.
Visual substitution: The visual sign of a compass is substituted for the letter *A* and an inverted cone is substituted for the letter *V.* (Designer: Harold Burch)

293.
Visual exaggeration: the irregular syntactic treatment of typographic signs exaggerates the process of taking things apart and putting things together. (Designer: Steff Geissbuhler)

the American premiere at the Depot in Urbana
of the play by Marcel Achard

translated by Sue Huseman Moretto
directed by Jose Moretto

October 31, November 1, 2, 3 1974
November 7, 8, 9, 10
at 8:00 pm, Friday and Saturday also at 10:30 pm

tickets at Record Service
704 South Sixth Champaign
and at the Depot 223 North Broadw
on nights of performance

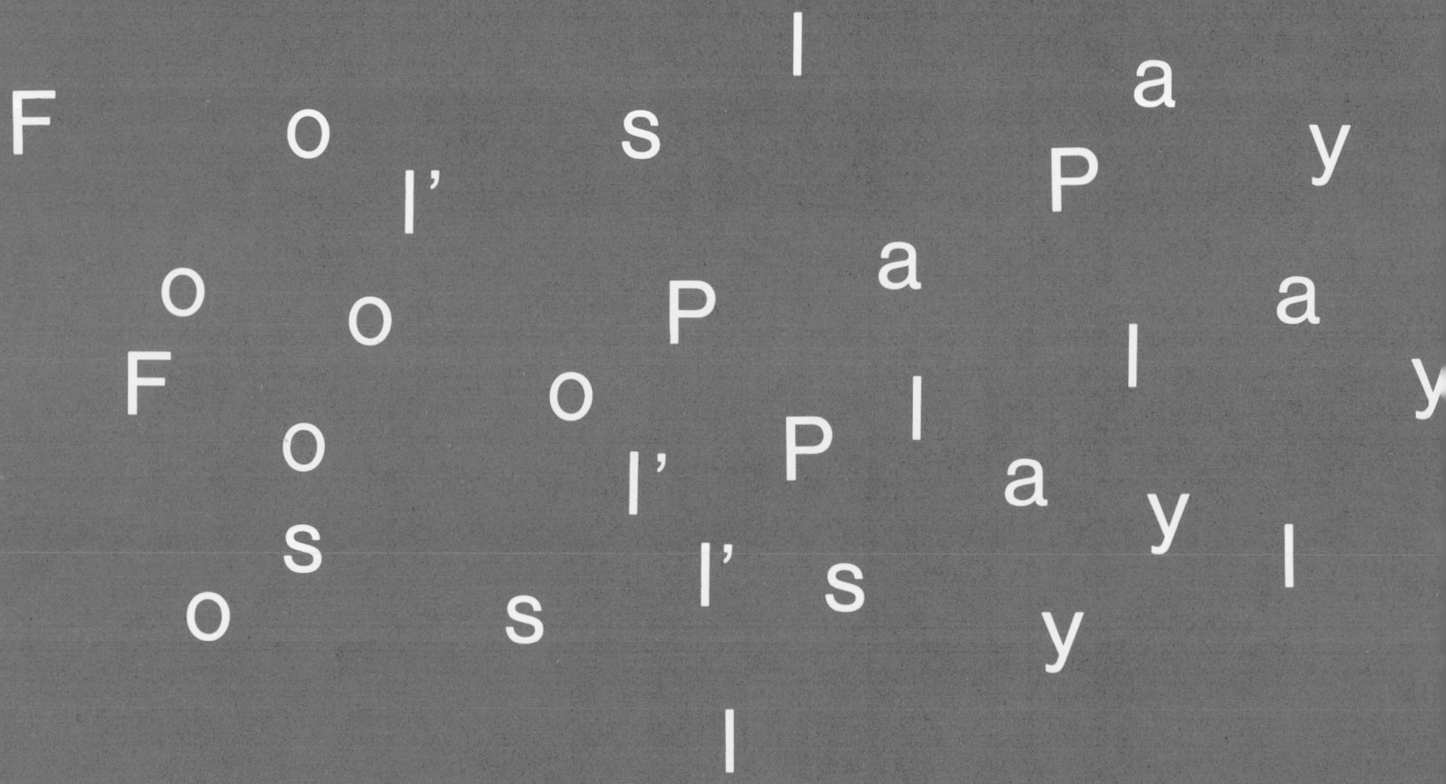

Fools Play

Fool's Play

Fool's Play

Fool's Play

295.
Form combination: Visual and verbal signs are combined into a single typographic statement, creating trademarks that suggest the nature of various industries: an electrical contractor, a maker of plastic fibers for carpets and draperies, and a lithographic printer. (Designer: Don Weller)

296.
Form combination: Verbal signs are combined with visual signs (cables). The resulting forms suggest the qualities of cable transmission. (Designers: Jerry L. Kuyper and Sheila de Bretteville)

297.
Parallel form: The Olivetti logotype and electronic calculator have similar visual characteristics which parallel each other. (Logotype design: Walter Ballmer)

298.
Verbal/visual correspondence: The syntactic qualities of this typographic sign correspond to the graffiti found in an urban environment. (Designer: Jeff Barnes)

299.
Verbal/visual correspondence: The visual characteristics of this typographic sign correspond to the form of a zipper. This is achieved by a repetition of letters and a horizontal shift within the word. (Designer: Richard Rumble)

296.

olivetti

297.

298.

city

294.
Visual exaggeration: The repetition and playful treatment of typographic forms effectively reinforces the content of the drama *Fool's Play,* for which this poster was designed. (Designer: David Colley)

ZIIIIIIIIIIIIPPPER

299.

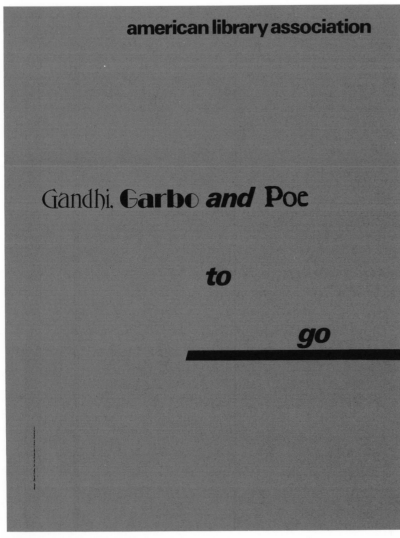

american library association

Gandhi. **Garbo** *and* Poe

to

go

300.

301.

300.
Verbal/visual correspondence:
The visual qualities of the typefaces chosen for the signs
Gandhi, Garbo, and *Poe* make
direct reference to time and
culture. The message is further
strengthened by the sounds
associated with the words.
(Designer: David Colley)
301.
Verbal/visual correspondence:
The visual repetition of this
word — unified by the shared
letters *u* and *n* — express the
concept of unity. (Designer:
Steff Geissbuhler)

Function and expression

Functionalism is a design term that has commonly been used to describe the utilitarian and pragmatic qualities inherent in designed objects. During the twentieth century, functionalism has generally been equated with purposeful, unornamented simplicity; however, functionalism is a subjective term that varies according to the needs of a user.

For example, if comfort in the design of a chair is defined as a soothing softness, an upholstered, automatic recliner, complete with footrest and vibrator, would exemplify a comfortable, functional chair.

In contrast to the automatic recliner is the red/blue chair, designed by Gerrit Rietveld in 1918, which is a central artifact of the de Stijl movement. This movement sought a restrained expression of universal harmony, and the creation of a new philosophy for living (Fig. 302). At first glance, the red/blue chair's hard, flat surfaces would seem to be very uncomfortable. This common reaction, however, is uninformed. Rietveld intended for his chair to promote alert mental activity through firm support. The seat and backrest planes are attached at only one edge; therefore, the naturally pliable wood adjusts to the user's weight. In this regard, the chair functions according to Rietveld's intentions. In an interior environment, Rietveld's red/blue chair has the presence and visual harmony of a piece of sculpture. The needs for a functional object (seating) *and* for aesthetic experience are fulfilled by this one piece.

In typography, function is the purposeful communication of information to a specific audience. Although the range of possible typographic-design solutions is infinite, the appropriateness of a solution always depends upon the purpose for which it was intended. Varying degrees of formal reduction or elaboration can be effective when solving specific typographic-design problems.

302.
Red/blue chair, 1918.
(Designer: Gerrit Rietveld)

305.
An announcement for a retro-spective exhibition of record album design has been influ-enced by Russian Constructiv-ism. A playful integration of horizontal and vertical typo-graphic elements contrasts with circular forms suggesting records. (Designer: Paula Scher)

304.
A vocabulary of functional typography is used in an ex-pressive and experimental manner to communicate the content of the typographic journal *Typografische Monatsblatter.* (Designer: Willi Kunz)

Formal reduction can be used to create optimum clarity and legibility, presenting complex informa-tion, such as news or scientific data, in a clear and straightforward manner. Orderly presentation guides the eye from one part to another, without a loss of interest in content (Figs. 303 and 304).

Another approach accomplishes its purpose through formal elaboration, creating visual impact. When appropriate, attention can be given to ex-perimental, expressive, and ornamental forms, in addition to verbal considerations. Ornament serves a variety of practical needs. Because it is semiotic, iconographic, and historical, it identifies the ob-ject with which it is associated. Ornament can place an object in time, reveal its purpose, and clarify its structure (Figs. 305–307). The formal elaboration of objects in architecture, industrial design, and the fine arts can significantly influence typographic development. Figures 71, 119, 180, and 308–10 possess strong ornamental qualities. Innovative typography can emerge when a de-signer fully understands communication needs and is able to assimilate a diversity of visual ideas.

On this subject, Ladislav Sutnar commented that "an eccentric visual scandal or visual shock of the outrageous and of the unexpected can catch the attention of the astonished eye…it may also de-light the eye to see a fresh design concept or a message so orderly presented as to make com-prehension fast and easy." A designer can avoid conventional solutions to typographic problems when innovation is appropriate. A single ap-proach to typographical design, induced by stylistic convention and predetermined formulas, is a routine activity lacking the vitality of meaningful typographic invention. Sound principles and a trained vision should supersede dependency upon preconceived formulas. For typography to be truly functional, satisfying the needs of an audience, a designer must understand both the verbal and the visual attributes of a typographic message.

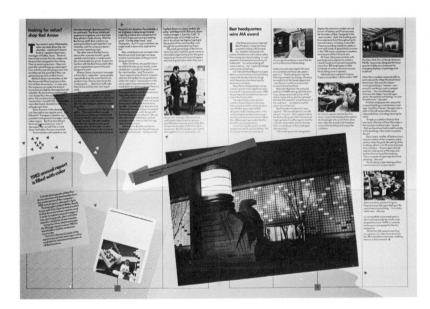

306.
Best Times, a Best Products employee publication, com-municates about corporate activities. Visual richness and reader interest are achieved through the use of abstract forms and color, photography, and typographic variety.

303.
The *Minneapolis Tribune* is an example of a functional news-paper design having legibility and clarity. All typographic elements conform to a well-defined grid, and a specific visual hierarchy determines the importance of each story. (De-sign director: Michael Carroll)

303.

TM
SGM
RSI

Typografische Monatsblätter
Schweizer Grafische Mitteilungen
Revue Suisse de l'Imprimerie

Nr. 2 3 4 5 6

309.
The Best Products corporate
headquarters makes a strong
decorative statement while
providing a functional work
environment. (Architect: Hardy
Holzman Pfeiffer Associates)

307.
A diversity of shape, tone, and
texture in this exhibition poster
parallels the range of visual art
on display. (Designer:
Wolfgang Weingart)
310.
The ornament of this late
nineteenth-century French
maquetry cabinet expresses
the spirit of its time.
(Designer: Eugene Gaillard)

308.
Lively geometric form and pattern characterize this folding
screen. (Designer: Daniel
Friedman)

4　Legibility

Typographic legibility is widely misunderstood and often neglected by designers. Yet it is a subject that requires careful study, and constant evaluation. Legibility represents those qualities and attributes inherent in typography that make type readable. These attributes make it possible for a reader to comprehend written forms with the least amount of difficulty.

Typographers and designers have a responsibility to communicate as clearly and appropriately as possible. This responsibility is suggested by Henry David Thoreau in *Walden:* "A written word is the choicest of relics. It is something at once more intimate with us and more universal than any other work of art."

aaddd d

As signs representing sounds in spoken language, letters are basic to legible typography. The primary purpose of a letterform is to convey a recognizable meaning to the mind. Therefore, letterforms must be designed with clarity, each being distinct within the alphabet. The contrast among individual characters makes it possible for the reader to decipher written information without confusion.

The most legible typefaces are those timeless examples characterized by three qualities upon which legibility is dependent: contrast, simplicity, and proportion. These typefaces exemplify beautiful and functional letterforms. A close look at typefaces such as Garamond, Baskerville, and Bodoni will reveal why their forms are as vital now as when they were first designed. (See the type specimens in chapter eight.) The use of well-designed typefaces, however, is no guarantee that typography will be legible. Effective typography depends upon such factors as the communications context and the subtle adjustment of letterforms and their spatial relationships, each of which may have an effect upon how easily typography is read. Making type legible is a masterful achievement, requiring a process of intelligent decision making.

In the strictest sense, legible typography is a means of communicating information objectively. However, typographic designers sometimes bend the traditional criteria of legibility for expressive purposes. Designers, with their instinctive curiosity, have experimented with typography, playing with forms, imposing new meaning, and changing the standards of typographic communication. Innovative typography always poses fresh questions, challenges edicts of the past, and redefines the concepts of legibility and functionality.

This chapter approaches legibility as an art of spatial synthesis. As an art, it is not absolute. Therefore, information derived from legibility research should be considered only a guideline. The knowledge designers have of legibility is based upon a legacy of typographic history and a keen awareness of the visible world. This knowledge will continually evolve, creating new standards for readability and functional typography.

Distinguishing characteristics of letters
The alphabet consists of twenty-six letters, each of which has evolved over the centuries to a unique place within this system of signs. This evolution has occurred gradually. It is no accident that the individual shapes of letterforms have developed out of a need to improve the communication process. As the alphabet has evolved, it has become a flexible system of signs in which all letters are distinct, yet all work together harmoniously as visible language.

In spite of the innumerable variations of size, proportion, weight, and elaboration in letterform design, the basic structure of each letterform must remain the same. For example, the capital *A* always consists of two oblique strokes joined at the top and connected by a horizontal stroke at their midsection. Sufficient contrast must exist between the letters in a font so that they can be easily distinguished (Fig. 311).

il
acegos
bdfhjmnpqrtu
kvwxyz

EFHILT
COQS
BDGJPRU
AKMNVWXYZ

Letters can be clustered into four groups according to their contrasting properties. These are letterforms with strokes that are vertical, curved, a combination of vertical and curved, or oblique (Fig. 312). From these groupings, one notices that letters are not only similar in many ways but that there are also some important differences. Obviously, letters with similar characteristics are more likely to be confused, while letters with distinct qualities provide contrast within a word. Letters within a word are most legible when they are taken, in equal number, from each group.

A closer look at the alphabet reveals additional characteristics distinguishing letters. The upper halves of letters provide more visual cues for letter recognition than the lower halves (Fig. 313). Likewise, the right halves of letters are more recognizable than the left halves (Fig. 314). Dominant letters within the alphabet that aid in word recognition are those that have either ascenders or descenders. Through tests, researchers have contributed valuable information about the comparative legibility of each letter in the alphabet. Findings vary only slightly. Lowercase letters can be rank-ordered according to their distinctiveness as follows: *d k m g h b p w u l j t v z r o f n a x y e i q c s.* This varies, however, with different typefaces.

The most frequently used letters, such as the vowels *a e i o u,* are among the most illegible, and *c g s x* are easily missed in reading. Other letters that often cause confusion and are mistaken for one another are *f i j l t.* For example, the words *fail, tail,* and *jail* each begin with letters of similar shape and could easily be misread. The eye could possibly perceive *f* as *t,* or *t* as *j* (Fig. 315). The designer should carefully study the words in display typography to identify such potential problems in legibility.

fail
tail
jail

As with the changing position
of the dancer, subtle changes
in the drawing of the forms
and counterforms significantly
affect perception.

316.

317.

DANCER
DANCER
DANCER

G
DANCER
DANCER
G

shape

SHAPE

318.
Word recognition is based on
word structure, a combination
of word shape (defined by the
contours of the letters) and
internal word pattern. The
word set in lowercase letters
is more distinct than the word
set in all capitals, because its
irregular word shape makes it
more recognizable.

The perception of a letter is based upon the form/counterform relationship. Counterforms are as significant to legibility as the shapes of the letters themselves. This principle relates to all aspects of visual phenomena. A dancer manipulates space with the body, "making shape," defining, and re-defining space (Fig. 316). If the shape of a letter is changed, so is the way in which that letter is perceived. Letter shapes are cues that distinguish one letter in the alphabet from another (Fig. 317).

Much controversy has surrounded the issue of the comparative legibility of serif and sans serif typefaces. One argument claims that serif text type is more readable because the serifs reinforce the horizontal flow of each line. Serif typefaces also offer more character definition: for example, the serif on the bottom horizontal stroke of a capital *E* accentuates the difference between it and a capital *F*. However, the relative legibility between serif and sans serif typefaces is negligible. Reader familiarity and the control of other legibility factors (to be discussed later) are far more significant than the selection of a serif or sans serif typeface. (See the text-type specimens in chapter eight to compare the legibility of serif and sans serif type.)

The nature of words
While individual letters as discrete units, affecting all other spatial and aesthetic considerations, are the basis for a discussion of legibility, one reads and perceives words and groups of words and not just letters. In discussing typographic legibility, Frederic Goudy observed that "a letter may not be considered apart from its kinsmen; it is a mere abstract and arbitrary form far remote from the original picture or symbol out of which it grew, and has no particular significance until it is employed to form part of a word."

There are two important factors involved in the reading process: word shape and internal pattern. Words are identified by their distinctive word shapes, strings of letters that are instantaneously perceived, permitting the reader to grasp content easily (Fig. 318). Counterforms create internal word patterns that provide cues for word recognition. When these internal spaces are altered sufficiently, the perceptual clarity of a word may also

O R D W
R D W O
D W O R
R O W D
W O R D
O W R D
319.

be altered. The weight of letters is vital to word recognition and influences an adequate internal pattern. The combination of word shape and internal pattern creates a word structure, an all-inclusive term describing the unique composition of each word (Fig. 319).

Capital and lowercase letters

If a text is set entirely in capital letters, it suffers a loss of legibility and the reader is placed at a significant disadvantage. Type set in this manner severely retards reading—more so than any other legibility factor. Figure 318 demonstrates that a word set in all capital letters is characterized by a straight horizontal alignment, creating an even word outline with letters of similar shape and size. A reader is not provided with the necessary visual cues that make words recognizable.

TEXT SET IN ALL CAPITAL LETTERS ALSO USES A SIGNIFICANTLY GREATER AMOUNT OF SPACE THAN TEXT SET IN LOWERCASE LETTERS OF THE SAME SIZE. AS MUCH AS 35 PERCENT MORE SPACE CAN BE CONSUMED WHEN USING ALL CAPITAL LETTERS.

On the other hand, text set in lowercase letters forms words that are distinct, based upon their irregular word shape and internal pattern. A variety of letter shapes, ascenders, and descenders provides rich contrasts that assure satisfactory perception. Once a specific word shape is perceived, it is stored in the reader's memory until the eye confronts it again while reading. A reader can become confused if a word takes on an appearance that differs from the originally learned word shape.

Interletter and interword spacing

The spacing of letterforms has a significant impact on legibility. Most readers are unaware of the typographic designer's attention to this detail. Minute spatial relationships are controlled to create not only readable but beautiful and harmonious typographic communication. It takes great skill to specify spaces between letters and words, determining proper spatial relationships. Letters must flow rhythmically and gracefully into words, and words into lines.

Typographic texture and tone are affected by the spacing of letters, words, and lines. When the texture and the spatial intervals between typographic elements are consistent, the result is an easily readable text. Texture is also affected by qualities unique to the design of specific typefaces. Sometimes designers arrange type for specific spatial effects, sensitively balancing norms of legibility with graphic impact. (See the text-type specimens in chapter eight.)

Too much or too little space between letters and words destroys the normal texture intended by the typeface designer. As you read this sentence, notice that the narrow letter and word spacing causes words to merge together visually. L i k e w i s e , t h e v e r y w i d e l e t t e r s p a c i n g o f t h i s s e n t e n c e a l s o d i s r u p t s t h e r e a d i n g p r o c e s s .

There is often a danger of misfit letter combinations, which, in earlier typesetting systems, such as linotype, could not be easily corrected. (If the type size is small and evenly textured, this is a minor problem.) With phototypesetting and digital typesetting, these details can be corrected easily. The kerning of specific letter combinations can be programmed into the typesetting system. As type is set, appropriate letterspacing appears automatically (Fig. 320).

319.
Letters can be grouped in a myriad of combinations. Those which are perceived as having meaning are words with which we have become familiar over time. They form a distinct and familiar shape.

Reading is disrupted by inappropriate wordspacing.

SPACING

SPACING

320.
Misfit letter combinations and irregular spacing can be a problem, particularly for display type. Optical adjustments should be made to achieve spatial consistency between elements.

Edwardo Johnston,o ao calligrapher, advocatedo ao wordo spaceo equalo to ao lowercaseo o.

Aaronr Burns,r ar contemporary typographer,r suggestsr wordr spacing equalr tor ar lowercaser r.

Space between letters and words should be proportional to the width of letters. This proportion is often open to personal judgment (Fig. 321). With experience and practice comes an understanding of the spacing that is suitable to a particular design project.

Type size, line length, and interline spacing
Critical to spatial harmony and legibility is an understanding of the triadic relationship of type size, line length, and interline spacing. When properly employed, these variables can improve the legibility of even poorly designed letterforms or enhance the legibility of those forms considered highly legible.

It is difficult to generalize about which sizes of type should be used, how long lines should be, or how much space should be inserted between lines. These decisions are based upon comparative judgments. The guidelines discussed in this section can never replace the type designer's sensitively trained eye for typographic detail. The normal reading distance for most printed matter is from twelve to fourteen inches, a fact to be kept in mind when making decisions about type size, since it affects the way in which a specific type size is perceived.

Text type that is too small or too large makes reading difficult. Small type reduces visibility by destroying counterforms, which affect word recognition, while large type can force a reader to perceive type in sections rather than as a whole. According to legibility research, the most legible sizes of text type at normal reading distances range from 9- to 12-point. This range results from the wide variation of x-height in different typefaces, that is, when typefaces of the same point size are

placed side by side, they may appear to be different sizes, because their x-heights vary radically. This is important to keep in mind when selecting typefaces and sizes.

An interesting comparison is the relationship between Univers 55 and Baskerville. Univers 55 has a very large x-height, with short ascenders and descenders. It appears much larger than Baskerville set in the same size, which has a smaller x-height and large ascenders and descenders. (See text column specimens in chapter eight.)

Type sizes larger than 12-point may require more fixation pauses, making reading uncomfortable and inefficient. A fixation pause occurs when the eye stops on a line of type during reading, actually perceiving the meaning of groups of words. When there are fewer fixation pauses, there is greater reading efficiency and comprehension. When text type is smaller than 9-point, internal patterns can break down, destroying legibility. The reading audience is also a major consideration. For example, children learning to read need large type sizes in simple formats, as do adults with poor eyesight.

An appropriate line length is essential for achieving a pleasant reading rhythm, allowing a reader to relax and concentrate on the content of the words. Overly short or long lines will tire a reader. Excess energy is expended when reading long lines, and it is difficult to find the next line. A short column measure requires the eye to change lines too often, and there is an inadequate supply of horizontal perceptual cues. Compare the legibility of this paragraph with the legibility of Figures 322 and 323.

An appropriate line length is essential for achieving a pleasant reading rhythm, allowing a reader to relax and concentrate on the content of the words. Overly short or long lines will tire a reader. Excess energy is expended when reading long lines, and it is difficult to find the next line. A short column measure requires the eye to change lines too often, and there is an inadequate supply of horizontal perceptual cues.

An appropriate line length is essential for achieving a pleasant reading rhythm, allowing a reader to relax and concentrate on the content of the words. Overly short or long lines will tire a reader. Excess energy is expended when reading long lines, and it is difficult to find the next line. A short column measure requires the eye to change lines too often, and there is an inadequate supply of horizontal perceptual cues.

Interline
spacing
intervals

324.

Interline
spacing
intervals

Certainly, every typographic problem has its own legibility requirements. The following data can serve as a point of departure in determining how to create legible typography. Line length is dependent upon both the size of type and the amount of space between lines. When working with the optimum sizes of 9-, 10-, 11-, and 12-point text type, a maximum of ten to twelve words (or sixty to seventy characters) per line would be acceptable. This would equal a line length of approximately 18 to 24 picas. An optimum line length for the average 10-point type is 19 picas.

The amount of interline spacing is dependent upon several factors. Generally, lines with no added space between them are read more slowly than lines with added space. Proper interline spacing carries the eye naturally from one line to the next. When there is inadequate space between lines, the eye takes in other lines as well. If lines are too widely spaced, a reader may have trouble locating the next line. As column measure increases, the interline spacing should also increase to maintain a proper ratio of column length to interline spacing.

Typefaces with larger x-heights need more interline spacing than those with smaller x-heights. Also, when working with display types, the frequency with which ascenders and descenders occur makes a difference. They can optically lessen the amount of white space between lines. Optical adjustments in display types should be made when spaces between lines appear inconsistent because of ascenders and descenders (Fig. 324). Generally, the maximum line length for text type with a small x-height — used without interline spacing — is about sixty-five characters. When text type with a large x-height is used without interline spacing, legibility is diminished when line length exceeds about fifty-two characters.

Research has shown that for the optimum sizes of text type (9-, 10-, 11-, and 12-point), one to four points of interline spacing can be effectively added between lines to increase legibility. Remember, this is not to say that type set outside these optimum specifications will be illegible, for critical judgment can ensure legible typography without inhibiting fresh approaches.

Weight

When considering the legibility of a typeface, the thickness (weight) of the strokes should be examined. A typeface that is too light or too heavy has diminished legibility. Light typefaces cannot be easily distinguished from their background, while a typeface that is too heavy has a tendency to lose its internal pattern of counterforms.

Weight can be used advantageously to provide contrast and clarity between typographic page elements such as titles, headlines, and subheads. A heavier or lighter weight can emphasize one piece of information over another, thereby making information more comprehensible.

Extreme thick and thin strokes within letters of a particular typeface make reading more difficult, preventing smooth transitions from one word or group of words to the next. Thin strokes are less visible, creating confusion with letters of similar shape. When a typeface with extreme contrasts between thick and thin strokes is used in a text setting, a dazzle or sparkle effect is created. The reader begins to have difficulty distinguishing the words, and legibility decreases significantly.

Character Width

The shape and size of the page or column can influence the selection of character width. For example, a condensed typeface might be selected for a narrow page or column, achieving proportional harmony and an adequate number of characters and words to the line.

The width of letters is also an important legibility factor. Generally, condensed type is more difficult to read. A narrower letter changes the form/counterform relationship, causing letters to have an extreme vertical posture that can alter eye movement and reading patterns, diminishing legibility.

Italics

Similar to other situations where typeforms deviate from a reader's expectations, italics impede reading. An extreme italic slant can slow the reading process and is disliked by many readers. However, italic type can be very effective when used as a means of providing emphasis.

Typefaces of median weight are most legible.

In text type, weight change significantly affects legibility.

In text type, legibility is affected when condensed or expanded typefaces are used.

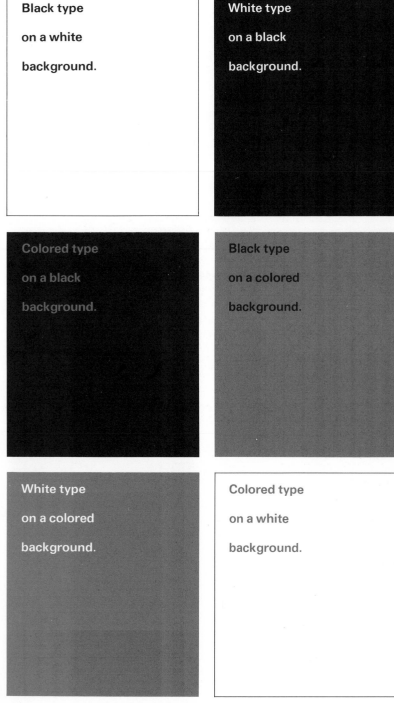

Black type on a white background.	White type on a black background.
Colored type on a black background.	Black type on a colored background.
White type on a colored background.	Colored type on a white background.

325.

Color combinations

When reading large amounts of text, people prefer black type on white backgrounds, and they are used to seeing this relationship. Large amounts of text are most legible as black on white, rather than the reverse. However, extreme black and white contrast can contribute to dazzle or sparkle. For example, reading a large amount of text on glossy bright-white paper is more difficult than reading the same text printed on uncoated paper. Type and its background can take various forms—from ink on paper to light on a cathode-ray tube. In all cases, the relationship between type and background is important to legibility.

If an appropriate type size and weight are chosen, the selection of a color combination for type and its ground is possible without a disturbing loss of legibility. Combinations of black, white, and color are often used for both type and ground (Fig. 325).

Justified and unjustified typography

Traditionally, it was common practice to set type in a justified alignment. This was done for reasons of efficiency; in addition, it was more familiar and was considered to be more refined. In the 1920s, designers began to question this typographic convention and experiment with alternative text-setting styles. Unjustified and asymmetrical typography began to find widespread acceptance. Among experimental typographic designers was Herbert Bayer, who said, "I have long believed that our conventional way of writing and setting type could be improved for easier reading. In my first typographic works in the early twenties, I started to abandon the flush-left-and-right system for short lines of text and have introduced the flush-left system, leaving a ragged-right outline."

There are appropriate reasons for setting either justified or unjustified typography, but type set flush left and ragged right promotes greater legibility. If properly used, flush-left, ragged-right typography provides visual points of reference that guide the eye smoothly down the page from line to line. Because each line is either shorter or longer than the next, the eye is cued from one to another. In a justified setting, all lines are of equal length. Lacking are visual cues that promote easy reading.

Compare the legibility of
the justified and unjustified
columns.

With the use of unjustified typography, wordspacing is even, creating a smooth rhythm and a consistent texture. The indiscriminate placement of additional space between words in order to justify lines causes awkward gaps or "rivers" in paragraphs, which are disruptive to reading. Hyphenations at the end of lines should be used whenever possible to keep wordspacing consistent.

When setting ragged-right text, care should be taken not to rag the type too much. Uncontrolled line breaks of erratic rhythm can create awkward spaces that inhibit reading. In ragged-right type, care should be given to the selection of interline spacing, for it influences legibility and appearance. Spatial consistency and rhythmic line breaks influence typographical decisions.

The breaking of lines can be determined by the author's meaning rather than by appearance. This method, sometimes referred to as "thought-unit" typography, arranges lines into discrete parts related to the meaning of the text. Ragged-right lines may be of any length, with line breaks that are logical and focus on the intended message of the writer (Fig. 326).

Paragraphs and indentations
An important goal for a designer is to distinguish typographically one thought from another, clarify content, and increase reader comprehension. Clear separation of paragraphs in a body of text is one way to accomplish this goal.

It is common practice in the design of books, magazines, and newspapers to indent each paragraph, usually with a moderate indentation of one to three ems. It is also typographic practice *not* to indent the first paragraph in an article, chapter, or advertisement so that the square corner of the first column can be maintained.

Paragraphs can also be separated by inserting additional space between them. This space should be proportional to the amount of interline spacing, which corresponds to the vertical measurement of the typographic grid. Paragraphs are often separated by one line space. This method should be avoided if the original copy is full of short,

choppy paragraphs. Spaces between such paragraphs could be very disturbing, consuming too much space. Indentations and additional linespace are also used to establish order within complex tabular matter, such as financial charts and scientific data.

Legibility and the grid
In discussing the grid, Josef Müller-Brockmann stated, "Information presented with clear and logically set out titles, subtitles, texts, illustrations, and captions will not only be read more quickly and easily, but the information will also be better understood and retained in memory." As a valuable framework for structuring typographic and pictorial elements, the grid produces a cohesiveness that can improve legibility and the communication of ideas.

In a rapidly changing information environment, designers must constantly reassess the nature of typographic legibility. As technology changes, so do communication techniques and methods. Today, legibility research must proceed beyond the realm of printed communications into the world of electronics, for words that once appeared primarily on paper are now found on the cathode-ray tube. Legibility concerns extend into all media, including videographics, television broadcasting, computer graphics, film, and laser graphics. Although the information found in this chapter relates mainly to printed communications, many of the principles and factors concerning typographic legibility apply to other media.

326.
Thought-unit typography
from the *Washburn College
Bible.* (Designer: Bradbury
Thompson)

1:1 In the beginning
God created the heaven and the earth.
2 And the earth was without form, and void;
and darkness was upon the face of the deep.
And the Spirit of God
moved upon the face of the waters.

3 And God said,
Let there be light:
and there was light.
4 And God saw the light, that it was good:
and God divided the light from the darkness.
5 And God called the light Day,
and the darkness he called Night.
And the evening and the morning
were the first day.

6 And God said,
Let there be a firmament
in the midst of the waters,
and let it divide the waters from the waters.
7 And God made the firmament,
and divided the waters
which were under the firmament
from the waters
which were above the firmament:
and it was so.

8 And God called the firmament Heaven.
And the evening and the morning
were the second day.

9 And God said,
Let the waters under the heaven
be gathered together unto one place,
and let the dry land appear:
and it was so.
10 And God called the dry land Earth;
and the gathering together of the waters
called he Seas:
and God saw that it was good.
11 And God said,
Let the earth bring forth grass,
the herb yielding seed,
and the fruit tree yielding fruit after his kind,
whose seed is in itself, upon the earth:
and it was so.
12 And the earth brought forth grass,
and herb yielding seed after his kind,
and the tree yielding fruit,
whose seed was in itself, after his kind:
and God saw that it was good.

The invention of typography has been called the beginning of the Industrial Revolution. It is the earliest mechanization of a handicraft: the hand-lettering of books. Typographic design has been closely bound to the evolution of technology, for the capabilities and limitations of typesetting systems have posed constraints upon the design process. At the same time, typesetting has offered creative challenges as designers have sought to explore the limitations of the available systems and to define their aesthetic and communicative potential.

From hand composition to today's electronically generated typography, it is important for designers to comprehend the nature and capabilities of typographic technologies, for this understanding provides a basis for a thoughtful blending of design and production.

Hand composition

The traditional method of setting foundry type by hand is similar to the method used by Gutenberg when he invented movable type in 1450. For centuries, hand composition was accomplished by assembling individual pieces of type (see Figure 202) into lines. A typographer would hold a composing stick (Fig. 327) in one hand while the other hand placed type selected from a type case (Fig. 328) into the stick. Type was set letter by letter, line by line, until the desired setting was achieved. When it was necessary to justify a line, additional spaces were created in the line by inserting metal spacing material between words. Letter-spacing was achieved by inserting very thin pieces of copper or brass between letters until words appeared to be evenly spaced. When additional space between lines was desired, strips of lead were inserted between the lines until the type column was the proper depth. By adding lead, the exact proportion and size of the column could be formed, assuring readability through consistent spacing.

Once type was set, it was "locked up" in a heavy rectangular steel frame called a chase (Fig. 329). This was done on a table called a stone. The type was surrounded by wood or metal spacing material, called furniture, and the contents of the chase were made secure by tightening steel wedgelike devices called quoins. After the type was secured

328.
Type case.

Chase

Wood furniture

Type

Quoins

329.
A chase containing type "locked-up" and ready for printing.

331.
Linotype matrix.

330.
Linotype machine.

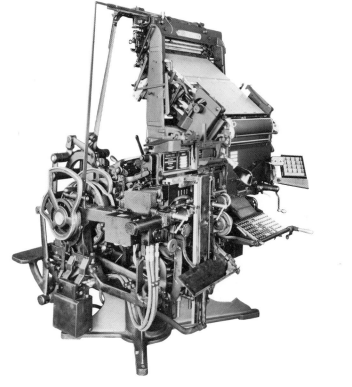

in the chase, it was ready to be transferred to a press for printing, and after printing, the individual pieces of type were distributed back into the type case by hand.

Hand composition was tedious and time consuming. When typesetting became automated as a result of the invention of Linotype and Monotype machines, hand composition was used only for setting small amounts of type or for display type. Currently, hand composition is obsolete as a practical means of setting type, but as an art form there has been a revival. Private presses produce limited-edition books and a variety of experimental materials by hand. Many of our typographic conventions and traditions have their origins in the rich heritage of handset metal type.

Linotype

One of the most profound developments in typesetting technology was the invention of the Linotype machine (Fig. 330) by Ottmar Mergenthaler in 1886. This machine represented the first great step toward typographic automation. Its name was coined because it produced a single line of type to a predetermined length specified by the keyboard operator.

The operation of the Linotype was based on the principle of a circulating matrix. Each time a key was pressed, a single brass matrix (Fig. 331) was released from an overhead magazine, divided into ninety vertical channels, each containing matrices for one character. The magazine was the character storage case for the machine. Once an entire line had been typed, the matrices moved into an automatic casting mechanism where the line of type was cast from molten lead. As each line was being cast, the operator typed the next line. After the casting process was complete, cast lines of type called slugs (Fig. 332) were ejected from the mold, and the matrices were automatically returned to their appropriate slot in the magazine for reuse.

The advantages of machine composition as compared to hand composition were obvious. It was faster and more accurate; the problem of type distribution (returning characters to the type case) was eliminated, for the cast lines of type were

332.
A linotype slug.

93

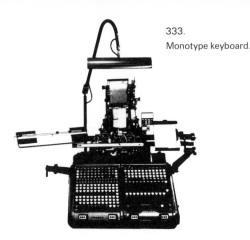

333.
Monotype keyboard.

simply melted, and the lead was reused. Justification of type was automatic, eliminating the tedious process of inserting spaces between letters and words. A standard Linotype could cast lines up to thirty picas in length.

An important development for linecasting type was the Teletypesetter. This perforated tape-driven machine—an attachment to Linotype and Intertype—was introduced in 1928. Tape that was punched by a machine similar to a standard typewriter could be generated from a distant office and transmitted to the linecaster by wire, which made the machine invaluable to news services.

Monotype

Another significant achievement leading to fully automated typesetting was the Monotype machine, invented by Tolbert Lanston in 1887. This machine cast one character at a time rather than an entire line. It was composed of two parts: a keyboard and a typecaster (Fig. 333). When an operator typed at a keyboard, a perforated paper tape was generated. This coded tape was used to drive the second part of the system—the typecaster. Compressed air, blown through the punched holes of this revolving spool of coded paper, determined which characters would be cast by the typecaster. Actual casting of type occurred when hot metal was forced into matrices from the matrix case (Fig. 334). Once the cast characters had cooled, they were placed into a metal tray called a galley, where the lines were assembled. Monotype lines could reach a maximum length of about sixty picas.

Monotype became an efficient way to set type for several reasons. Corrections could be made by changing individual letters instead of complete lines. Therefore, complex typesetting, such as scientific data and tabular information, was easier. The Monotype matrix case held many more characters than a Linotype magazine, and the casting machine was relatively fast, casting one hundred fifty characters per minute. Since the system consisted of two separate machines, an operator could generate type away from the clatter of the casting machine. In fact, several operators could keyboard information for later setting.

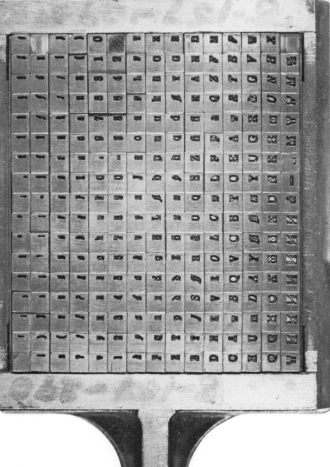

334.
Monotype matrix case.

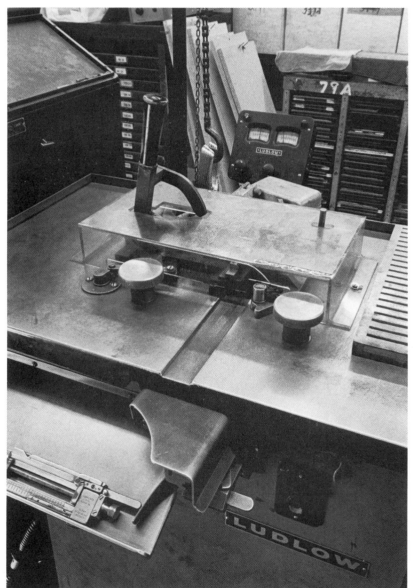

Ludlow

Ludlow, a semiautomatic linecaster, is another machine that found a place in the development of automated typesetting (Fig. 335). Unlike the Linotype and Monotype, the Ludlow did not have a keyboard but combined both hand and machine production. An operator took matrices from a matrix case similar to a handset type case and placed them into a special composing stick, one by one. The stick would automatically justify or center lines by inserting blank matrices where necessary. Once a line of matrices was assembled, it was placed into a casting device where it was automatically cast into slugs. If a correction was necessary, matrices were inserted into the stick, cast, locked up, and printed. Although partially automated, this process was time consuming. Distributing the matrices back into the type case by hand added to the production time.

Type produced by the Ludlow machine ranged from 6- to 144-point. Its major use was to produce display type for headlines and other purposes requiring larger typefaces. As was true in the case of handset composition, the Ludlow was neither practical nor efficient for setting large volumes of type.

335.
Ludlow linecaster.

Phototypesetting

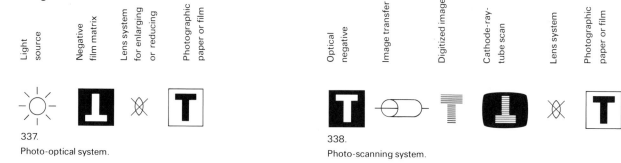

Light source
Negative film matrix
Lens system for enlarging or reducing
Photographic paper or film

337.
Photo-optical system.

Optical negative
Image transfer
Digitized image
Cathode-ray-tube scan
Lens system
Photographic paper or film

338.
Photo-scanning system.

Although some research in the area of phototype-setting had been done as early as the 1880s, the practicality of this new form of typesetting was not fully recognized until the close of World War II. Printing technology advanced from letterpress to the photographic process of offset lithography; typesetting underwent a similar technological change.

Phototypesetting and digital typesetting are currently the primary methods of setting type in the graphic arts. Since the development of Intertype's Fotosetter and Mergenthaler's Linofilm, the first generation of keyboard phototypesetters, introduced in 1950, numerous other systems have been developed (Fig. 336). Typesetting speed, character definition, and ergonomics (the relationship between man and machine) have continued to improve. Despite varying degrees of electronic sophistication among systems, phototypesetting can be divided into two basic classes: photo-optical systems and photo-scanning systems.

Photo-optical systems
Photo-optical systems store characters in the form of a master font on film, discs, grids, strips,

or drums (Fig. 337). These negative images are the "matrices" of phototypesetting systems. They are optically projected onto photographic film or paper. A variety of type sizes can be obtained from a single master font in most systems. An operator enters text and specifications at an editing terminal. Advanced computer technology is used to control this typesetting process.

Photo-scanning systems
Photo-scanning systems store characters in the form of a master font, not unlike those of photo-optical systems (Fig. 338). However, characters are not photographically projected onto film or paper; rather, they are scanned electronically and broken down into either dots or lines. These digitized characters are then projected onto a cathode-ray tube from which they are optically projected onto photographic paper or film. Once the characters have been digitally generated, their appearance can easily be altered. Weight, width, and slant can be changed automatically. Photo-scanning systems operate at much higher speeds than photo-optical systems.

336.
Linofilm machine.

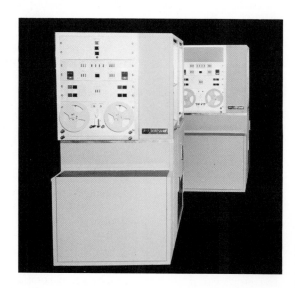

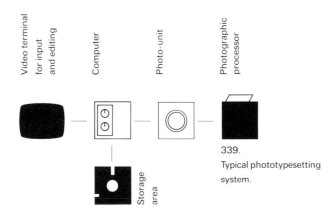

Video terminal for input and editing

Computer

Photo-unit

Photographic processor

Storage area

339.
Typical phototypesetting system.

System components

Typically, a phototypesetting system is composed of five parts, which perform input, output, editing, and storage functions (Fig. 339).

Keyboard and visual display terminal (VDT). Copy is typed at the keyboard and viewed on the VDT. Although keyboards vary from one system to another, their basic function is to enter and edit text. While a phototypesetter keyboard is similar to a typewriter's keyboard, additional keys are provided to perform special functions. The editing capabilities of a terminal save considerable time and effort. Words, lines, and paragraphs can be added, deleted, and moved from one area of the screen to another with ease. Changes can be made at the keyboard before type is processed.

Storage area. Storage is a very important part of the editing system of a phototypesetter and may or may not be a part of the VDT. Input is stored temporarily in the computer's memory or permanently on a magnetic disk or on tape. If at a later date the type needs to be altered, the contents of the disk or tape are simply loaded into the computer and changes are made at the keyboard.

Computer. This component, which is connected to the VDT, relays signals between the keyboard, the screen, memory, photo-unit, and processor.

Photo-unit. The photo-unit is the part of the system that actually generates type. A photo-optic system, for example, would optically expose an entire character from a photographic negative onto paper or film.

Processor. After type has been set, the exposed film or paper is developed in a photographic processor. This may be a part of the typesetter, or it may be a separate unit.

A machine that combines all the above components into one unit is called a direct-entry phototypesetter. These machines are very popular for a number of reasons. They are small, affordable, easy to operate, and capable of handling difficult typesetting demands. Since input and output are shared by a single unit, a direct-entry machine can be used as a word processor and editing terminal

that produces high-quality type. Some units can connect with other word-processing terminals, enabling input from more than one operator. Other units have full-page display capabilities. Called area-composition terminals, these units enable complete page makeup and presentation on a visual display terminal.

Phototypesetting systems, especially those of newspapers and other large publishers, can be part of complex and extensive networks, with links to word processors and mainframe computers. Text generated at one location can be transferred to another via telephone modem or satellite.

The advantages of phototypesetting over hot-metal composition are obvious. Phototypesetters are highly flexible and very fast. The typical photo-typesetter can set as many as five hundred characters per second, while hot-metal machines may set only five characters per second. Hot-metal machines are operated mechanically; phototype-setters are controlled and operated electronically. Type generated from a phototypesetting system takes up very little physical space because its final form is a film or paper proof. In contrast, the space required to store lead slugs is enormous. Another major advantage of phototypesetting is that text input uses computerized editing capabilities. This speeds up the process of entering the text considerably, as corrections are made electronically at the keyboard.

Typography created by phototypesetting is free of the physical restrictions inherent in lead type. There is flexibility in the spacing of typographic elements through kerning, letterspacing, overlapping, interline spacing, and special effects such as runarounds (type that runs around another element such as a photograph or illustration). A designer should understand the capabilities and limitations of typesetting technology so that it can be controlled and used to a greater advantage.

Display photographic typesetting

Light source

Negative
film font

Lens system

Film or paper

Processing
tray, allowing
immediate
viewing of type

341.
Typical display photographic
typesetter.

A rapid increase in the use of display photographic typesetting during the 1960s brought new design capabilities to the designer in display typography (Fig. 340). As with keyboard phototypesetters, a light source projects the image of a letterform from the film font through a lens system onto photographic paper or film. There is no keyboard; each character from the film font is brought into position by the operator using hand controls. Because the operator is able to see the recently set characters as they develop photographically, letterspacing can be precisely controlled (Fig. 341).

The numerous design advantages of display photographic systems led to their becoming the dominant method for headline typesetting within a few years. Instead of being bound by the sizes of handset composition, the designer could now specify any enlargement or reduction of the master font — which has capitals about one inch high — from twice up to four times down with perfect sharpness. Unlike metal display fonts, which have a limited number of characters, display phototype offers an unlimited supply. Spacing flexibility was a major innovation, for display type could now overlap, touch, and be set at any interletter-spacing interval specified by the designer. The constraints of blocks of metal yielded to the elasticity of photographic processes, and innovative designers rapidly explored new possibilities. The lens system enables letterform distortion. Characters can be expanded, condensed, italicized, and even backslanted (Fig. 342). The tremendous expense of introducing new metal typefaces, requiring punches, matrices, and cast letters in each size, was replaced by one economical film font. As a result, the introduction of new typefaces and revivals of earlier styles greatly increased.

Normal		aaaaaaaa
Expanded	8%	aaaaaaaa
	16%	aaaaaaaa
	24%	aaaaaa
Condensed	8%	aaaaaaaaa
	16%	aaaaaaaaaa
	24%	aaaaaaaaaa
Backslant	10%	aaaaaaaa
	16%	aaaaaaaa
	24%	aaaaaaaa
Italic	10%	aaaaaaaa
	16%	aaaaaaaa
	24%	aaaaaaaa

340.
Display photographic
typesetter.

The digital computer, in combination with the high-resolution cathode-ray tube (CRT) and laser, is revolutionizing the communications industry. Because digital computers have no mechanical parts and are entirely composed of electronic components, they set and process type at speeds never thought possible. In addition, the text type from digital typesetters has now been developed to rival the quality of phototype.

Knowledge of digital-computer functions is critical to an understanding of digital typesetting. A digital computer is an electronic device that uses electricity to process information. It can perform repetitive logical and arithmetic operations and store the results of those operations in memory. A computer system is composed of hardware, software, and firmware. Hardware consists of the physical components of a computer; software is the program data which controls the operation of the hardware; firmware is software in hardware form.

The computer component that controls all other parts, performs logical operations, and stores information is the central processing unit (CPU). All components that do not belong to the CPU are called peripherals. A typical digital-typesetting system is composed of a CPU and various peripherals that perform functions necessary to the setting of type—for example, editing and storing text, displaying text on a screen, and printing typeset copy.

A CPU consists of three interdependent components: arithmetic-logic unit (ALU), main memory, and control unit. These three components work together to control the operations of the computer. The ALU performs both arithmetic and logical functions such as adding two numbers together and determining which of two numbers is the greatest. In the main memory, called the random-access memory (RAM), data is stored and retrieved by the control unit. This unit also governs the functions of ALU and RAM. Consisting of these three parts, the CPU is the brain of a computer. It controls all functions, including the generation and setting of type in a digital-typesetting system.

A digital-computer system is based on the biconditional state of electronic circuitry. An electronic line can exist in only one of two states: it is either on or off. Each on/off state represents one binary digit or bit, enabling a computer to operate within the laws of the binary-number system. The binary system is a base-2 numbering system using only two numbers, 0 and 1. These numbers coincide with the biconditionals: off and on, respectively. The binary system is the exclusive language of any digital computer.

A computer communicates and processes information through the use of data structures. These are bits that have been grouped together into various configurations large enough to store significant information. The smallest bit structure is a byte, which consists of a group of bits linked together, such as the ASCII code (American Standard Code of Information Interchange, an information code in which the numbers zero to one hundred twenty-seven represent alphanumeric characters on the keyboard). These data structures are binary codes representing characters or numbers. Translating our alphanumeric characters into the binary system enables computers and people to communicate.

In digital typesetting, when the operator punches a key to enter a letter or issue a command (such as line length or paragraph indent), the computer receives it as a binary code. Once information has been entered, it can be stored, edited, and sent to a peripheral device for typesetting.

A digital-typesetting system encodes typographic characters digitally on a grid, defining the shape of each letter as a certain number of distinct points. Every detail of a letter is defined, including horizontal strokes, vertical strokes, and curves. The coded characters are stored electronically as digital instructions designating the x and y coordinates of the character on the grid. These instructions are then sent to a CRT, where the character is generated onto the screen.

A CRT is much like a television set. It has a vacuum tube with a cathode at one end and a plate of phosphorus and aluminum at the other. When

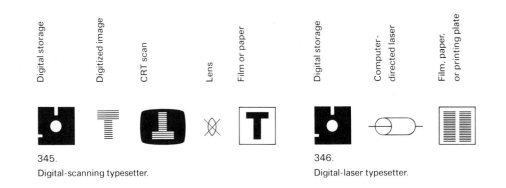

Digital storage

Digitized image

CRT scan

Lens

Film or paper

Digital storage

Computer-directed laser

Film, paper, or printing plate

345.
Digital-scanning typesetter.

346.
Digital-laser typesetter.

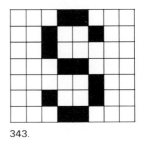

the CRT receives the digital instructions from the computer, defining the shape of the characters, the cathode emits a beam, which scans the tube in a series of parallel, back-and-forth sweeps. The cathode beam is programmed to be either on or off, depending upon the design of the letterforms that have been digitally encoded into the computer. When the beam is on, it excites the phosphorus and aluminum plate. The light emitted by the plate defines each character being typeset. The type is then digitally exposed to photographic paper.

The level of resolution in digital letterforms is an important consideration. Basically, the more dots or lines used to describe a letterform, the higher the resolution becomes. Because letters are constructed on a grid, the curved lines consist of a series of stair-stepped contours (Fig. 343). When more dots are used to represent a curve, the curve appears smoother to the eye. Large characters require more dots than do small characters to achieve a refined appearance. The quality of a letterform is determined not only by its original design, but also by its digital resolution (Fig. 344). The designer of digital type must consider digital technology and its effect upon the resolution of letterforms.

One major difference between digital type and phototype is the manner in which type is stored. Rather than storing master fonts on photographic disks, drums, grids, or strips, digital master fonts can be stored electronically as bit patterns on a magnetic disk. Some machines are capable of storing hundreds of fonts, with each size stored independently.

Scanning and laser systems
There are two classes of digital typesetters: digital-scanning systems and digital-laser systems. In digital-scanning systems (Fig. 345), photographic characters are digitally scanned and recorded electronically on a magnetic disk or tape. The characters are translated into a grid of extremely high resolution and are transmitted as a set of instructions to a CRT. Next, the characters are generated onto the CRT by a series of scan lines. The letterform images are then projected from the CRT onto paper, film, or an electrostatic drum. Because the

output type is digital, it can be modified automatically to reflect a number of typographic variations. For example, it can be made heavier, lighter, slanted, condensed, or expanded at the command of the operator.

Digital-laser systems (Fig. 346) also store characters digitally, but do not employ a CRT to generate characters. A laser beam scans photographic paper as it reads digital information stored in the typesetter. As the paper is scanned, a series of dots forming the characters are exposed to the paper. The information controlling the laser includes the typographic font and spacing, such as hyphenation, justification, kerning, and letterspacing.

Because digital typesetting is so fast, it is particularly suited to industries requiring the processing of enormous amounts of information, such as news services and publishing companies. However, smaller offices and type houses are also using digital type because of its efficiency.

Direct-entry digital typesetters (Fig. 347) are similar to direct-entry phototypesetters, for they are both self-contained. However, direct-entry digital typesetters are much faster and more versatile. Because they generate modified characters and a wider range of sizes and spatial intervals, direct-entry digital typesetters bring greater flexibility to the typesetting process (Fig. 348).

343.

344.
Examples of digital letterforms, demonstrating decreasing resolution, from top to bottom, as the number of elements is reduced.

Video terminal
for input and editing

Computer

CRT or
laser scan

Photographic
processor

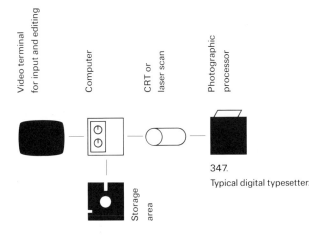

347.
Typical digital typesetter.

Storage
area

348.
An infinite variety of letterform alteration is possible with
digital typesetters.

ABabABabABabABabA

ABabABabABabABabABabAB

ABCabcABCabcABCabcABCab

ABCabcABCabcABCabcABCabcABCab

ABCabcABCabcABCabcABCabcABCabcABCabcAB

ABCDabcdABCDabcdABCDabcdABCDabcdABCDabcd

ABCDEabcdeABCDEabcdeABCDEabcdeABCDEabcdeABCDEabc

ABCDEFabcdefABCDEFabcdefABCDEFabcdefABCDEFabcdefABCDEFabcdef

ABCDEFGabcdefgABCDEFGabcdefgABCDEFGabcdefgABCDEFGabcdefgABC

ABCDEFGHabcdefghABCDEFGHbcdefghABCDEFGHabcdefghABCDEFGHabcdefghABCDE

ABCDEFGHIJabcdefghijABCDEFGHIJabcdefghijABCDEFGHIJabcdefghijABCDEFGHIJabcdefghijABCDEFGHIJa

ABCDEFGHIJKLabcdefghijklABCDEFGHIJKLabcdefghijklABCDEFGHIJKLabcdefghijklABCDEFGHIJKLabcdefghijklABCDEFGHIJKLabcdefghijkl

Each major typographic process has its own place in the evolution of technology. Increased efficiency, control, flexibility, and the design of letterforms have been affected by continuous research and innovation. The nature of the typographic image has been changed as well (Fig. 349). The microphotographs by Mike Cody demonstrate the differences. Letterpress printing of metal type impressed the letterform into the fibers of the paper. Phototype, usually printed by offset lithography, provides a precise image with a comparatively smooth contour. As the microphotographic enlargement shows, digital type evidences the stepped contour caused by the digitization of the image into discrete elements. In the most advanced digital-typesetting systems, the discrete elements are so small that they become indiscernible to the naked eye.

Technology develops rapidly, and designers must work to keep abreast of innovations that influence the design process and the typographic image. Designers should view typographers as partners in the design process, for their specialized knowledge of the typesetting system and its capabilities, along with an understanding of typographic refinements, can help the designer achieve the desired quality of typographic communication.

349.
Microphotographic enlargement of letterforms.

Metal type on newsprint.

Metal type on coated paper.

Phototype.

Digital type.

The rapid advance of technology and the expanding role of visual and audiovisual communication in contemporary society have created new challenges for typographic education. Faced with the complex communications environment and the changes that are occurring and are anticipated, how can a designer nurture sensitivity to typographic form and communication? An appreciation of our typographic heritage, an ability to meet the standards of contemporary design practice, and an innovative spirit in facing the challenges of tomorrow are required.

The following assignments, ranging from basic theoretical exercises to complex applied projects, provide an overview of contemporary typographic design education. Responsible design education is composed of perceptual and conceptual development, technical training, and an ability to solve complex design problems. These projects were selected with emphasis upon building the perceptual and conceptual abilities that provide a foundation for effective and innovative typographic-design practice.

Generation of a typographical sign
from a gestural mark

P. Lyn Middleton

North Carolina
State University

Students were asked to make gestural question marks (Figs. 350–52), giving consideration to the visual-design qualities of their sketches. Proportion, stroke weight, negative space, and details such as the relationship of the dot to the curved gesture were evaluated. One of the student's question marks was selected and became the basis for designing a freehand typographic sign.

Students generated a variety of graphic signs, exploring a range of forms that can function as a question mark. Executing the typographic version develops visual and manual acuity, and an understanding of the differences between written and typographic signs.

350.
Designer: Alexandre Lock.
351.
Designer: Maxine Mills
352.
Designer: Angela Stewart

350.

351.

352.

Letter/digit configurations

Urban letterform studies

Rob Carter

Virginia Commonwealth
University

Thomas Detrie

Guest Lecturer
Winter Session in Basel
Rhode Island
School of Design

Visual configurations were invented by combining a letter from the English alphabet with a single-digit number (Figs. 353–56). Scale, proportion, weight, and shape relationships between two different signs were explored.

Objectives of this exercise include introducing letterform drawing and drafting skills, using typographic joinery to unify the two distinct forms into a visual gestalt, and understanding the variety of spatial relationships that can exist among characters.

353.
Designer: Linda Evans
354.
Designer: Colene Kirwin
355.
Designer: Virginia Commonwealth University Sophomore
356.
Designer: Virginia Commonwealth University Sophomore

357.

Letterforms in an old section of a European town were studied and documented through drawing, rubbings, and found material. A black-and-white letter composition was developed, depicting graphic qualities found in the assigned area (Fig. 357).

On a formal level, compositional issues such as dynamic asymmetrical composition and form-counterform relations are explored. On an interpretive level, the ambiance of a historical area is translated into a typographic configuration.

353.

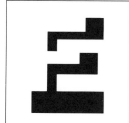

354.

355.

356.

357.
Designer: J. P. Williams

Inventing sign systems

Greg Prygrocki

North Carolina
State University

358.

359.

A set of nine signs were invented (Figs. 358–59). Each was required to be a distinctive mark, with unique optical characteristics, yet harmonious with all the other signs and clearly recognizable as part of the set.

The focus of this project is to make students aware of the properties that bring unity to any typographic system. These include stroke weight and direction, stress, form repetition, and intersection.

358.
Designer: Joe Easter
359.
Designer: Paul Dean

Letterform analysis

Ben Day

Boston University

A modular grid of horizontal, vertical, and diagonal units was established and used to draw variations of a letterform (Fig. 360). The sans serif *E* has been transformed into expanded and condensed variations. A grid sequence from four to twelve vertical units and from five to ten horizontal units was used. In Figure 361, the form has been elaborated upon by opening the space between the vertical stroke and the three horizontal strokes.

The purpose of this project is to understand the allowable tolerence for the alteration of letterform proportions without losing sign legibility. In addition, the internal structure of a letter is analyzed and manipulated. This project introduces students to the formal variety that is possible and to the process of logo design.

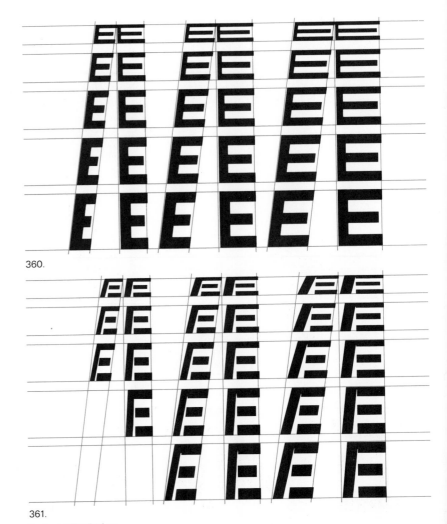

360.

361.
Designer: Tim Barker

Interpretive compositions

Christopher Ozubko

University of Washington
at Seattle

2.

363.

364.

Each student generated compositions using found typography, attempting to express specific emotional states (Figs. 362–64).

This introductory problem enables students to experiment with type size, weight, and style; spacing and clustering; progression, repetition, and pattern; and texture, movement, and contrast. The interpretive potential of formal typographic qualities relating to implied content is emphasized.

362.
Individuality, Designer: Kyle Wiley
363.
Exuberance, Designer: Richard di Furia
364.
Celebration, Designer: Laurie Greischel

Greg Prygrocki

North Carolina
State University

Gordon Salchow

University of Cincinnati

An understanding of the structural nature of letterforms was investigated by using form repetition to create a clearly definable pattern (Figs. 365 and 366). Through the rotation and repetition of letterforms, the student can acquire increased sensitivity to letterform structure and skill in alignment.

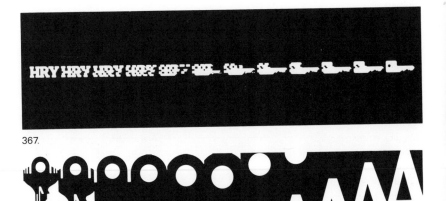

367.

365.
Designer: Elizabeth
McPherson

A letter has been altered in a series of steps until it is transformed into a simple object, an abstract shape, or another letterform (Figs. 367–69). An understanding of typographic sequencing, permutation, and kinetic properties is developed. Students can gain an awareness of form and counterform relationships and the unity that can be created in complex configurations.

368.

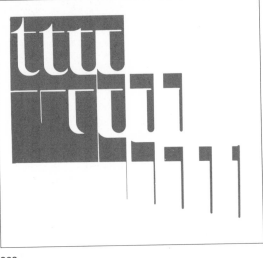

369.

366.
Designer: Kim Marlatt

367.
Designer: University of
Cincinnati Sophomore
368.
Designer: University of
Cincinnati Sophomore
369.
Designer: University of
Cincinnati Sophomore

Visual organization and grid structures

Greg Prygrocki

North Carolina State University

Students developed linear grid structures, then created a series of plates, organizing found typographic materials into spatial compositions based upon this underlying structure (Figs. 370 and 371).

This project introduces the grid structure as a formal design element. The grid module is the basic compositional unit, bringing order to the arrangement. Students consider contrast, structure, positive and negative space, balance, texture and tone, and rhythm as design properties.

370.

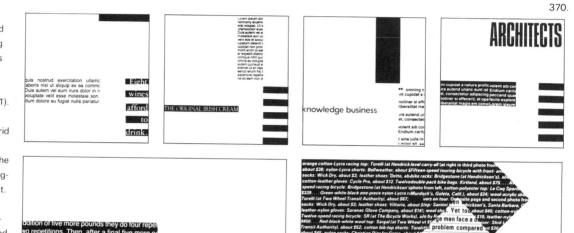

370.
Designer: Craig McLawhorn
371.
Designer: Matt Monk

371.

**Unity of form
and communication**

Christopher Ozubko

University of Washington
at Seattle

After selecting a historical
event as subject, students were
asked to develop a typographic
message using the visual properties of type and space to
amplify content (Figs. 372–75).
This project develops an understanding of the inventive potential of typographic form.
As a message carrier, typography can intensify and expand
content and meaning.

372.
Designer: Steve Cox
373.
Designer: Kyle Wiley
374.
Designer: Bill Jolley
375.
Designer: Susan Dewey

372.

the worlds deepest submarine

nov

17

1973

dive

32,820ft

373.

Amelia Earhart   July 2 1937   Disappeared in flight over the Atlantic Ocean

ChristianBarnardFirstSuccessful   Transplant12/3/67

Heart

374.

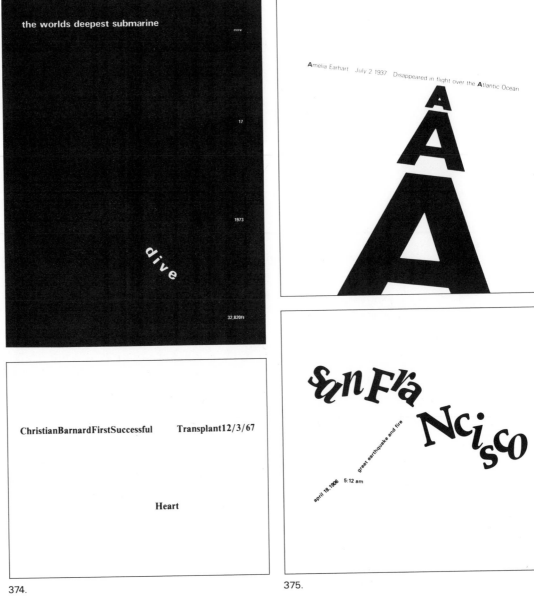

SanFra Ncisco

april 18, 1906   5:12 am   great earthquake and fire

375.

**Typographic variations
through changing parameters**

Rob Carter

Virginia Commonwealth
University

376.

377.

378.

379.

380.

Using descriptive copy from a small newspaper advertisement, students designed a series of typographic messages. These variations were generated through changing problem parameters in a progressive series. Parameters for the examples shown here are as follows: same type size and weight (Fig. 376); same type size, different weight (Fig. 377); different type size and weight (Fig. 378); different size and weight, varied letter-spacing for emphasis (Fig. 379); and interpretive manipulation of type to reinforce the message (Fig. 380).

The objective is to make students aware that a visual hierarchy can be created by changing typographic parameters. Students learn that an infinite number of possible solutions to each problem is available. A typographic designer can generate and evaluate these possible solutions for their communicative effectiveness.

376.
Designer: Michelle Teten
377.
Designer: Michelle Teten
378.
Designer: James Creps
379.
Designer: Michelle Teten
380.
Designer: Colene Kirwin

Experimental compositions
with found typography

Katherine McCoy

Cranbrook Academy of Art

Using all of the typography found on a product label, a grid-based composition was produced exploring size relationships, spatial interval, and weight (Fig. 381). A second composition was generated with more dynamic movement and scale change (Fig. 382). Visual notations were made of each, analyzing eye movement, massing, and structure (Figs. 383 and 384). Tone, texture, and shape are substituted for the typographic elements.

This project is designed to encourage an understanding of the abstract properties inherent in existing typographic forms. An exploratory attitude toward space and visual organization is developed.

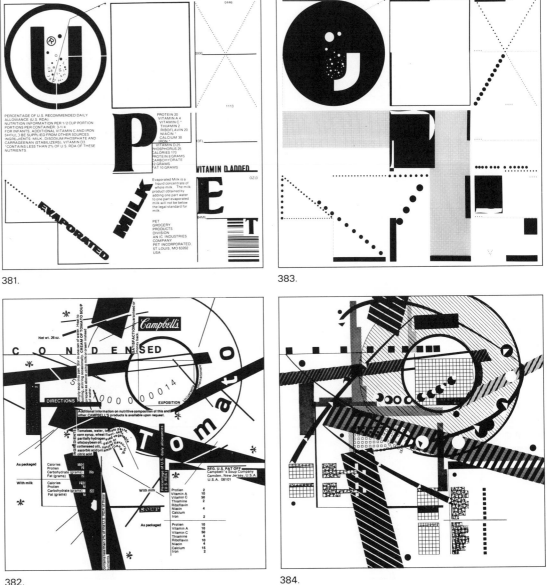

381.

383.

382.

384.

381–384.
Designer: Ryoji Ohashi

Poem and news combinations

Jan Boterman

Gerrit Rietveld Academy
Amsterdam

Using a standard-size sheet of paper, folded at one-third its size, students were challenged to lay out two contrasting communications — a poem and a news item — on the same subject. Time and sequence were introduced through the use of the folded sheet. In Figure 385, a line of poetry, "He that knows that enough is enough, always has enough," is combined with a newspaper headline: *Meer Geld* ("More money"). Figure 386 shows a sound poem of repeating sounds that translate, "That small round part is dealt out." The second item describes the type of poem structure that is present in the sound poem.

The keystone of this project is an editorial and syntactical problem: combine two messages into a single typographic expression while maintaining their uniqueness. Production was by letterpress. Selection of paper stock and ink color appropriate to the message were important considerations.

385.

386.

385.
Designer: Allan Tan
386.
Designer: Rijk Boerma

Typographic cubes

Calendar typography

R. Roger Remington

Rochester Institute
of Technology

Josef Godlewski

Indiana University

A visual presentation combining typography, images, and symbols was created as an extension of a self-assessment study by advanced design students (Figs. 387–89). The students made a formal analysis of their past experiences and future goals. This part of the project stressed research and information gathering. The collected materials were evaluated for their communicative effectiveness in a complex design.

Transforming diverse information into a three-dimensional cube poses a complex design problem. Each side of the cube functions as part of a totality; the four contiguous sides are graphically and communicatively integrated.

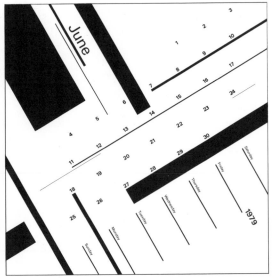

387.

388.

389.

387.
Designer: Beth April Smolev
388.
Designer: Katherine St. James
389.
Designer: Bruce Morgan

Calendar pages were designed using typographic elements to organize the space and direct eye movement on the page (Fig. 390). Emphasis was placed upon experimentation, creating unity and movement on each page and developing a visual elaboration over twelve pages. A grid structure was established and used to achieve diversity and order within a sequence of twelve designs. Graphic elements were limited to typography and rules.

This assignment enables students to explore interrelationships between graphic elements and the surrounding space.

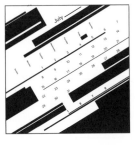

390.
Designer: Jean
Brueggenjohann

Interpretive typography: form and content

John DeMao

University of Illinois
at Chicago

Using only typography, students arrived at appropriate interpretations of the essential character of a renowned work of literature (Figs. 391–93). They were asked to respond to the story by manipulating letterforms in a figurative and expressive way.

Distortion and alteration of letterforms achieve visual dynamics and intensify the meaning of the title. An awareness of the potential correspondence between typographic form and verbal content is developed.

391.
Designer: Mark Signorio
392.
Designer: Cindy Kim
393.
Designer: Karl Knauz

391.

392.

393.

Typeface history posters

Type specimen book page

Jan Baker

Rhode Island
School of Design

Jean Brueggenjohann

Boston University

396.

Each student in the class was assigned a typeface to study and use in a poster design, communicating its essential characteristics (Figs. 394 and 395). Letterforms that reveal the unique properties of the typeface were emphasized. The typeface name and entire alphabet were required components of the design.

This project enables students to establish a visual hierarchy in a poster format, while introducing them to the visual characteristics of typefaces.
394.
Designer: Holly Hurwitz
395.
Designer: Luci Goodman

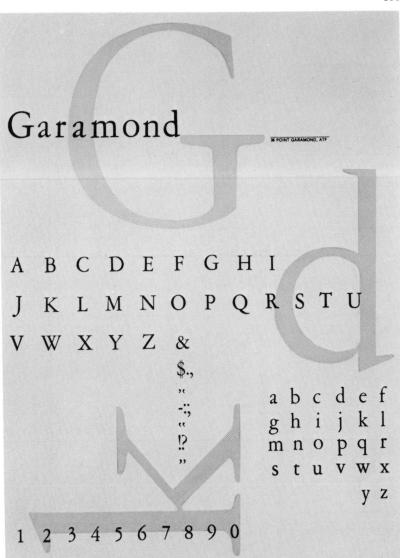

Garamond

394.

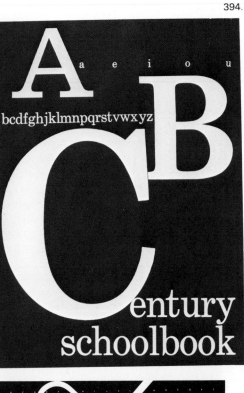

395.

A specimen book page was developed using the typeface name, complete upper- and lowercase alphabets, numbers, punctuation, and display letterforms selected to convey the visual properties of the font (Fig. 396).

Objectives of this project include: the establishment and use of a simple grid, the clustering of elements to create typographic densities, and expressing the nature of the typeface through an overall patterning. A one-color repro-

duction restriction enables the students to explore the potential of screen tints.
396.
Designer: Joyce Hempstead

Jan Baker

Rhode Island
School of Design

David Colley

University of Illinois
at Champaign-Urbana

An abecedarian primer was designed and printed by letterpress (Fig. 397). Each student researched a topic, then developed a sequence of twenty-six pages presenting information about the subject. The example shown presents the historical evolution of each letterform in the alphabet; other student research included music, animals, the Amazon, and teaching the alphabet to preschool children.

Combining display and text type into cohesive page layouts, integrating the left- and right-hand pages, and creating a visual flow in a serial progression are project objectives. Students learn how to translate their subject research into a typographic format.
397.
Designer: Susan Limoncelli

A series of posters was designed to encourage local high school students to attend symphony concerts (Fig. 398). Emphasis was placed on writing interpretive copy and selecting typefaces appropriate to that message. Diversity of expression to parallel the concert season was an important consideration. (These posters were printed by offset and donated to the symphony.)

This project introduces the student to the importance of the message in typographic communication. Language devices including metaphor, sound repetition, and rhyme were used to make the content memorable. The relationship of form and meaning was addressed; the nature of each composer's music was considered in the selection of typeface, size, placement, and color. In the examples shown, typographic dissonance in the Stockhausen poster parallels the composer's musical dissonance; word substitution occurs in the the Brahms poster; and an auditory double meaning is found in the Bach poster.
398.
Designers: University of Illinois undergraduate students

398.

397.

117

Type chronology booklet

R. Roger Remington

Rochester Institute
of Technology

A comparative study of ten
typefaces was made by each
student. The information was
organized chronologically in a
booklet with four pages devoted to each typeface. In Figure
399, the opening spread juxta-
poses descriptive text and a
complete font opposite a large
letterform. The following
spread contains a historical
application of the type opposite a contemporary application created by the student.

This project develops research
skills, an understanding of
typographic history, and an
ability to work with different
typefaces. Large amounts of
complex data are organized; a
consistent format is developed;
diversity is created within this
format.

399.
Designer: Heinz Klinkon

Thematic exhibition posters

Alston Purvis
and Jean Brueggenjohann

Boston University

An extensive research project investigated the traditions of design in early New England. The results were presented in a series of exhibition posters (Fig. 400). Emphasis was placed upon the integration of images and type into cohesive compositions.

In this advanced self-initiated project, the student made use of principles of grid organization to bring unity to each poster. Since the artifacts shown varied widely in design and format, major compositional axes (composed of a horizontal flow line one-third from the top and a central vertical division) were used as a structural theme unifying the series.

400.
Designer: Suzanne Perry

Ben Day

Virginia Commonwealth
University

Student teams researched an epoch of European cultural history, then formulated an itinerary for a journey through Europe to major sites. A visual and verbal timeline was designed, outlining the journey for a potential traveler. Each timeline begins with a map of Europe and ends with a poster composition of the final destination. Figure 401 shows a segment of a tour of early cultures; in Figure 402 the final destination on a tour of early twentieth-century architecture is seen.

Background and pictorial research, image selection, and organization of complex data on a grid are addressed in this project. Functional communicative considerations and expressive graphic interpretation are emphasized.

401.

402.

401.
Designer: Lark Pfleegor
402.
Designer: Michael Fanizza

Case Studies
in Typographic Design

Many of the educational projects in the preceding chapter represent theoretical and exploratory investigations. They are structured to teach typographic history, theory, spatial concepts, form, and meaning. The goal of typographic education is to prepare young designers for the complexity of applied problem solving. The case studies presented in this chapter describe specific typographic design problems encountered in professional practice. The nature of each problem is analyzed, and the rationale for the solution is discussed.

These six studies cover a wide range of typographic design: a visual identification system, an exhibition catalog, a newspaper redesign, permutations of a title page, motion-picture titles, and a periodical. Each of the examples presents a different aspect of the broad scope of typography in our contemporary communications environment, and each fulfills a human communicative need with functional clarity and sensitivity.

A new logotype and graphic standards for the National Aeronautics and Space Administration were created by the design firm Danne and Blackburn Inc., of New York City. A graphic-standards manual was developed to instruct individuals throughout the NASA organization on the proper application of the unified visual-communications system. The continued evolution and implementation of this design system has been the responsibility of NASA graphics coordinator Robert Schulman. By designating an individual at each NASA location (usually the section head of the graphics department) with responsibility for implementation and maintenance of the graphics system, Schulman was able to develop a network of professionals who are closely involved in NASA visual communications on a daily basis.

The first element in a visual-identity system is the visual identifier: a sign, symbol, or uniquely designed word called a *logotype.* It is used in a consistent, repetitive manner to establish and maintain a unified image and immediate identification. The NASA logotype is the dominant element in the visual-communications system (Fig. 403). In it the agency initials are reduced to their most elemental forms. The resulting simplicity enables the logotype to be reduced to small sizes and to be readily identified from afar on signs, aircraft, and vehicles. The angled junctions of strokes in the capital *N* and the apexes of the *A*s are replaced by curved forms. This reduces the contrast between the letterforms, making the *N* and *A*s more harmonious with the *S.* The strokes are all of one width, evoking qualities of unity and technical precision. The crossbars from the two *A* forms are deleted, giving them a vertical thrust which suggests rocketry

406.

and space flight. The sum of these design devices is visual cohesiveness and expressiveness. Although the stylization is very pronounced, readability and legibility are maintained.

A key to the effectiveness of the NASA system is the consistent use of the agency name and the identification of NASA centers. Subtle visual relationships are important. The name is set in Helvetica Light, which has letterforms compatible to the logotype but has definite weight contrast (Fig. 404). The stroke weight of the logotype, the

403.

National Aeronautics and
Space Administration

National Aeronautics and
Space Administration

John F. Kennedy Space Center

x- height of the lowercase letters, and the spatial interval between the bottom of the logotype and the topmost lowercase letters are virtually identical in measure. This repetition of spatial interval links the logotype and identifying name together. When the name of a NASA center is added to the logotype, contrast is achieved through the use of Helvetica Medium (Fig. 405). Note that the interval between the agency name and the center name is a one-line space. However, this is measured to the x-height of the lowercase letters of the center name (*not* the top of the capitals) to achieve optical, rather than mathematical, evenness of the spatial intervals.

Two colors are designated for use in NASA graphics: a warm, lively red and a medium shade of warm gray. The consistent use of color is another unifying element in the visual-communications system. Careful guidelines govern the use of color and ban incorrect graphic treatments, such as outlining the logo, superimposing a pattern or texture over the logo, running it uphill, adding perspective shadows, or placing it in a circle, square, or plaque. Formulation of these regulations is critical to the success of the visual-identification program. Without clear and concise guidelines detailing all typographic treatments for visual identification, personnel throughout NASA's worldwide system might deviate, resulting in a dilution of the system's effectiveness.

Publications are the largest visual-communications area. The *NASA Graphic Standards Manual* specifies criteria for routine printed material. For example, stationery has a logotype of 5/6-inch capital height with 10/12 Helvetica Light and Medium upper- and lowercase typography (Fig. 406). Secondary typography is always set in 7/8 Helvetica Light upper- and lowercase typography. The left margin of the typography establishes the typing margin. Line spaces are used instead of paragraph indents. This combines typography and typewriting into a unified presentation.

The NASA logotype is often used as a "stem word" in conjunction with Helvetica type to form publication titles (Fig. 407). This technique is limited to ongoing periodicals and requires approval of

NASA Tech Briefs

National
Aeronautics and
Space
Administration

407.

408.

Before   After

409.

National Aeronautics and Space Administration   NASA

←

Logistics Division	415
Management Systems Division	412
Medical Division	426
Office of the Director	401
Personnel Management	423

→

Budget Division	432
Civil Rights Staff	465
Executive Officer	455

4

Langley Research Center

the NASA graphics coordinator to ensure appropriate treatment. In some organizations, the graphic-standards manuals rigidly specify grid structures and text-type sizes for all publications. At NASA, the manual provides general guidance to allow a measure of flexibility in the design of publications. The logotype and accompanying typographic elements must be used consistently to create a strong, integrated family of publications. The level of graphic improvement and consistent identification achieved by the NASA program is evidenced by the redesign of a mission operation report (Fig. 408) and in the application of the system to routine printing materials. While Helvetica is designated as the primary typeface, the manual recommends Futura, Garamond, and Times Roman as possible alternatives in special cases where the character of one of these faces might be more appropriate. The *NASA Graphic Standards Manual* presents grid systems for use in publication design (See Figures 273–75).

Environmental applications include signage, vehicle identification, and aircraft. The NASA system involves simple, functional signs employing flush-left, ragged-right Helvetica (Fig. 409). In accordance with governmental regulations, vehicle identification consists of four elements: government-use identification, logotype, agency identification, and installation identification (Fig. 410). Careful design specifications are also detailed for NASA aircraft (Fig. 411). A white fuselage top, a blue stripe around the aircraft perimeter, a gray fuselage underside, and a red NASA logo on the tail are consistent design elements. This basic scheme adapts well to a wide range of aircraft. However, the proportions of the stripes vary widely when applied to aircraft sizes and shapes from small single-engine aircraft to the Boeing 747 photographed carrying the space shuttle *Enterprise* (Fig. 412). Spacecraft marking, of necessity, is different on each vehicle. Flight engineers and scientists designated only a few areas on each spacecraft for graphics.

411.

412.

As shown on the *Enterprise,* the NASA logo, American flag, "United States," and vehicle name are carefully placed to conform with technical requirements and to be harmonious with the overall form and shape of the spacecraft. The NASA logo is in gray to avoid visual conflict with the red stripes of the flag. The logotype and Helvetica Medium typeface ensure continuity with all other NASA graphics.

The NASA visual-identification system has proven strong and resilient. It is both consistent and easily identifiable, yet the system has allowed for a wide variety of applications over the years.

410.

An exhibition catalog for *Fluxus Etc.*

For a major exhibition presenting work from two decades by the Fluxus group of artists, designers Katherine McCoy, Lori Barnett, Lyn Silarski, and Ken Windsor were commissioned to design a four-hundred-page exhibition catalog. The Fluxus experimental art group was founded in 1962 by George Maciunas. International in scope and nurtured by the early twentieth-century art movements, Fluxus issued several manifestos, published inexpensive editions of artist's works, musical scores, and documentation of events. It provided a focus for experimentation that challenged accepted notions about art and the art experience.

The catalog provides a record of hundreds of works from the exhibition. In addition, it serves as a permanent documentation of the Fluxus movement. The challenge facing the design team was to organize a large quantity of diverse information into a legible and coherent format, while capturing the vitality and spirit of the Fluxus movement. The catalog is divided into five sections: a history of Fluxus, including philosophy, attitudes, influences, and purposes; a portfolio of over five hundred Fluxus Editions and related works; a presentation of Fluxus periodicals and documents; an illustrated record of Fluxus performance events; and a chronology of Fluxus performances.

Clearly, a format design was needed that could unify the breadth of information and imagery, while allowing design flexibility. A format was developed for nine-by-ten-inch pages, using primary and secondary divisions of space. Each page has four vertical columns, with a secondary division of eight columns. Horizontal structure is achieved with a "floating" modular spatial division, which accommodates a diversity of content, form, and scale. Fluxus was greatly involved with process; therefore, the design process of this catalog has been revealed by printing the grid structure for the pages in a subtle, screened tint. Thus, the construction lines for the pages are visible and become design elements. Unity is achieved through the repetition of a vertical black band down the left-hand side of each page. Key information appears on this band. A ruled line transverses the top of

413.

414.

415.

each page, with the page number placed in the top left-hand corner. Consistent use of condensed sans serif type lends further unity.

The front and back covers signify the content and mood of the publication. The front cover reproduces a 1963 photograph by George Maciunas, depicting a front door with a figure peering through the mail slot (Fig. 413). The image communicates on several levels. It invites the reader to enter the world of Fluxus. The weathered, knobless door with a latch hanging below the mail slot without apparent purpose evokes a Dada-like visual irony, and the person peering from within is an ambiguous image, defying a specific interpretation. The stepped red box (containing the title) and the black band on the right establish the typographic format and graphic theme within. The back cover expresses a parallel but contrasting visual theme (Fig. 414).

The complete history of Fluxus is presented through contributions by artists and poets from around the world. Manifestos (Fig. 415) and philosophic observations (Fig. 416) by members of the group are reproduced as full-page statements. The poetic energy and visual texture of the originals are preserved.

The section-divider pages are solid black, in contrast to the lighter tone and texture of the book (Figs. 417 and 418). Stepped contour shapes provide spaces for each section's title typography.

The section entitled "Fluxus Editions and Related Works" presents an illustrated checklist of five hundred thirty items (Fig. 419). Unity within complexity is achieved by the repetition of similar graphic elements. The designers placed the catalog numbers in small white rectangles along the left-hand black bands. In the first grid column, typography identifies the artist, title, date, and dimensions of the work. Media and descriptive copy are placed in the second column. Rules are used to divide

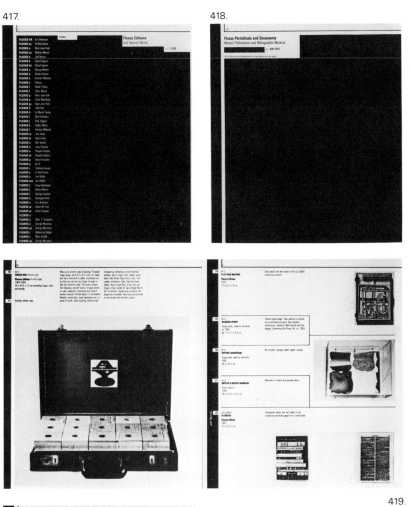

417.

418.

419.

416.

each page clearly into zones separating the works. The reader quickly understands the system and can connect the typography and images without difficulty.

This format continues into the sections presenting periodicals, documents, and performances, where illustrations include posters, invitations, and other artifacts relating to the events (Fig. 420). A playful typographic vitality, expressive of the nature of the performances, characterizes these materials.

The final section is a typographic presentation of a "working document," a chronology of the Fluxus movement (Fig. 421). The reader must turn the book to read the information. The primary division of space splits each page into two long columns upon which the programs are listed, separated by heavy rules. Three columns divide each program into areas for artists, work, and performers. As in the catalog material, use of a bolder typeface gives appropriate emphasis to titles.

In determining the typographic schema and format of this book, the designers have been sensitive to the nature of the exhibition and the attitudes and philosophies of the Fluxus art movement. The exploratory innnovations of the Fluxus group made appropriate the design team's decision to create a book that displays its grid organization. In addition, the flexibility of the modular spatial divisions clearly separates each work from others on the page. It allows page arrangements and grid manipulations to reflect the diversified content.

421.

420.

The redesign of the *Minneapolis Tribune*

422.

Although a form of newspaper appeared by 1609 in Augsburg, Germany, the newspaper as we know it is a product of the Industrial Revolution. The invention of the telegraph in the mid-nineteenth century enabled information to be transmitted over long distances instantaneously; the invention of the Linotype in 1886 increased typesetting productivity sevenfold. For nearly a century, newspapers have provided readers with information from around the world within hours after events have occurred.

Until the 1970s, most newspapers were content to leave design matters to editors and makeup people as a matter of expediency. The 1951 front page from the *Minneapolis Morning Tribune* (Fig. 422) demonstrates that, in spite of the tremendous technological advances and design innovations of the twentieth century, most newspapers had changed little from their nineteenth-century antecedents. Writing about newspapers, designer Philip Ritzenberg observed that "…virtually the entire industry clings to archaic graphic forms. While newspaper journalism continues to change and grow, the average newspaper itself still resembles a bulletin board hung with shreds of information, disorder passing for spontaneity, stridency passing for immediacy…." A newspaper must combine design and legibility with effective reportage if it is to maintain its position in a visually-oriented culture of instantaneous electronic communications.

Since the mid-1970s, major newspapers have turned to graphic designers for assistance in upgrading the organization and readability of their pages. The redesign of the *Minneapolis Tribune,* which was at the forefront of this design revolution, was accomplished under the direction of graphic designer Frank Ariss. The paper's continuing graphic evolution has been in the hands of Michael Carroll.

The *Minneapolis Tribune* logotype as it evolved over a century reflects efforts to improve it, while keeping it consistent with the traditional design (Fig. 423). In one fell swoop, Ariss catapulted the *Tribune* into the present. His symbol design for

use on *Tribune* vehicles, stationery, section headings, and so on, evokes a web of paper coming off a cylinder press (Fig. 424). It also mirrors the curved form of an open newspaper being held by a reader (Fig. 425).

Mindful that computerized typography and electronic page composition were on the horizon, Ariss used the "graphic engineering" of a grid structure to bring consistent, logical reorganization to every page. This grid has six 12½-pica-wide columns with one-pica gutters (Fig. 426). Each page is divided vertically into 167 units, which are 9½ points deep (the depth of the *Tribune's* text type). By sizing all elements correctly and placing them precisely on the grid, the staff formats every page within the parameters of the design system (Fig. 427).

Page layout is based on the "flush-left principle." Pages are built from the upper-left-hand corner, and each element (headlines, photographs, text) is placed on the page from the upper-left-hand corner of the space it occupies. One unit of space (9½ points) is used to separate related elements on the page, and two units of space (19 points) are

1867

Tribune

1921

Tribune

1932

Tribune

1969

Tribune

1971

Tribune

423.

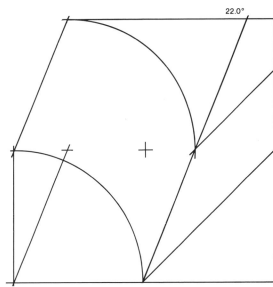

22.0°

424.
Construction schema for symbol.

425.

129

used to separate unrelated elements. As a result, a group of related elements, such as a headline, photograph with caption, and news article are combined into a unit on the page. This separation of editorial material by spatial intervals creates a clean, attractive, and readable page. The flush-left principle functions well with our custom of reading left to right. The *Tribune*'s computerized typesetters are programmed to set headline type in a flush-left mode.

The traditional clutter of newspaper design is caused in part by the potpourri of type sizes and styles used for headlines and the variety of type and column widths. The *Tribune* created visual order by using one text type (Bedford Roman with bold) and one headline type (Helvetica with bold). Helvetica Bold headlines are used for hard news stories, and the regular weight is used for features. Twelve sizes of each (from 12 to 80 point) give editors wide latitude in planning the visual hierarchy and relative importance of stories and features on each page.

The computer typesetters are coded to set all headlines in conformity with the grid. For example, in a headline composed of two lines of 30-point type, the typesetter adds 6½ points of interline space. The headline is 66½ points deep, filling seven of the 9½-point grid units. Precise specifications have been developed for picture captions, jump headlines (where a story continues onto another page), bylines, and other recurring typographic matter.

The *Tribune* uses an abundance of photographs, charts, maps, and illustrations to support and expand editorial content. Careful consideration is given to the graphic qualities of pictorial elements to achieve consistency throughout the newspaper.

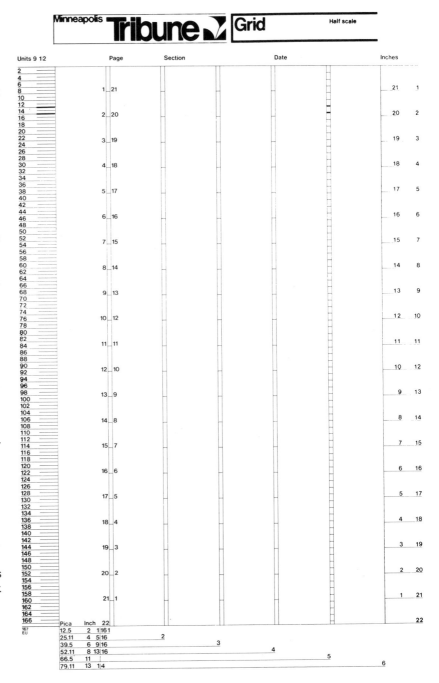

426.

427.

428.

Each special-feature section is purposefully designed to have a visual character and personality appropriate to its content. Michael Carroll comments that the "Special sections *look* special — different from the news section." The difference does not, however, break with the major design principles: Helvetica headline type, spacing intervals, and modular grid design. Special-section covers are simpler and more pictorial (Fig. 428). Carroll used the term *floating grid* to describe the greater spatial freedom in placing the typography and images on these pages.

The range of potential solutions to a typographic problem is seemingly infinite. Variations, permutations, and transformations can be developed, exploring changes in both fundamental aspects and subtle details. In this case study, designer Thomas Detrie has developed a sequence of solutions for a title-page design. Detrie's approach to the design process is based on his beliefs that "solutions come from within the problem" and "ideas come from working with the material and are not supplied or preconceived."

The problem-solving sequence is a three-stage design process: preliminary exploration, message investigation, and visualization of solutions. In his preliminary exploration, Detrie considered the nature and content of the problem and made sketches to explore possible directions. Typographic information (title, subtitle, authors, and publisher) was assigned priority. Detrie raised the question, "For the book *Basic Typography,* what is basic to typography that can be signified in a visual solution?" His answer established parameters appropriate to the given problem: a right-angled system, black on white, printed and unprinted areas, and a clear message. These considerations became the criteria for the investigation.

To investigate the range of typographic possibilities for the clear presentation of the manuscript, actual type was set and used in the initial visualizations for accuracy. A sans serif face was chosen, and the message was printed in three sizes and two weights for use as raw material in these typographic studies. While maintaining the message priorities determined in the first stage, a variety of visual solutions were executed. Decisions were made through subtle comparisons of type sizes and weights to select those that provided the best visual balance and message conveyance. Detrie did not place the type upon a predetermined grid; rather, he allowed the organizational structure to evolve from the process of working with the type proofs. Selecting the basic typographic arrangement was an intermediate step in the design process (Fig. 429).

Next, Detrie developed a series of variations of this arrangement by investigating the application of horizontal and vertical lines, positive and negative shapes with positive type, and positive and negative shapes with positive and reversed type. Figure 429 shows nine permutations with the application of vertical lines to the basic typographic schema. Permutations range from type alone to the addition of linear and rectilinear elements to a solid black page with reversed type (Fig. 430). A graded arrangement of twenty-four of the many solutions is shown in Figure 431. Observe the horizontal and vertical sequencing.

Unlimited solutions are possible in typographic design, and selection becomes an integral part of the design process. Not every possible solution is appropriate; the designer must continually evaluate each one against the problem criteria. The significance of Detrie's investigations lay in the workings of the design process.

This project commenced in the postgraduate program in graphic design at the Basel School of Design, Switzerland. The encouragement and criticism of Wolfgang Weingart is gratefully acknowledged.

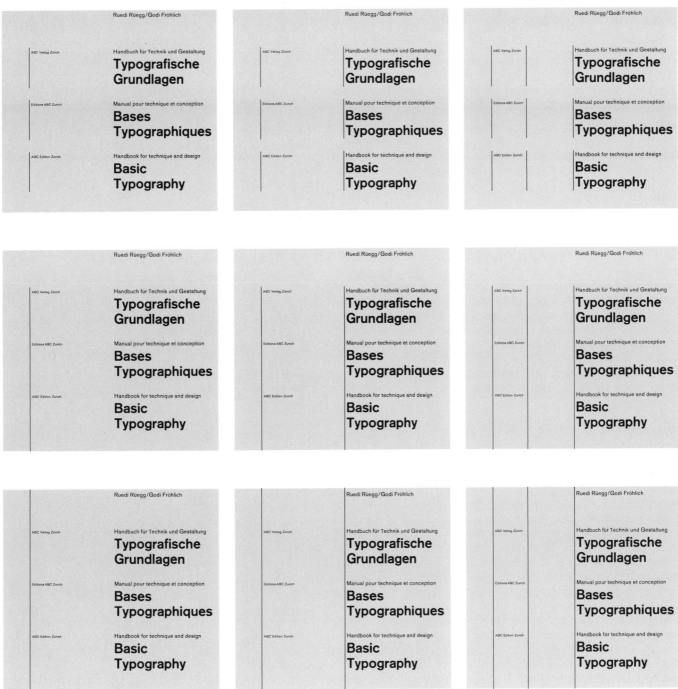

429.

430.

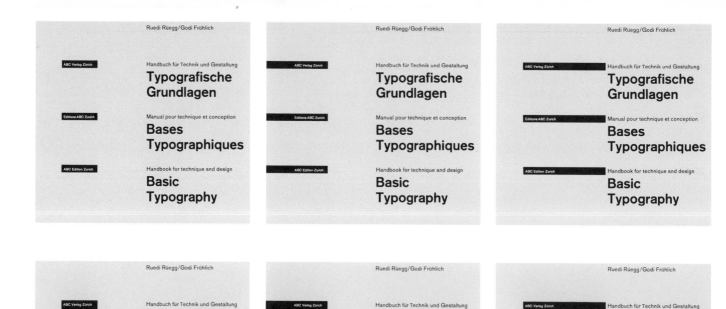

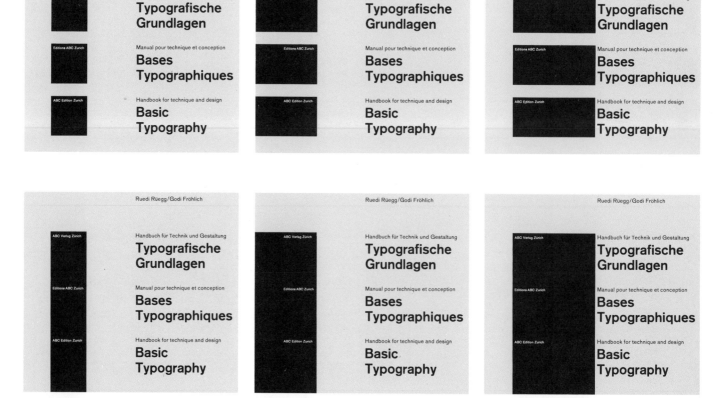

431.

Referring to a movie advertisement that used letterforms "painted by light," typographic historian Beatrice Warde wrote that "after forty centuries of the necessarily static Alphabet, I saw what its members could do in the fourth dimension of Time, 'flux,' movement. You may well say that I was electrified." Through advanced animation and computer-graphics techniques, graphic designers are transforming typographic communication into kinetic sequences that might almost be called "visual music."

Richard Greenberg, Director/Designer of R/Greenberg Associates in New York City, has emerged as a leading innovator on the frontier of cinematic graphic design for film titles, movie previews, special effects, and television commercials. Greenberg considers film titles to be a "visual metaphor" for the movie that follows, setting "the *tone* of the movie. You have to take the people who have just arrived at the theater and separate them from their ordinary reality—walking on the street, waiting in line; you bring them *into* the movie. You want to tell them how to react: that it's all right to laugh, that they are going to be scared, or that something serious is going on."

In the titles for the Warner Bros. film *Superman —the Movie,* bright blue names and the Superman emblem streak through space like comets,

stop for a moment, then evaporate into deep space (Fig. 432). The speed and power of this film's fantasy superhero are evoked. This effect is accomplished by tracking rear-illuminated typography in front of an open camera lens. Each frame captures a streak of light that starts and stops slightly before the light streak recorded on the next frame. When shown at twenty-four frames per second, this series of still images is transformed into a dynamic expression of zooming energy.

A very different mood is expressed by Greenberg in his title designs for the PolyGram Pictures production *Making Love* (Fig. 433). Four red dots appear on the black screen and begin to move, forming abstract lines. As the sequence continues, the word *LOVE* emerges and fills the screen in elegant sans serif letterforms having slightly tapered terminals. Then widely letterspaced capitals spell out the first word of the title.

For the Warner Bros. movie *Altered States,* the title sequence opens with a wide-angle image of a researcher in an isolation tank (Fig. 434). Superimposed over this image, the two words of the title —transparent, as if they are windows cut from a black background—overlap each other as they slowly move across the screen. The film credits are superimposed in white typography in front of this lively pattern of typographic forms and

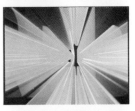

432.

counterforms. Behind the title the background slowly darkens while the camera pulls away from it, causing the letterforms to become smaller and smaller. Finally, the complete title, *Altered States,* appears in its entirety before the totally black screen. In the title, set in Avant Garde Demi, the right stroke of each capital *A* is deleted. The repetition of this unusual configuration unifies the two words and serves to make the title a unique and memorable signification.

An ominous and mysterious mood is created in the title sequence for the Twentieth Century-Fox production *Alien* (Fig. 435). As the camera tracks across a barren landscape, the title emerges before the void of deep space. One by one, small white rectangles appear and undergo a metamorphosis, forming a five-letter title letterspaced across the screen. In a dynamic change of scale and orientation for the audience, the landscape transforms into the egg of an alien. The sequence closes as an internal blast of light rips through the shell of the egg. The dramatic intensity of this final scene is strengthened by its contrast with the quietude of the initial sequence.

In contrast to the otherworldy aura created by the *Alien* film titles, Greenberg's film trailer and television promotion for the Universal Studios production *Jaws 3-D* combines straightforward ocean

433.

434.

footage and typographic animation with documentary conviction (Fig. 436). The trailer begins with a black screen. The first stroke of the roman numeral III fades in, revealing a calm sky and placid ocean as the voiceover speaks of the terror of the original *Jaws* motion picture. Next, another stroke fades in as the voiceover recalls the excitement of *Jaws II.* Then the center stroke fades in, revealing a distant figure moving through the ocean toward the viewer. As the viewer becomes aware that the figure is a shark's fin, the middle stroke of the roman numeral bursts outward, filling the frame with the menacing form. As the shark's fin turns, it becomes the curve of the letter *J* in the *Jaws 3-D* logo. The perspective configuration of the logo becomes a powerful signification of dimensionality, an appropriate expression of the intense spatial illusionism of the 3-D cinematography used in this film.

The time-space orientation of kinetic media enables the typographic designer to add motion, scale change, sequence, and metamorphosis to alphabet communication. As demonstrated by the work of Richard Greenberg, this opens new vistas of expressive communication.

436.

435.

138

Sensitive typographic treatment of a specific subject can often be found in publication design. A fine example of the marriage of typography — titles, text, and captions — to a particular content is displayed in the elegant full-color journal *Nautical Quarterly.*

This carefully crafted publication includes visual and written descriptions of yacht racing, regattas, boating safety, marine lore, and artifacts. The exemplary visuals are primarily photographs, with a rich texture of teak decks, taut sails, and blue skies. The text describes various marine traditions and locations from Gloucester to Sausalito.

Creative Director Martin Pedersen and his staff have designed a publication that reflects precise editing and thoughtful art direction. The readers — yachtsmen, skippers, and marine enthusiasts in general — are treated to articles presented with delicately balanced images and legible typography. Assembling multiple-component page spreads is a difficult task, requiring a thorough understanding of the subject and a design program that is flexible enough to accommodate a range of material.

Typically, a title page for a story article consists of the title, one or more images, text, borders, and rules. The article "The Indomitable Wander Bird" features a bold headline and has the text *(top)* and illustration *(below)* printed in a subtle screen tint of black (Fig. 437). The stenciled initial capital *A* and the small figure of a man act in combination with the ship to balance the page (Fig. 438). The tension created by this juxtaposition is relieved by the ample white space at the bottom. The *A* is blue, adding yet another visual accent to this straightforward yet lively title page. The example illustrates as well that a variety of typefaces can be combined successfully when care is given to their relative sizes, weights, and placement.

Pages are characterized by consistent margins, which are almost always reinforced by a fine border rule. A repetitive element is the *Nautical Quarterly* logotype, centered and reversed, in a

437.
A bold Egyptian headline is combined with stencil and Old Style typefaces for graphic diversity.
438.
This diagram demonstrates the principle of compensation; the careful placement and linking of elements to form an asymmetrical, balanced equilibrium.

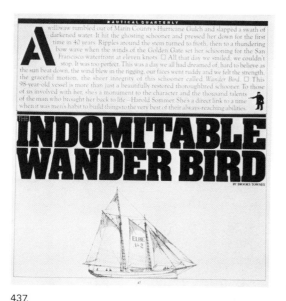

437.

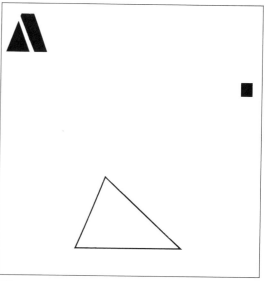

438.

439.

441.
This layout departs from the
standard format. Graphic connections to the other pages
are formed by: the text size;
the stencil letterform; inser-
tion of elements into a rec-
tangle of typography; and the
surrounding white space.

440.

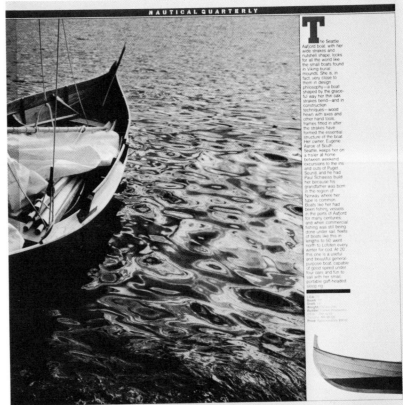

bar rule at the top of most pages (Fig. 439). Captions are set with a narrow column measure and
are often lengthy (Fig. 440). They can run a full
page in depth and function as both caption and text.
The organization of a publication involves establishing a visual hierarchy for each layout. Typography must fit the number of pages available for
editorial material, and take into account the arrangement and sequencing of pages. This means
that adjustments must be made in the sizing of
various typographic and pictorial components to
represent content graphically. These adjustments
are made possible by the flexibility within the grid
system, and determine to a large extent the overall
appearance of the magazine. For example, the full
text columns and relatively small photographs in
weekly newsmagazines project a very different
visual ambiance than the large photographs and
generous use of white space found in *Nautical
Quarterly.* The identity of any periodical is established by planned connections between components. Thus, a publication's format becomes a
familiar one for its readers.

While Pedersen and his staff have developed a
very consistent page format, they are willing to
depart from this system to achieve variety and to
express the content of special subject matter. In
an article about sharks (Fig. 441), the rules and
borders are abandoned for a dramatic cropping
of a full-page bleed illustration. A strong horizontal
movement is extended across the right-hand page
by the typography.

Nautical Quarterly is a journal of typographic
distinction. The success of its design can be at-
tributed to the designer's concern for visual hierarchy, attention to the linking and sequencing of
typographic elements, and careful selection of
typefaces and sizes for overall continuity.

441.

The typographic specimens in this chapter were selected from outstanding type families to provide examples of major classifications: Old Style, Transitional, Modern, Egyptian, and Sans Serif. Old Style is represented by ITC Garamond, a recent redesign with a large x-height and a weight range popular in recent decades. By contrast, the specimens of Baskerville, the Transitional face displayed here, have the letter proportions of traditional typography. The strong geometric stress and thick-and-thin strokes of the Modern category are demonstrated by Bodoni. Egyptian is represented by specimens of a recent type family, ITC Lubalin Graph, which has slab serifs and the geometric construction found in much twentieth-century design. The Univers family, known for the design cohesion among its members, represents the Sans Serif category.

More extensive specimens of ITC Garamond and Univers than of the other families are shown. They are typical of the two most widely used categories. Enlarged fonts are included for study and tracing purposes. Text specimens are shown with one-, two-, and three-point interline spacing. Eight full columns of text type are included for comparison and for layout purposes. Additional display fonts are shown in approximately 30-point type. These materials have been carefully selected to provide a compendium of the essential qualities of typographic form.

ORONTII FINEI

DELPHINATIS, REGII MATHEMA=
TICARVM PROFESSORIS, DE
ARITHMETICA PRACTICA
LIBRI QVATVOR.

LIBER PRIMVS, DE INTEGRIS: HOC EST,
eiuſdem ſpeciei, ſiue denominationis tractat numeris.

De fructu, atq dignitate ipſius Arithmeticæ: Proœmium.

1

NTER LIBERALES MA=
thematicas, quæ ſolæ diſciplinæ vocátur,
Arithmeticam primum locum ſibi vendi=
caſſe: nemo ſanæ mentis ignorat. Eſt enim
Arithmetica omnium aliarum diſciplina=
rum mater, & nutrix antiquiſſima: nume=
rorū qualitates, vim, & naturam, ac id ge=
nus alia demonſtrans, quæ abſolutum vi=
dentur reſpicere numerum . Cuius prin=
cipia tanta excellunt ſimplicitate , vt nul=
lius artis videatur indigere ſuffragio: ſed cunctis opituletur artibus. Ad
cuius puritatem illud etiam plurimum facit: quoniam nulla diuinitati
adeò cónexa eſt diſciplina, quantùm Arithmetica. Nam vnitas omniū
numerorū radix & origo, in ſe, à ſe, ac circum ſeipſam vnica vel impar=
tibilis permanet: ex cuius tamen coaceruatione, omnis cóſurgit & ge=
neratur, omniſque tandem in eam reſoluitur numerus. Quemadmo=
dum cuncta quæ ſeu diſcreta, ſiue compoſita inſpectentur Vniuerſo, à
ſummo rerum conditore in definitum digeſta, redactáve ſunt, & demū
reſoluenda numerum. Quot autem vtilitates cognita, quótve laby=
rinthos ignota præbeat Arithmetica: conſpicere facile eſt. Numerorū
etenim ratione ſublata, tollitur & muſicarum modulationū intelligen=
tia: geometricorum , cæleſtiúmve arcanorum ſubtilis aufertur ingreſ=
ſio: tollitur & vniuerſa Philoſophia , ſiue quæ diuina, ſeu quæ contem=
platur humana: imperfecta relinquitur legū adminiſtratio, vtpote, quæ

Dignitas arithmeticę.

2

Fructus arithmeticę.

A. iij.

Old Style   **ITC Garamond**

442.

Page three, *Arithmetica* by Oronce Fine, printed by Simon de Colines in Paris, 1535.

Although Old Style typefaces trace their development to the printers of the Italian Renaissance, their heritage extends to an earlier time, for Roman inscriptional letterforms inspired their capital-letter design. The Caroline Minuscules from medieval manuscripts inspired writing styles during the fifteenth century, and these became the model for Old Style lowercase letters.

Many Old Style typefaces bear the name of Claude Garamond, a leading typeface designer and punchcutter working in Paris when the book *Arithmetica* was printed (Fig. 442). In the heading material, the designer used bold capitals for the author's name, two sizes of capitals for the title,

and italics for a subhead. The spatial intervals between these units have been established with great care. Fleurons (printer's flowers), paragraph marks, a woodcut headpiece, and a large initial bring vibrancy to this elegant example of French Renaissance book design.

ITC Garamond, presented here, was designed by Tony Stan for the International Typeface Corporation. The first four fonts in the family were issued in 1975. ITC Garamond has a large x-height and shortened ascenders and descenders. The complete type family has sixteen fonts, light, book, bold, and ultra, each with an italic, and a companion series of eight condensed versions.

abcdefgh
ijklmnop
qrstuvw
xyz$1234
567890,.;:!?

ABCDEF
GHIJKL
MNOPQ
RSTUV
WXYZ&

abcdefghijklmn

opqrstuvwxyz

ABCDEFGHIJK

LMNOPQRSTU

VWXYZ$12344

567890(,"'"-;:!)?&

72 Point

abcdefghijklmn
opqrstuvwxyz
ABCDEFGHIJK
LMNOPQRSTU
VWXYZ$1234
567890(,'""-;.:!)?&

abcdefghijklmnopq
rstuvwxyzABCD
EFGHIJKLMNOPQ
RSTUVWXYZ$123
4567890(.,""""-;.:!)?&

abcdefghijklmnopqrstu
vwxyzABCDEFGHIJK
LMNOPQRSTUVWXYZ
$12344567890(.,""""-;.:!)?&

abcdefghijklmnopq
rstuvwxyzABCDE
FGHIJKLMNOPQR
STUVWXYZ$1234
567890(,'""-;:!)?&&

abcdefghijklmnopqrstu
vwxyzABCDEFGHIJK
LMNOPQRSTUVWXYZ
$12344567890(,'""-;:!)?&&

abcdefghijklmnopqrstuvwxyz
ABCDEFGHIJKLMNOPQRSTUV
WXYZ$12344567890 (.,""''-;:!)?&

abcdefghijklmnopqrstuvwxyz
ABCDEFGHIJKLMNOPQRSTUVW
XYZ$12344567890 (.,""''-;:!)?&

abcdefghijklmnopqrstuvwxyz
ABCDEFGHIJKLMNOPQRSTUVWXYZ
$12344567890 (.,""''-;:!)?&

abcdefghijklmnopqrstuvwxyz
ABCDEFGHIJKLMNOPQRSTUVWXYZ
$12344567890 (.,""''-;:!)?&

36 Point

abcdefghijklmnopqrstuvwxyz
ABCDEFGHIJKLMNOPQRSTU
VWXYZ$1234567890(,'""-;:!)?&

30 Point

abcdefghijklmnopqrstuvwxyz
ABCDEFGHIJKLMNOPQRSTUVW
XYZ$1234567890(,'""-;:!)?&

24 Point

abcdefghijklmnopqrstuvwxyz
ABCDEFGHIJKLMNOPQRSTUVWXYZ
$1234567890(,'""-;:!)?&

18 Point

abcdefghijklmnopqrstuvwxyz
ABCDEFGHIJKLMNOPQRSTUVWXYZ
$1234567890(,'""-;:!)?&

72 Point

abcdefghijklmno
pqrstuvwxyz
ABCDEFGHIJKL
MNOPQRSTUV
WXYZ$123456
7890(,'""–-;:!)?&

ITC Garamond Bold

(,’“”-;:!)?&

72 Point

abcdefghijklm
nopqrstuvwx
yzABCDEFGH
IJKLMNOPQ
RSTUVWXYZ
$1234567890

abcdefghijklmnopqrstuv
wxyzABCDEFGHIJKL
MNOPQRSTUVWXYZ
$1234567890 (.,"""-;:!)?&

abcdefghijklmnopqrstuvwxyz
ABCDEFGHIJKLMNOPQRSTUVWXYZ
$1234567890 (.,"""-;:!)?&

abcdefghijklmnopqrstuvwxyz
ABCDEFGHIJKLMNOPQRSTUVWXYZ
$1234567890 (.,"""-;:!)?&

(.,""''-;:!)?&

abcdefghijklmnopqrs
tuvwxyzABCDEFGH
IJKLMNOPQRSTUVW
XYZ$1234567890

abcdefghijklmnopqrstuvwxyz
ABCDEFGHIJKLMNOPQRSTUVW
XYZ$1234567890(.,""''-;:!)?&

abcdefghijklmnopqrstuvwxyz
ABCDEFGHIJKLMNOPQRSTUVWXYZ
$1234567890(.,""''-;:!)?&

72 Point

abcdefghijkl
mnopqrstuv
wxyzABCDEF
GHIJKLMNO
PQRSTUVW
XYZ$123456

abcdefghijklmnop
qrstuvwxyzABCDEF
GHIJKLMNOPQRST
UVWXYZ$123456
7890 (.,"""-;:!)?&

abcdefghijklmnopqrstuvwxyz
ABCDEFGHIJKLMNOPQRSTUV
WXYZ$12344567890 (.,"""-;:!)?&

abcdefghijklmnopqrstuvwxyz ABCDEFGHIJKL
MNOPQRSTUVWXYZ$12344567890 (.,"""-;:!)?&

abcdefghijklmnopqr
stuvwxyzABCDEFGH
IJKLMNOPQRSTUV
WXYZ$1234567890
(.,'""-;:!)?&

abcdefghijklmnopqrstuvw
xyzABCDEFGHIJKLMNOPQRS
TUVWXYZ$12344567890
(.,""''-;:!)?&

abcdefghijklmnopqrstuvwxyz

ABCDEFGHIJKLMNOPQRSTUVWXYZ

$12344567890 (.,""''-;:!)?&

abcdefghijklmnopqrstuvwxyz
ABCDEFGHIJKLMNOPQRSTUVWXYZ
$12344567890 (.,""''-;:!)?&

abcdefghijklmnopq
rstuvwxyzABCDE
FGHIJKLMNOPQRS
TUVWXYZ$12345
67890(.,""''-;:!)?&

abcdefghijklmnopqrstuvw
xyz ABCDEFGHIJKLMNOPQ
RSTUVWXYZ $12345678
90 (.,""''-;:!)?&

abcdefghijklmnopqrstuvwxyz
ABCDEFGHIJKLMNOPQRSTUVWXYZ
$12344567890 (.,""''-;:!)?&

abcdefghijklmnopqrstuvwxyz
ABCDEFGHIJKLMNOPQRSTUVWXYZ
$12344567890 (.,""''-;:!)?&

72 Point

abcdefghijklmn
opqrstuvwxyz
ABCDEFGHIJKLM
NOPQRSTUVWX
YZ$1234456789O
(.,""''-;:!)?&

abcdefghijklmnopqrstu
vwxyzABCDEFGHIJKLMN
OPQRSTUVWXYZ$12344
567890 (.,""''-;:!)?&

abcdefghijklmnopqrstuvwxyz
ABCDEFGHIJKLMNOPQRSTUVWXYZ
$12344567890 (.,""''-;:!)?&

abcdefghijklmnopqrstuvwxyz
ABCDEFGHIJKLMNOPQRSTUVWXYZ
$12344567890 (.,""''-;:!)?&

(.,''""„"–-;:!)?&

72 Point

abcdefghijklmnop
qrstuvwxyz ABCD
EFGHIJKLMNOPQ
RSTUVWXYZ $1234
4567890

abcdefghijklmnopqrstuv
wxyzABCDEFGHIJKLMNOP
QRSTUVWXYZ$12345678
90(.,'""''-;:!)?&

abcdefghijklmnopqrstuvwxyz
ABCDEFGHIJKLMNOPQRSTUVWXYZ
$12344567890(.,'""''-;:!)?&

abcdefghijklmnopqrstuvwxyz
ABCDEFGHIJKLMNOPQRSTUVWXYZ
$12344567890(.,'""''-;:!)?&

abcdefghijklmnopqrstuvwxyz
ABCDEFGHIJKLMNOPQRSTUVWXYZ
$1234567890(.,'"-;:!)?&

abcdefghijklmnopqrstuvwxyz
ABCDEFGHIJKLMNOPQRSTUVWXYZ
$1234567890(.,'"-;:!)?&

abcdefghijklmnopqrstuvwxyz
ABCDEFGHIJKLMNOPQRSTUVWXYZ
$1234567890(.,'"-;:!)?&

abcdefghijklmnopqrstuvwxyz
ABCDEFGHIJKLMNOPQRSTUVWXYZ
$1234567890(.,'"-;:!)?&

ITC Garamond Light

The whole duty of Typography, as of Calligraphy, is to communicate to the imagination, without loss by the way, the thought or image intended to be communicated by the Author. And the whole duty of beautiful typography is not to substitute for the beauty or interest of the thing thought and intended to be conveyed by the symbol, a beauty or interest of its own, but, on the one hand, to win access for that communication by the clearness and beauty of the vehicle, and on the other hand, to take advantage of every pause or stage in that communication to interpose some characteristic & restful beauty in its own art. We thus have a reason for the clearness and beauty of the text as a whole, for the especial beauty of the first or introductory page and of the title, and for the especial beauty of the headings of chapters, capital or initial letters, and so on, and an opening for the illustrator as we shall see by and by. Further, in the case of Poetry, verse, in my opinion, appeals by its form to the eye, as well as to *the ear, and should be placed on the page so that its structure*
8/9

The whole duty of Typography, as of Calligraphy, is to communicate to the imagination, without loss by the way, the thought or image intended to be communicated by the Author. And the whole duty of beautiful typography is not to substitute for the beauty or interest of the thing thought and intended to be conveyed by the symbol, a beauty or interest of its own, but, on the one hand, to win access for that communication by the clearness and beauty of the vehicle, and on the other hand, to take advantage of every pause or stage in that communication to interpose some characteristic & restful beauty in its own art. We thus have a reason for the clearness and beauty of the text as a whole, for the especial beauty of the first or introductory page and of the title, and for the especial beauty of the headings of chapters, capital or initial letters, and so on, and an opening for the illustrator as we shall see by and by. Further, in the case of Poetry, *verse, in my opinion, appeals by its form to the eye, as well as to*
8/10

The whole duty of Typography, as of Calligraphy, is to communicate to the imagination, without loss by the way, the thought or image intended to be communicated by the Author. And the whole duty of beautiful typography is not to substitute for the beauty or interest of the thing thought and intended to be conveyed by the symbol, a beauty or interest of its own, but, on the one hand, to win access for that communication by the clearness and beauty of the vehicle, and on the other hand, to take advantage of every pause or stage in that communication to interpose some characteristic & restful beauty in its own art. We thus have a reason for the clearness and beauty of the text as a whole, for the especial beauty of the first or introductory page and of the title, and for the especial beauty of the headings of chapters, *capital or initial letters, and so on, and an opening for the illus-*
8/11

The whole duty of Typography, as of Calligraphy, is to communicate to the imagination, without loss by the way, the thought or image intended to be communicated by the Author. And the whole duty of beautiful typography is not to substitute for the beauty or interest of the thing thought and intended to be conveyed by the symbol, a beauty or interest of its own, but, on the one hand, to win access for that communication by the clearness and beauty of the vehicle, and on the other hand, to take advantage of every pause or stage in that communication to interpose some characteristic & restful beauty in its own art. We thus have a reason for the clearness and beauty of the text as a whole, for the especial beauty of the first or introductory page and of the title, and for the especial beauty of the headings of chapters, capital or *initial letters, and so on, and an opening for the illustrator*
9/10

The whole duty of Typography, as of Calligraphy, is to communicate to the imagination, without loss by the way, the thought or image intended to be communicated by the Author. And the whole duty of beautiful typography is not to substitute for the beauty or interest of the thing thought and intended to be conveyed by the symbol, a beauty or interest of its own, but, on the one hand, to win access for that communication by the clearness and beauty of the vehicle, and on the other hand, to take advantage of every pause or stage in that communication to interpose some characteristic & restful beauty in its own art. We thus have a reason for the clearness and beauty of the text as a whole, for the especial beauty of *the first or introductory page and of the title, and for the*
9/11

The whole duty of Typography, as of Calligraphy, is to communicate to the imagination, without loss by the way, the thought or image intended to be communicated by the Author. And the whole duty of beautiful typography is not to substitute for the beauty or interest of the thing thought and intended to be conveyed by the symbol, a beauty or interest of its own, but, on the one hand, to win access for that communication by the clearness and beauty of the vehicle, and on the other hand, to take advantage of every pause or stage in that communication to interpose some characteristic & restful beauty in its own art. We thus have a reason for the clearness and *beauty of the text as a whole, for the especial beauty of*
9/12

abcdefghijklmnopqrstuvwxyz
ABCDEFGHIJKLMNOPQRSTUVWXYZ
$1234567890(.,'"-;:!)?&

abcdefghijklmnopqrstuvwxyz
ABCDEFGHIJKLMNOPQRSTUVWXYZ
$1234567890(.,'"-;:!)?&

abcdefghijklmnopqrstuvwxyz
ABCDEFGHIJKLMNOPQRSTUVWXYZ
$1234567890(.,'"-;:!)?&

abcdefghijklmnopqrstuvwxyz
ABCDEFGHIJKLMNOPQRSTUVWXYZ
$1234567890(.,'"-;:!)?&

The whole duty of Typography, as of Calligraphy, is to communicate to the imagination, without loss by the way, the thought or image intended to be communicated by the Author. And the whole duty of beautiful typography is not to substitute for the beauty or interest of the thing thought and intended to be conveyed by the symbol, a beauty or interest of its own, but, on the one hand, to win access for that communication by the clearness and beauty of the vehicle, and on the other hand, to take advantage of every pause or stage in that communication to interpose some characteristic & restful beauty in its own art. We thus have a reason for the clearness *and beauty of the text as a whole, for the especial*
10/11

The whole duty of Typography, as of Calligraphy, is to communicate to the imagination, without loss by the way, the thought or image intended to be communicated by the Author. And the whole duty of beautiful typography is not to substitute for the beauty or interest of the thing thought and intended to be conveyed by the symbol, a beauty or interest of its own, but, on the one hand, to win access for that communication by the clearness and beauty of the vehicle, and on the other hand, to take advantage of every pause or stage in that communication to interpose some characteristic & restful beauty in *its own art. We thus have a reason for the clearness*
10/12

The whole duty of Typography, as of Calligraphy, is to communicate to the imagination, without loss by the way, the thought or image intended to be communicated by the Author. And the whole duty of beautiful typography is not to substitute for the beauty or interest of the thing thought and intended to be conveyed by the symbol, a beauty or interest of its own, but, on the one hand, to win access for that communication by the clearness and beauty of the vehicle, and on the other hand, to take advantage of every pause or stage in that communication *to interpose some characteristic & restful beauty in*
10/13

The whole duty of Typography, as of Calligraphy, is to communicate to the imagination, without loss by the way, the thought or image intended to be communicated by the Author. And the whole duty of beautiful typography is not to substitute for the beauty or interest of the thing thought and intended to be conveyed by the symbol, a beauty or interest of its own, but, on the one hand, to win access for that communication by the clearness and beauty of the *vehicle, and on the other hand, to take ad* -
12/13

The whole duty of Typography, as of Calligraphy, is to communicate to the imagination, without loss by the way, the thought or image intended to be communicated by the Author. And the whole duty of beautiful typography is not to substitute for the beauty or interest of the thing thought and intended to be conveyed by the symbol, a beauty or interest of its own, but, on the one hand, to win access for that communi- *cation by the clearness and beauty of the*
12/14

The whole duty of Typography, as of Calligraphy, is to communicate to the imagination, without loss by the way, the thought or image intended to be communicated by the Author. And the whole duty of beautiful typography is not to substitute for the beauty or interest of the thing thought and intended to be conveyed by the symbol, a beauty or interest of its own, but, on the *one hand, to win access for that communi-*
12/15

abcdefghijklmnopqrstuvwxyz
ABCDEFGHIJKLMNOPQRSTUVWXYZ
$1234567890(.,'"-;:!)?&

abcdefghijklmnopqrstuvwxyz
ABCDEFGHIJKLMNOPQRSTUVWXYZ
$1234567890(.,'"-;:!)?&

abcdefghijklmnopqrstuvwxyz
ABCDEFGHIJKLMNOPQRSTUVWXYZ
$1234567890(.,'"-;:!)?&

abcdefghijklmnopqrstuvwxyz
ABCDEFGHIJKLMNOPQRSTUVWXYZ
$1234567890(.,'"-;:!)?&

ITC Garamond Book

The whole duty of Typography, as of Calligraphy, is to communicate to the imagination, without loss by the way, the thought or image intended to be communicated by the Author. And the whole duty of beautiful typography is not to substitute for the beauty or interest of the thing thought and intended to be conveyed by the symbol, a beauty or interest of its own, but, on the one hand, to win access for that communication by the clearness and beauty of the vehicle, and on the other hand, to take advantage of every pause or stage in that communication to interpose some characteristic & restful beauty in its own art. We thus have a reason for the clearness and beauty of the text as a whole, for the especial beauty of the first or introductory page and of the title, and for the especial beauty of the headings of chapters, capital or initial letters, and so on, and an opening for the illustrator as we shall see by and by. Further, in the case of Poetry, verse, *in my opinion, appeals by its form to the eye, as well as to the*
8/9

The whole duty of Typography, as of Calligraphy, is to communicate to the imagination, without loss by the way, the thought or image intended to be communicated by the Author. And the whole duty of beautiful typography is not to substitute for the beauty or interest of the thing thought and intended to be conveyed by the symbol, a beauty or interest of its own, but, on the one hand, to win access for that communication by the clearness and beauty of the vehicle, and on the other hand, to take advantage of every pause or stage in that communication to interpose some characteristic & restful beauty in its own art. We thus have a reason for the clearness and beauty of the text as a whole, for the especial beauty of the first or introductory page and of the title, and for the especial beauty of the headings of chapters, capital or initial letters, and so on, and an opening for the illustrator *as we shall see by and by. Further, in the case of Poetry, verse,*
8/10

The whole duty of Typography, as of Calligraphy, is to communicate to the imagination, without loss by the way, the thought or image intended to be communicated by the Author. And the whole duty of beautiful typography is not to substitute for the beauty or interest of the thing thought and intended to be conveyed by the symbol, a beauty or interest of its own, but, on the one hand, to win access for that communication by the clearness and beauty of the vehicle, and on the other hand, to take advantage of every pause or stage in that communication to interpose some characteristic & restful beauty in its own art. We thus have a reason for the clearness and beauty of the text as a whole, for the especial beauty of the first or introductory page and of the title, and *for the especial beauty of the headings of chapters, capital*
8/11

The whole duty of Typography, as of Calligraphy, is to communicate to the imagination, without loss by the way, the thought or image intended to be communicated by the Author. And the whole duty of beautiful typography is not to substitute for the beauty or interest of the thing thought and intended to be conveyed by the symbol, a beauty or interest of its own, but, on the one hand, to win access for that communication by the clearness and beauty of the vehicle, and on the other hand, to take advantage of every pause or stage in that communication to interpose some characteristic & restful beauty in its own art. We thus have a reason for the clearness and beauty of the text as a whole, for the especial beauty of the first or introductory page and of the title, and for the especial beauty of the headings *of chapters, capital or initial letters, and so on, and*
9/10

The whole duty of Typography, as of Calligraphy, is to communicate to the imagination, without loss by the way, the thought or image intended to be communicated by the Author. And the whole duty of beautiful typography is not to substitute for the beauty or interest of the thing thought and intended to be conveyed by the symbol, a beauty or interest of its own, but, on the one hand, to win access for that communication by the clearness and beauty of the vehicle, and on the other hand, to take advantage of every pause or stage in that communication to interpose some characteristic & restful beauty in its own art. We thus have a reason for the clearness and beauty of the text as a whole, for the *especial beauty of the first or introductory page and*
9/11

The whole duty of Typography, as of Calligraphy, is to communicate to the imagination, without loss by the way, the thought or image intended to be communicated by the Author. And the whole duty of beautiful typography is not to substitute for the beauty or interest of the thing thought and intended to be conveyed by the symbol, a beauty or interest of its own, but, on the one hand, to win access for that communication by the clearness and beauty of the vehicle, and on the other hand, to take advantage of every pause or stage in that communication to interpose some characteristic & restful beauty in its own art. We thus have a reason for *the clearness and beauty of the text as a whole, for*
9/12

abcdefghijklmnopqrstuvwxyz
ABCDEFGHIJKLMNOPQRSTUVWXYZ
$1234567890(.,'"-;:!)?&

abcdefghijklmnopqrstuvwxyz
ABCDEFGHIJKLMNOPQRSTUVWXYZ
$1234567890(.,'"-;:!)?&

abcdefghijklmnopqrstuvwxyz
ABCDEFGHIJKLMNOPQRSTUVWXYZ
$1234567890(.,'"-;:!)?&

abcdefghijklmnopqrstuvwxyz
ABCDEFGHIJKLMNOPQRSTUVWXYZ
$1234567890(.,'"-;:!)?&

The whole duty of Typography, as of Calligraphy, is to communicate to the imagination, without loss by the way, the thought or image intended to be communicated by the Author. And the whole duty of beautiful typography is not to substitute for the beauty or interest of the thing thought and intended to be conveyed by the symbol, a beauty or interest of its own, but, on the one hand, to win access for that communication by the clearness and beauty of the vehicle, and on the other hand, to take advantage of every pause or stage in that communication to interpose some characteristic & restful beauty in its own art. We thus have *a reason for the clearness and beauty of the text*
10/11

The whole duty of Typography, as of Calligraphy, is to communicate to the imagination, without loss by the way, the thought or image intended to be communicated by the Author. And the whole duty of beautiful typography is not to substitute for the beauty or interest of the thing thought and intended to be conveyed by the symbol, a beauty or interest of its own, but, on the one hand, to win access for that communication by the clearness and beauty of the vehicle, and on the other hand, to take advantage of every pause or stage in that communication to interpose some character-*istic & restful beauty in its own art. We thus have*
10/12

The whole duty of Typography, as of Calligraphy, is to communicate to the imagination, without loss by the way, the thought or image intended to be communicated by the Author. And the whole duty of beautiful typography is not to substitute for the beauty or interest of the thing thought and intended to be conveyed by the symbol, a beauty or interest of its own, but, on the one hand, to win access for that communication by the clearness and beauty of the vehicle, and on the other hand, to take advantage of every pause or stage in *that communication to interpose some char-*
10/13

The whole duty of Typography, as of Calligraphy, is to communicate to the imagination, without loss by the way, the thought or image intended to be communicated by the Author. And the whole duty of beautiful typography is not to substitute for the beauty or interest of the thing thought and intended to be conveyed by the symbol, a beauty or interest of its own, but, on the one hand, to win access for that communication by the *clearness and beauty of the vehicle, and*
12/13

The whole duty of Typography, as of Calligraphy, is to communicate to the imagination, without loss by the way, the thought or image intended to be communicated by the Author. And the whole duty of beautiful typography is not to substitute for the beauty or interest of the thing thought and intended to be conveyed by the symbol, a beauty or interest of its own, but, on the one hand, to win *access for that communication by the*
12/14

The whole duty of Typography, as of Calligraphy, is to communicate to the imagination, without loss by the way, the thought or image intended to be communicated by the Author. And the whole duty of beautiful typography is not to substitute for the beauty or interest of the thing thought and intended to be conveyed by the symbol, a beauty or interest *of its own, but, on the one hand, to win*
12/15

abcdefghijklmnopqrstuvwxyz
ABCDEFGHIJKLMNOPQRSTUVWXYZ
$1234567890(.,'"-;:!)?&

abcdefghijklmnopqrstuvwxyz
ABCDEFGHIJKLMNOPQRSTUVWXYZ
$1234567890(.,'"-;:!)?&

abcdefghijklmnopqrstuvwxyz
ABCDEFGHIJKLMNOPQRSTUVWXYZ
$1234567890(.,'"-;:!)?&

abcdefghijklmnopqrstuvwxyz
ABCDEFGHIJKLMNOPQRSTUVWXYZ
$1234567890(.,'"-;:!)?&

ITC Garamond Bold

The whole duty of Typography, as of Calligraphy, is to communicate to the imagination, without loss by the way, the thought or image intended to be communicated by the Author. And the whole duty of beautiful typography is not to substitute for the beauty or interest of the thing thought and intended to be conveyed by the symbol, a beauty or interest of its own, but, on the one hand, to win access for that communication by the clearness and beauty of the vehicle, and on the other hand, to take advantage of every pause or stage in that communication to interpose some characteristic & restful beauty in its own art. We thus have a reason for the clearness and beauty of the text as a whole, for the especial beauty of the first or introductory page and of the title, and for the especial beauty of the headings of chapters, capital or initial *letters, and so on, and an opening for the illustrator*
8/9

The whole duty of Typography, as of Calligraphy, is to communicate to the imagination, without loss by the way, the thought or image intended to be communicated by the Author. And the whole duty of beautiful typography is not to substitute for the beauty or interest of the thing thought and intended to be conveyed by the symbol, a beauty or interest of its own, but, on the one hand, to win access for that communication by the clearness and beauty of the vehicle, and on the other hand, to take advantage of every pause or stage in that communication to interpose some characteristic & restful beauty in its own art. We thus have a reason for the clearness and beauty of the text as a whole, for the especial beauty of the first or introductory page and of the title, and for the especial *beauty of the headings of chapters, capital or initial*
8/10

The whole duty of Typography, as of Calligraphy, is to communicate to the imagination, without loss by the way, the thought or image intended to be communicated by the Author. And the whole duty of beautiful typography is not to substitute for the beauty or interest of the thing thought and intended to be conveyed by the symbol, a beauty or interest of its own, but, on the one hand, to win access for that communication by the clearness and beauty of the vehicle, and on the other hand, to take advantage of every pause or stage in that communication to interpose some characteristic & restful beauty in its own art. We thus have a reason for the clearness and beauty of the text as a *whole, for the especial beauty of the first or intro-*
8/11

The whole duty of Typography, as of Calligraphy, is to communicate to the imagination, without loss by the way, the thought or image intended to be communicated by the Author. And the whole duty of beautiful typography is not to substitute for the beauty or interest of the thing thought and intended to be conveyed by the symbol, a beauty or interest of its own, but, on the one hand, to win access for that communication by the clearness and beauty of the vehicle, and on the other hand, to take advantage of every pause or stage in that communication to interpose some characteristic & restful beauty in its own art. We thus have a reason for the clearness and beauty of the text as a whole, for *the especial beauty of the first or introductory*
9/10

The whole duty of Typography, as of Calligraphy, is to communicate to the imagination, without loss by the way, the thought or image intended to be communicated by the Author. And the whole duty of beautiful typography is not to substitute for the beauty or interest of the thing thought and intended to be conveyed by the symbol, a beauty or interest of its own, but, on the one hand, to win access for that communication by the clearness and beauty of the vehicle, and on the other hand, to take advantage of every pause or stage in that communication to interpose some characteristic & restful beauty *in its own art. We thus have a reason for the*
9/11

The whole duty of Typography, as of Calligraphy, is to communicate to the imagination, without loss by the way, the thought or image intended to be communicated by the Author. And the whole duty of beautiful typography is not to substitute for the beauty or interest of the thing thought and intended to be conveyed by the symbol, a beauty or interest of its own, but, on the one hand, to win access for that communication by the clearness and beauty of the vehicle, and on the other hand, to take advantage of every pause or stage in that communication to *interpose some characteristic & restful beauty*
9/12

abcdefghijklmnopqrstuvwxyz
ABCDEFGHIJKLMNOPQRSTUVWXYZ
$1234567890(.,'"-;:!)?&

abcdefghijklmnopqrstuvwxyz
ABCDEFGHIJKLMNOPQRSTUVWXYZ
$1234567890(.,'"-;:!)?&

abcdefghijklmnopqrstuvwxyz
ABCDEFGHIJKLMNOPQRSTUVWXYZ
$1234567890(.,'"-;:!)?&

abcdefghijklmnopqrstuvwxyz
ABCDEFGHIJKLMNOPQRSTUVWXYZ
$1234567890(.,'"-;:!)?&

The whole duty of Typography, as of Callig-raphy, is to communicate to the imagina-tion, without loss by the way, the thought or image intended to be communicated by the Author. And the whole duty of beautiful typography is not to substitute for the beauty or interest of the thing thought and intended to be conveyed by the symbol, a beauty or interest of its own, but, on the one hand, to win access for that communi-cation by the clearness and beauty of the vehicle, and on the other hand, to take ad-vantage of every pause or stage in that com-*munication to interpose some characteris-*

10/11

The whole duty of Typography, as of Callig-raphy, is to communicate to the imagina-tion, without loss by the way, the thought or image intended to be communicated by the Author. And the whole duty of beautiful typography is not to substitute for the beauty or interest of the thing thought and intended to be conveyed by the symbol, a beauty or interest of its own, but, on the one hand, to win access for that communi-cation by the clearness and beauty of the vehicle, and on the other hand, to take ad-*vantage of every pause or stage in that com-*

10/12

The whole duty of Typography, as of Callig-raphy, is to communicate to the imagina-tion, without loss by the way, the thought or image intended to be communicated by the Author. And the whole duty of beautiful typography is not to substitute for the beauty or interest of the thing thought and intended to be conveyed by the symbol, a beauty or interest of its own, but, on the one hand, to win access for that communi-cation by the clearness and beauty of the *vehicle, and on the other hand, to take ad-*

10/13

The whole duty of Typography, as of Calligraphy, is to communicate to the imagination, without loss by the way, the thought or image intended to be communicated by the Author. And the whole duty of beautiful typography is not to substitute for the beauty or interest of the thing thought and intended to be conveyed by the symbol, a beauty or interest of its own, but, on the one *hand, to win access for that com-*

12/13

The whole duty of Typography, as of Calligraphy, is to communicate to the imagination, without loss by the way, the thought or image intended to be communicated by the Author. And the whole duty of beautiful typography is not to substitute for the beauty or interest of the thing thought and intended to be conveyed by the symbol, a beauty or in-*terest of its own, but, on the one*

12/14

The whole duty of Typography, as of Calligraphy, is to communicate to the imagination, without loss by the way, the thought or image intended to be communicated by the Author. And the whole duty of beautiful typography is not to substitute for the beauty or interest of the thing thought and intended to be con-*veyed by the symbol, a beauty or in-*

12/15

Im VERLAG DES BILDUNGSVERBANDES der Deutschen Buchdrucker,
Berlin SW 61, Dreibundstr. 5, erscheint demnächst:

JAN TSCHICHOLD
Lehrer an der Meisterschule für Deutschlands Buchdrucker in München

DIE NEUE TYPOGRAPHIE

**Handbuch für die gesamte Fachwelt
und die drucksachenverbrauchenden Kreise**

Das Problem der neuen gestaltenden Typographie hat eine lebhafte
Diskussion bei allen Beteiligten hervorgerufen. Wir glauben dem Bedürf-
nis, die aufgeworfenen Fragen ausführlich behandelt zu sehen, zu ent-
sprechen, wenn wir jetzt ein Handbuch der **NEUEN TYPOGRAPHIE**
herausbringen.

Es kam dem Verfasser, einem ihrer bekanntesten Vertreter, in diesem
Buche zunächst darauf an, den engen Zusammenhang der neuen
Typographie mit dem **Gesamtkomplex heutigen Lebens** aufzuzei-
gen und zu beweisen, daß die neue Typographie ein ebenso notwendi-
ger Ausdruck einer neuen Gesinnung ist wie die neue Baukunst und
alles Neue, das mit unserer Zeit anbricht. Diese geschichtliche Notwen-
digkeit der neuen Typographie belegt weiterhin eine kritische Dar-
stellung der **alten Typographie**. Die Entwicklung der **neuen Male-
rei**, die für alles Neue unserer Zeit geistig bahnbrechend gewesen ist,
wird in einem reich illustrierten Aufsatz des Buches leicht faßlich dar-
gestellt. Ein kurzer Abschnitt „**Zur Geschichte der neuen Typographie**" leitet zu dem wichtigsten Teile des Buches, den **Grundbegriffen
der neuen Typographie** über. Diese werden klar herausgeschält,
richtige und falsche Beispiele einander gegenübergestellt. Zwei wei-
tere Artikel behandeln „**Photographie und Typographie**" und
„**Neue Typographie und Normung**".

Der Hauptwert des Buches für den Praktiker besteht in dem zweiten
Teil „**Typographische Hauptformen**" (siehe das nebenstehende
Inhaltsverzeichnis). Es fehlte bisher an einem Werke, das wie dieses Buch
die schon bei einfachen Satzaufgaben auftauchenden gestalterischen
Fragen in gebührender Ausführlichkeit behandelte. Jeder Teilabschnitt
enthält neben **allgemeinen typographischen Regeln** vor allem die
Abbildungen aller in Betracht kommenden **Normblätter** des Deutschen
Normenausschusses, alle andern (z. B. postalischen) **Vorschriften** und
zahlreiche Beispiele, Gegenbeispiele und Schemen.

Für jeden Buchdrucker, insbesondere jeden Akzidenzsetzer, wird „Die
neue Typographie" ein **unentbehrliches Handbuch** sein. Von nicht
geringerer Bedeutung ist es für Reklamefachleute, Gebrauchsgraphiker,
Kaufleute, Photographen, Architekten, Ingenieure und Schriftsteller,
also für alle, die mit dem Buchdruck in Berührung kommen.

INHALT DES BUCHES

Werden und Wesen der neuen Typographie
Das neue Weltbild
Die alte Typographie (Rückblick und Kritik)
Die neue Kunst
Zur Geschichte der neuen Typographie
Die Grundbegriffe der neuen Typographie
Photographie und Typographie
Neue Typographie und Normung

Typographische Hauptformen
Das Typosignet
Der Geschäftsbrief
Der Halbbrief
Briefhüllen ohne Fenster
Fensterbriefhüllen
Die Postkarte
Die Postkarte mit Klappe
Die Geschäftskarte
Die Besuchskarte
Werbsachen (Karten, Blätter, Prospekte, Kataloge)
Das Typoplakat
Das Bildplakat
Schildformate, Tafeln und Rahmen
Inserate
Die Zeitschrift
Die Tageszeitung
Die illustrierte Zeitung
Tabellensatz
Das neue Buch

Bibliographie
Verzeichnis der Abbildungen
Register

typ. tschichold

Das Buch enthält über 125 Abbildungen, von
denen etwa ein Viertel **zweifarbig** gedruckt ist,
und umfaßt gegen **200** Seiten auf gutem Kunst-
druckpapier. Es erscheint im Format DIN A 5 (148×
210 mm) und ist biegsam in Ganzleinen gebunden.

Preis bei Vorbestellung bis 1. Juni 1928: **5.**00 RM
durch den Buchhandel nur zum Preise von **6.**50 RM

Bestellschein umstehend ➡

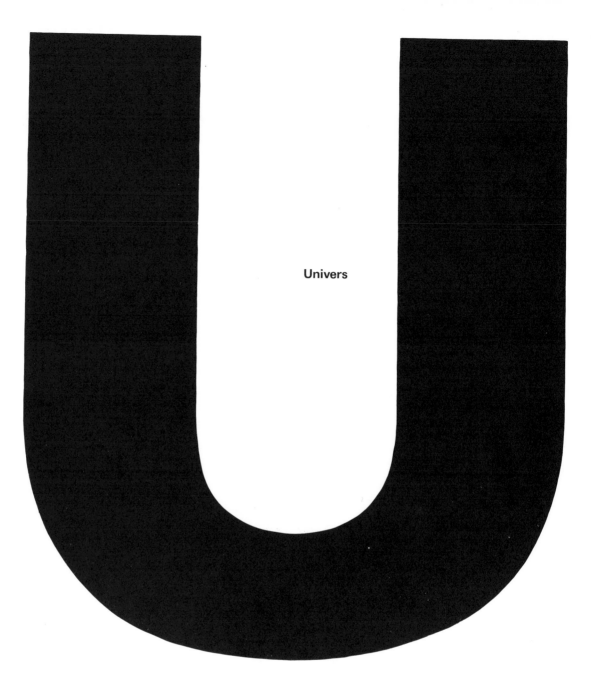

Sans Serif

Univers

443.

Prospectus designed by Jan Tschichold for his book, *Die Neue Typographie,* 1928.

Sans Serif typefaces have elemental letterforms stripped of serifs and decorations. Although sans serifs first appeared early in the nineteenth century, their use accelerated during the 1920s. "Form follows function" became the design dictum, and the functional simplicity of sans serif typefaces led many designers to look upon them as the ideal typographic expression of a scientific and technological century.

In Jan Tschichold's influential book, *Die Neue Typographie,* he advocated a new functional style for a rational era. In the prospectus for the book, he used sans serif type as an expression of the age (Fig. 443). The page also demonstrates asymmetrical balancing of elements on a grid system, visual contrasts of type size and weight, and the importance of spatial intervals and white space as design elements.

During the 1950s, Univers and Helvetica were both designed as more contemporary versions of Akzidenz Grotesque, a German turn-of-the-century sans serif. Compare the text setting and the display specimens of Helvetica with their Univers counterparts. There are subtle differences in the drawing of many letterforms. The Univers family (shown here) is renowned for its remarkable graphic unity, which enables the typographic designer to use all twenty-one fonts together as a flexible, integrated typographic system.

abcdefghi
jklmnopq
rstuvwx
yz $1234
567890!?

72 Point

abcdefghijklmnop
qrstuvwxyz AB
CDEFGHIJKLMN
OPQRSTUVW
XYZ$12345678
90(.,""''-;:!)?&

(.,""'"""-;:!])?&

abcdefghijklmn
opqrstuvwxyz
ABCDEFGHIJKL
MNOPQRSTU
VWXYZ$1234
567890

abcdefghijklmnopqr
stuvwxyzABCDEF
GHIJKLMNOPQRST
UVWXYZ$123456
7890(.,""''-;:!)?&

abcdefghijklmnopqrstuv
wxyzABCDEFGHIJKLMN
OPQRSTUVWXYZ$123
4567890(.,""''-;:!)?&

abcdefghijklmnopq
rstuvwxyzABCD
EFGHIJKLMNOPQ
RSTUVWXYZ$123
4567890(.,""""-;:!)?&

abcdefghijklmnopqrstuv
wxyzABCDEFGHIJKL
MNOPQRSTUVWXYZ
$1234567890(.,""""-;:!)?&

---

36 Point

abcdefghijklmnopqrstuvwxyz
ABCDEFGHIJKLMNOPQRSTUVW
XYZ$1234567890(.,""''-;:!)?&

---

30 Point

abcdefghijklmnopqrstuvwxyz
ABCDEFGHIJKLMNOPQRSTUVWXYZ
$1234567890(.,""''-;:!)?&

---

24 Point

abcdefghijklmnopqrstuvwxyz
ABCDEFGHIJKLMNOPQRSTUVWXYZ
$1234567890(.,""''-;:!)?&

---

18 Point

abcdefghijklmnopqrstuvwxyz
ABCDEFGHIJKLMNOPQRSTUVWXYZ
$1234567890(.,""''-;:!)?&

Univers 65

36 Point

abcdefghijklmnopqrstuvwxyz
ABCDEFGHIJKLMNOPQRSTUV
WXYZ $1234567890(.,‘’“”-;:!)?&

30 Point

abcdefghijklmnopqrstuvwxyz
ABCDEFGHIJKLMNOPQRSTUVWXYZ
$1234567890(.,‘’“”-;:!)?&

24 Point

abcdefghijklmnopqrstuvwxyz
ABCDEFGHIJKLMNOPQRSTUVWXYZ
$1234567890(.,‘’“”-;:!)?&

18 Point

abcdefghijklmnopqrstuvwxyz
ABCDEFGHIJKLMNOPQRSTUVWXYZ
$1234567890(.,‘’“”-;:!)?&

72 Point

abcdefghijklmnop
qrstuvwxyz AB
CDEFGHIJKLMN
OPQRSTUVW
XYZ$12345678
90 (.,'''''-;.:!)?&

(.,'""''-;:!)?&

72 Point

abcdefghijklmn
opqrstuvwxyz
ABCDEFGHIJKL
MNOPQRSTU
VWXYZ$12345
67890

48 Point

abcdefghijklmnopqrstuvw
xyzABCDEFGHIJKLMNOP
QRSTUVWXYZ$123456
7890 (.,""";::!)?&

30 Point

abcdefghijklmnopqrstuvwxyz
ABCDEFGHIJKLMNOPQRSTUVWXYZ
$1234567890 (.,""";::!)?&

18 Point

abcdefghijklmnopqrstuvwxyz
ABCDEFGHIJKLMNOPQRSTUVWXYZ
$1234567890 (.,""";::!)?&

48 Point

abcdefghijklmnopqrst
uvwxyzABCDEFGHIJKL
MNOPQRSTUVWXYZ
$1234567890(.,'""-;:!)?&

30 Point

abcdefghijklmnopqrstuvwxyz
ABCDEFGHIJKLMNOPQRSTUVWXYZ
$1234567890(.,'""-;:!)?&

18 Point

abcdefghijklmnopqrstuvwxyz
ABCDEFGHIJKLMNOPQRSTUVWXYZ
$1234567890(.,'""-;:!)?&

Univers 47

abcdefghijklmnopqrstuvwxyz
ABCDEFGHIJKLMNOPQRSTUVWXYZ
$1234567890(.,'"-;:!)?&

abcdefghijklmnopqrstu
vwxyzABCDEFGHIJKLM
NOPQRSTUVWXYZ $12
34567890(.,'"-;:!)?&

abcdefghijklmnopqrstuvwxyz
ABCDEFGHIJKLMNOPQRSTUVWXYZ
$1234567890(.,""''`-;:!)?&

72 Point

abcdefghijklmnopqrstuvw
xyzABCDEFGHIJKLM
NOPQRSTUVWXYZ$123
4567890(.,""''`-;:!)?&

abcdefghijklmnopqrstuvwxyz
ABCDEFGHIJKLMNOPQRSTUVWXYZ
$1234567890 (.,"""-;:!)?&

72 Point

abcdefghijklmno
pqrstuvwxyzABC
DEFGHIJKLMNO
PQRSTUVWX
YZ$1234567890
(.,""""-;:!)?&

Univers 46

18 Point

abcdefghijklmnopqrstuvwxyz
ABCDEFGGHIJKLMNOPQRSTUVWXYZ
$11234567890(.,""''-;:!)?&&

72 Point

abcdefghijklmno
pqrstuvwxyzAB
CDEFGGHIJKL
MNOPQRSTUV
WXYZ$112345
67890(.,""''-;:!)?&&

abcdefghijklmnopqrstuvwxyz
ABCDEFGGHIJKLMNOPQRSTUVWXYZ
$1234567890 (.,"""-;:!)?&

abcdefghijklmnopq

rstuvwxyzABCDEFGG

HIJKLMNOPQRSTU

VWXYZ$123

4567890(.,"""-;:!)?&

Univers 58

18 Point

abcdefghijklmnopqrstuvwxyz
ABCDEFGHIJKLMNOPQRSTUVWXYZ
$1234567890(.,''""-;:!)?&

72 Point

abcdefghijklmnopqr
stuvwxyz ABCDEFGH
IJKLMNOPQRSTU
VWXYZ $12345678
90(.,''""-;:!)?&

abcdefghijklmnopqrstuvwxyz
ABCDEFGHIJKLMNOPQRSTUVWXYZ
$11234567890(.,""''-;:!)?&

abcdefghijklmnop
qrstuvwxyzABCDE
FGHIJKLMNOPQR
STUVWXYZ$11234
567890(.,""''-;:!)?&

abcdefghijklmnopqrstuvwxyz
ABCDEFGHIJKLMNOPQRSTUVWXYZ
$1234567890 (.,""''-;:!)?&

abcdefghijklmnop

qrstuvwxyzABCDE

FGHIJKLMNOPQ

RSTUVWXYZ$123

4567890(.,""''-;:!)?&

abcdefghijklmnopqrstuvwxyz
ABCDEFGHIJKLMNOPQRSTUVW
XYZ$1234567890(.,'"-;:!)?&

72 Point

abcdefghijklm
nopqrstuvwx
yzABCDEFGHI
JKLMNOPQR
STUVWXYZ
$1234(.,'"-;:!)?&

abcdefghijklmnopqrstuvwxyz
ABCDEFGHIJKLMNOPQRSTUVWX
YZ $1234567890 (.,'''-;:!)?&

abcdefghijklm

nopqrstuvwx

yz ABCDEFGHI

JKLMNOPQR

STUVWXYZ

$1234(.,'''-;:!)?&

abcdefghijklmnopqrstuvw
xyz ABCDEFGHIJKLMNOPQ
RSTUVWXYZ $1234567890
(.,""""-;:!)?&&

abcdefghijk
lmnopqrstu
vwxyz ABC
DEFGHIJKL
MNOPQRST
UVWXYZ $

24 Point

abcdefghijklmnopqrstuvwxyz
ABCDEFGGHIJKLMNOPQRSTUVWXYZ
$1234567890 (.,'""-;:!)?&

72 Point

1234567890
(.,'""-;:!)?&&

72 Point

abcdefghijklmnopqrstuvwxyz

ABCDEFGGHIJKLMNOPQRSTUVWXYZ

$1234567890 (.,'""-;:!)?&

abcdefghijklmnopqrstuvwxyz
ABCDEFGHIJKLMNOPQRSTUVWXYZ
$1234567890(.,'"-;:!)?&

abcdefghijklmnopqrstuvwxyz
ABCDEFGHIJKLMNOPQRSTUVWXYZ
$1234567890(.,'"-;:!)?&

abcdefghijklmnopqrstuvwxyz
ABCDEFGHIJKLMNOPQRSTUVWXYZ
$1234567890(.,'"-;:!)?&

abcdefghijklmnopqrstuvwxyz
ABCDEFGHIJKLMNOPQRSTUVWXYZ
$1234567890(.,'"-;:!)?&

Univers 45

The whole duty of Typography, as of Calligraphy, is to communicate to the imagination, without loss by the way, the thought or image intended to be communicated by the Author. And the whole duty of beautiful typography is not to substitute for the beauty or interest of the thing thought and intended to be conveyed by the symbol, a beauty or interest of its own, but, on the one hand, to win access for that communication by the clearness and beauty of the vehicle, and on the other hand, to take advantage of every pause or stage in that communication to interpose some characteristic & restful beauty in its own art. We thus have a reason for the clearness and beauty of the text as a whole, for the especial beauty of the first or introductory page and of the title, and for the especial beauty of the headings of chapters, capital or initial letters, and so on, and an opening for the illustrator as we shall see by and *by. Further, in the case of Poetry, verse, in my opinion,*
8/9

The whole duty of Typography, as of Calligraphy, is to communicate to the imagination, without loss by the way, the thought or image intended to be communicated by the Author. And the whole duty of beautiful typography is not to substitute for the beauty or interest of the thing thought and intended to be conveyed by the symbol, a beauty or interest of its own, but, on the one hand, to win access for that communication by the clearness and beauty of the vehicle, and on the other hand, to take advantage of every pause or stage in that communication to interpose some characteristic & restful beauty in its own art. We thus have a reason for the clearness and beauty of the text as a whole, for the especial beauty of the first or introductory page and of the title, and for the especial beauty of the *and an opening for the illustrator as we shall see by and*
8/10

The whole duty of Typography, as of Calligraphy, is to communicate to the imagination, without loss by the way, the thought or image intended to be communicated by the Author. And the whole duty of beautiful typography is not to substitute for the beauty or interest of the thing thought and intended to be conveyed by the symbol, a beauty or interest of its own, but, on the one hand, to win access for that communication by the clearness and beauty of the vehicle, and on the other hand, to take advantage of every pause or stage in that communication to interpose some characteristic & restful beauty in its own art. We thus have a reason for the clearness and beauty of the text as a whole, for the especial beauty of the first or introductory *page and of the title, and for the especial beauty of the*
8/11

The whole duty of Typography, as of Calligraphy, is to communicate to the imagination, without loss by the way, the thought or image intended to be communicated by the Author. And the whole duty of beautiful typography is not to substitute for the beauty or interest of the thing thought and intended to be conveyed by the symbol, a beauty or interest of its own, but, on the one hand, to win access for that communication by the clearness and beauty of the vehicle, and on the other hand, to take advantage of every pause or stage in that communication to interpose some characteristic & restful beauty in its own art. We thus have a reason for the clearness and beauty of the text as a whole, for the especial *title, and for the especial beauty of the headings of*
9/10

The whole duty of Typography, as of Calligraphy, is to communicate to the imagination, without loss by the way, the thought or image intended to be communicated by the Author. And the whole duty of beautiful typography is not to substitute for the beauty or interest of the thing thought and intended to be conveyed by the symbol, a beauty or interest of its own, but, on the one hand, to win access for that communication by the clearness and beauty of the vehicle, and on the other hand, to take advantage of every pause or stage in that communication to interpose some characteristic & restful beauty in its own art. We thus have a reason for the clearness *and beauty of the text as a whole, for the especial*
9/11

The whole duty of Typography, as of Calligraphy, is to communicate to the imagination, without loss by the way, the thought or image intended to be communicated by the Author. And the whole duty of beautiful typography is not to substitute for the beauty or interest of the thing thought and intended to be conveyed by the symbol, a beauty or interest of its own, but, on the one hand, to win access for that communication by the clearness and beauty of the vehicle, and on the other hand, to take advantage of every pause or stage in that communication to interpose some characteristic & restful beauty in its own art. We thus have a reason for the clearness
9/12

abcdefghijklmnopqrstuvwxyz
ABCDEFGHIJKLMNOPQRSTUVWXYZ
$1234567890(.,'"-;:!)?&

abcdefghijklmnopqrstuvwxyz
ABCDEFGHIJKLMNOPQRSTUVWXYZ
$1234567890(.,'"-;:!)?&

abcdefghijklmnopqrstuvwxyz
ABCDEFGHIJKLMNOPQRSTUVWXYZ
$1234567890(.,'"-;:!)?&

abcdefghijklmnopqrstuvwxyz
ABCDEFGHIJKLMNOPQRSTUVWXYZ
$1234567890(.,'"-;:!)?&

The whole duty of Typography, as of Callig-raphy, is to communicate to the imagination, without loss by the way, the thought or image intended to be communicated by the Author. And the whole duty of beautiful typography is not to substitute for the beauty or interest of the thing thought and intended to be conveyed by the symbol, a beauty or interest of its own, but, on the one hand, to win access for that communication by the clearness and beauty of the vehicle, and on the other hand, to take advantage of every pause or stage in that com-munication to interpose some characteristic *& restful beauty in its own art. We thus have a*

10/11

The whole duty of Typography, as of Callig-raphy, is to communicate to the imagination, without loss by the way, the thought or image intended to be communicated by the Author. And the whole duty of beautiful typography is not to substitute for the beauty or interest of the thing thought and intended to be conveyed by the symbol, a beauty or interest of its own, but, on the one hand, to win access for that communication by the clearness and beauty of the vehicle, and on the other hand, to take advantage of every pause or stage in that com-*munication to interpose some characteristic*

10/12

The whole duty of Typography, as of Callig-raphy, is to communicate to the imagination, without loss by the way, the thought or image intended to be communicated by the Author. And the whole duty of beautiful typography is not to substitute for the beauty or interest of the thing thought and intended to be conveyed by the symbol, a beauty or interest of its own, but, on the one hand, to win access for that communication by the clearness and beauty of the vehicle, and on the other hand, to take *advantage of every pause or stage in that*

10/13

The whole duty of Typography, as of Calligraphy, is to communicate to the imagination, without loss by the way, the thought or image intended to be communicated by the Author. And the whole duty of beautiful typography is not to substitute for the beauty or in-terest of the thing thought and intended to be conveyed by the symbol, a beauty or interest of its own, but, on the one hand, to win access for that *communication by the clearness and*

12/13

The whole duty of Typography, as of Calligraphy, is to communicate to the imagination, without loss by the way, the thought or image intended to be communicated by the Author. And the whole duty of beautiful typography is not to substitute for the beauty or in-terest of the thing thought and intended to be conveyed by the symbol, a beauty or interest of its own, but, on *the one hand, to win access for that*

12/14

The whole duty of Typography, as of Calligraphy, is to communicate to the imagination, without loss by the way, the thought or image intended to be communicated by the Author. And the whole duty of beautiful typography is not to substitute for the beauty or in-terest of the thing thought and intended to be conveyed by the symbol, a *beauty or interest of its own, but, on*

12/15

abcdefghijklmnopqrstuvwxyz
ABCDEFGHIJKLMNOPQRSTUVWXYZ
$1234567890(.,'"-;:!)?&

abcdefghijklmnopqrstuvwxyz
ABCDEFGHIJKLMNOPQRSTUVWXYZ
$1234567890(.,'"-;:!)?&

abcdefghijklmnopqrstuvwxyz
ABCDEFGHIJKLMNOPQRSTUVWXYZ
$1234567890(.,'"-;:!)?&

abcdefghijklmnopqrstuvwxyz
ABCDEFGHIJKLMNOPQRSTUVWXYZ
$1234567890(.,'"-;:!)?&

Univers 55

The whole duty of Typography, as of Calligraphy, is to communicate to the imagination, without loss by the way, the thought or image intended to be communicated by the Author. And the whole duty of beautiful typography is not to substitute for the beauty or interest of the thing thought and intended to be conveyed by the symbol, a beauty or interest of its own, but, on the one hand, to win access for that communication by the clearness and beauty of the vehicle, and on the other hand, to take advantage of every pause or stage in that communication to interpose some characteristic & restful beauty in its own art. We thus have a reason for the clearness and beauty of the text as a whole, for the especial beauty of the first or introductory page and of the title, and for the especial beauty of the headings of chapters, capital or initial letters, and so on, and an *opening for the illustrator as we shall see by and by.*
8/9

The whole duty of Typography, as of Calligraphy, is to communicate to the imagination, without loss by the way, the thought or image intended to be communicated by the Author. And the whole duty of beautiful typography is not to substitute for the beauty or interest of the thing thought and intended to be conveyed by the symbol, a beauty or interest of its own, but, on the one hand, to win access for that communication by the clearness and beauty of the vehicle, and on the other hand, to take advantage of every pause or stage in that communication to interpose some characteristic & restful beauty in its own art. We thus have a reason for the clearness and beauty of the text as a whole, for the especial beauty of the first or introductory page and of the title, and for the especial beauty of the headings *of chapters, capital or initial letters, and so on, and an*
8/10

The whole duty of Typography, as of Calligraphy, is to communicate to the imagination, without loss by the way, the thought or image intended to be communicated by the Author. And the whole duty of beautiful typography is not to substitute for the beauty or interest of the thing thought and intended to be conveyed by the symbol, a beauty or interest of its own, but, on the one hand, to win access for that communication by the clearness and beauty of the vehicle, and on the other hand, to take advantage of every pause or stage in that communication to interpose some characteristic & restful beauty in its own art. We thus have a reason for the clearness and beauty of the text as a whole, for the *especial beauty of the first or introductory page and*
8/11

The whole duty of Typography, as of Calligraphy, is to communicate to the imagination, without loss by the way, the thought or image intended to be communicated by the Author. And the whole duty of beautiful typography is not to substitute for the beauty or interest of the thing thought and intended to be conveyed by the symbol, a beauty or interest of its own, but, on the one hand, to win access for that communication by the clearness and beauty of the vehicle, and on the other hand, to take advantage of every pause or stage in that communication to interpose some characteristic & restful beauty in its own art. We thus have a reason for the clearness and beauty of the text as a whole, for the especial beauty of the first or introductory page and of the title, and for the es-
9/10

The whole duty of Typography, as of Calligraphy, is to communicate to the imagination, without loss by the way, the thought or image intended to be communicated by the Author. And the whole duty of beautiful typography is not to substitute for the beauty or interest of the thing thought and intended to be conveyed by the symbol, a beauty or interest of its own, but, on the one hand, to win access for that communication by the clearness and beauty of the vehicle, and on the other hand, to take advantage of every pause or stage in that communication to interpose some characteristic & restful beauty in its own art. We thus have a *reason for the clearness and beauty of the text as*
9/11

The whole duty of Typography, as of Calligraphy, is to communicate to the imagination, without loss by the way, the thought or image intended to be communicated by the Author. And the whole duty of beautiful typography is not to substitute for the beauty or interest of the thing thought and intended to be conveyed by the symbol, a beauty or interest of its own, but, on the one hand, to win access for that communication by the clearness and beauty of the vehicle, and on the other hand, to take advantage of every pause or stage in that communication to interpose some characteristic *& restful beauty in its own art. We thus have a*
9/12

abcdefghijklmnopqrstuvwxyz
ABCDEFGHIJKLMNOPQRSTUVWXYZ
$1234567890(.,'"-;:!)?&

abcdefghijklmnopqrstuvwxyz
ABCDEFGHIJKLMNOPQRSTUVWXYZ
$1234567890(.,'"-;:!)?&

abcdefghijklmnopqrstuvwxyz
ABCDEFGHIJKLMNOPQRSTUVWXYZ
$1234567890(.,'"-;:!)?&

abcdefghijklmnopqrstuvwxyz
ABCDEFGHIJKLMNOPQRSTUVWXYZ
$1234567890(.,'"-;:!)?&

The whole duty of Typography, as of Calligraphy, is to communicate to the imagination, without loss by the way, the thought or image intended to be communicated by the Author. And the whole duty of beautiful typography is not to substitute for the beauty or interest of the thing thought and intended to be conveyed by the symbol, a beauty or interest of its own, but, on the one hand, to win access for that communication by the clearness and beauty of the vehicle, and on the other hand, to take advantage of every pause or stage in that communication to interpose some char-*acteristic & restful beauty in its own art. We*
10/11

The whole duty of Typography, as of Calligraphy, is to communicate to the imagination, without loss by the way, the thought or image intended to be communicated by the Author. And the whole duty of beautiful typography is not to substitute for the beauty or interest of the thing thought and intended to be conveyed by the symbol, a beauty or interest of its own, but, on the one hand, to win access for that communication by the clearness and beauty of the vehicle, and on the other hand, *that communication to interpose some char-*
10/12

The whole duty of Typography, as of Calligraphy, is to communicate to the imagination, without loss by the way, the thought or image intended to be communicated by the Author. And the whole duty of beautiful typography is not to substitute for the beauty or interest of the thing thought and intended to be conveyed by the symbol, a beauty or interest of its own, but, on the one hand, to win access for that communication by the clearness and beauty of the vehicle, and on the other hand, *to take advantage of every pause or stage in*
10/13

The whole duty of Typography, as of Calligraphy, is to communicate to the imagination, without loss by the way, the thought or image intended to be communicated by the Author. And the whole duty of beautiful typography is not to substitute for the beauty or interest of the thing thought and intended to be conveyed by the symbol, a beauty or interest of its own, but, on the one hand, to win access for that *communication by the clearness and*
12/13

The whole duty of Typography, as of Calligraphy, is to communicate to the imagination, without loss by the way, the thought or image intended to be communicated by the Author. And the whole duty of beautiful typography is not to substitute for the beauty or interest of the thing thought and intended to be conveyed by the symbol, a beauty or interest of its own, but, on *the one hand, to win access for that*
12/14

The whole duty of Typography, as of Calligraphy, is to communicate to the imagination, without loss by the way, the thought or image intended to be communicated by the Author. And the whole duty of beautiful typography is not to substitute for the beauty or interest of the thing thought and intended to be conveyed by the symbol, *a beauty or interest of its own, but, on*
12/15

abcdefghijklmnopqrstuvwxyz
ABCDEFGHIJKLMNOPQRSTUVWXYZ
$1234567890(.,'"-;:!)?&

abcdefghijklmnopqrstuvwxyz
ABCDEFGHIJKLMNOPQRSTUVWXYZ
$1234567890(.,'"-;:!)?&

abcdefghijklmnopqrstuvwxyz
ABCDEFGHIJKLMNOPQRSTUVWXYZ
$1234567890(.,'"-;:!)?&

abcdefghijklmnopqrstuvwxyz
ABCDEFGHIJKLMNOPQRSTUVWXYZ
$1234567890(.,'"-;:!)?&

Univers 65

The whole duty of Typography, as of Calligraphy, is to communicate to the imagination, without loss by the way, the thought or image intended to be communicated by the Author. And the whole duty of beautiful typography is not to substitute for the beauty or interest of the thing thought and intended to be conveyed by the symbol, a beauty or interest of its own, but, on the one hand, to win access for that communication by the clearness and beauty of the vehicle, and on the other hand, to take advantage of every pause or stage in that communication to interpose some characteristic & restful beauty in its own art. We thus have a reason for the clearness and beauty of the text as a whole, for the especial beauty of the first or introductory page and of the title, and for the especial *beauty of the headings of chapters, capital or*
8/9

The whole duty of Typography, as of Calligraphy, is to communicate to the imagination, without loss by the way, the thought or image intended to be communicated by the Author. And the whole duty of beautiful typography is not to substitute for the beauty or interest of the thing thought and intended to be conveyed by the symbol, a beauty or interest of its own, but, on the one hand, to win access for that communication by the clearness and beauty of the vehicle, and on the other hand, to take advantage of every pause or stage in that communication to interpose some characteristic & restful beauty in its own art. We thus have a reason for the clearness and beauty of the text as a whole, for the especial beauty of the first or intro-*ductory page and of the title, and for the especial*
8/10

The whole duty of Typography, as of Calligraphy, is to communicate to the imagination, without loss by the way, the thought or image intended to be communicated by the Author. And the whole duty of beautiful typography is not to substitute for the beauty or interest of the thing thought and intended to be conveyed by the symbol, a beauty or interest of its own, but, on the one hand, to win access for that communication by the clearness and beauty of the vehicle, and on the other hand, to take advantage of every pause or stage in that communication to interpose some characteristic & restful beauty in its own art. We thus have a rea-*son for the clearness and beauty of the text as a*
8/11

The whole duty of Typography, as of Calligraphy, is to communicate to the imagination, without loss by the way, the thought or image intended to be communicated by the Author. And the whole duty of beautiful typography is not to substitute for the beauty or interest of the thing thought and intended to be conveyed by the symbol, a beauty or interest of its own, but, on the one hand, to win access for that communication by the clearness and beauty of the vehicle, and on the other hand, to take advantage of every pause or stage in that communication to interpose some characteristic & restful beauty in its own art. We *beauty of the text as a whole, for the especial*
9/10

The whole duty of Typography, as of Calligraphy, is to communicate to the imagination, without loss by the way, the thought or image intended to be communicated by the Author. And the whole duty of beautiful typography is not to substitute for the beauty or interest of the thing thought and intended to be conveyed by the symbol, a beauty or interest of its own, but, on the one hand, to win access for that communication by the clearness and beauty of the vehicle, and on the other hand, to take advantage of every pause or stage in that communication to interpose some char-*acteristic & restful beauty in its own art. We*
9/11

The whole duty of Typography, as of Calligraphy, is to communicate to the imagination, without loss by the way, the thought or image intended to be communicated by the Author. And the whole duty of beautiful typography is not to substitute for the beauty or interest of the thing thought and intended to be conveyed by the symbol, a beauty or interest of its own, but, on the one hand, to win access for that communication by the clearness and beauty of the vehicle, and on the other hand, to take advantage of every pause or stage in *that communication to interpose some char-*
9/12

abcdefghijklmnopqrstuvwxyz
ABCDEFGHIJKLMNOPQRSTUVWXYZ
$1234567890(.,'"-;:!)?&

abcdefghijklmnopqrstuvwxyz
ABCDEFGHIJKLMNOPQRSTUVWXYZ
$1234567890(.,'"-;:!)?&

abcdefghijklmnopqrstuvwxyz
ABCDEFGHIJKLMNOPQRSTUVWXYZ
$1234567890(.,'"-;:!)?&

abcdefghijklmnopqrstuvwxyz
ABCDEFGHIJKLMNOPQRSTUVWXYZ
$1234567890(.,'"-;:!)?&

The whole duty of Typography, as of Calligraphy, is to communicate to the imagination, without loss by the way, the thought or image intended to be communicated by the Author. And the whole duty of beautiful typography is not to substitute for the beauty or interest of the thing thought and intended to be conveyed by the symbol, a beauty or interest of its own, but, on the one hand, to win access for that communication by the clearness and beauty of the vehicle, and on the other hand, to take advantage of *every pause or stage in that communica-*

10/11

The whole duty of Typography, as of Calligraphy, is to communicate to the imagination, without loss by the way, the thought or image intended to be communicated by the Author. And the whole duty of beautiful typography is not to substitute for the beauty or interest of the thing thought and intended to be conveyed by the symbol, a beauty or interest of its own, but, on the one hand, to win access for that communication by the clearness and beauty of the vehicle, and *on the other hand, to take advantage of*

10/12

The whole duty of Typography, as of Calligraphy, is to communicate to the imagination, without loss by the way, the thought or image intended to be communicated by the Author. And the whole duty of beautiful typography is not to substitute for the beauty or interest of the thing thought and intended to be conveyed by the symbol, a beauty or interest of its own, but, on the one hand, to win access for that communication by the *clearness and beauty of the vehicle, and*

10/13

The whole duty of Typography, as of Calligraphy, is to communicate to the imagination, without loss by the way, the thought or image intended to be communicated by the Author. And the whole duty of beautiful typography is not to substitute for the beauty or interest of the thing thought and intended to be conveyed by the symbol, a beauty or interest of its own, but, *on the one hand, to win access for*

12/13

The whole duty of Typography, as of Calligraphy, is to communicate to the imagination, without loss by the way, the thought or image intended to be communicated by the Author. And the whole duty of beautiful typography is not to substitute for the beauty or interest of the thing thought and intended to be conveyed by the symbol, a *beauty or interest of its own, but,*

12/14

The whole duty of Typography, as of Calligraphy, is to communicate to the imagination, without loss by the way, the thought or image intended to be communicated by the Author. And the whole duty of beautiful typography is not to substitute for the beauty or interest of the thing thought and intended to *be conveyed by the symbol, a*

12/15

GEORGICON.

LIBER SECUNDUS.

Hactenus arvorum cultus, et sidera cœli:
Nunc te, Bacche, canam, nec non silvestria tecum
Virgulta, et prolem tarde crescentis olivæ.
Huc, pater o Lenæe; (tuis hic omnia plena
5 Muneribus: tibi pampineo gravidus autumno
Floret ager; spumat plenis vindemia labris)
Huc, pater o Lenæe, veni; nudataque musto
Tinge novo mecum direptis crura cothurnis.
    Principio arboribus varia est natura creandis:
10 Namque aliæ, nullis hominum cogentibus, ipsæ
Sponte sua veniunt, camposque et flumina late
Curva tenent: ut molle siler, lentæque genistæ,
Populus, et glauca canentia fronde salicta.
Pars autem posito surgunt de semine: ut altæ
15 Castaneæ, nemorumque Jovi quæ maxima frondet
Aesculus, atque habitæ Graiis oracula quercus.
Pullulat ab radice aliis densissima silva:
Ut cerasis, ulmisque: etiam Parnassia laurus
Parva sub ingenti matris se subjicit umbra.
20 Hos natura modos primum dedit: his genus omne
Silvarum, fruticumque viret, nemorumque sacrorum.
Sunt alii, quos ipse via sibi repperit usus.
Hic plantas tenero abscindens de corpore matrum

Transitional

Baskerville

444.
Title page for the second book of Virgil's *Georgics,* designed and printed by John Basker-ville, 1757.

Transitional typefaces appeared during the eigh-teenth century, a period of typographic evolution. Designers gradually increased the contrast be-tween thick-and-thin strokes, made serifs sharper and more horizontal, and increased the vertical stress of rounded letterforms. By the century's end, Old Style typefaces had evolved into the Modern styles with hairline serifs and geometric proportions: typefaces designed in the middle of this period of change were *transitional.*

Simplicity and understated elegance were achieved through the use of John Baskerville's masterful Transitional typefaces, seen in the title page of Virgil's *Georgics* (Fig. 444). Generous margins,

letterspaced display type, and thoughtfully con-sidered interline and word spacing are present. The great Roman poet is presented to the reader with clarity and dignity in a book that "went forth to astonish all the librarians of Europe."

If the words *Transitional* and *Baskerville* have become interwoven in the lexicon of typography, it is because the Transitional typefaces produced by John Baskerville of Birmingham, England have an unsurpassed beauty and harmony. Many Transitional typefaces in use today, including the specimens shown, are closely modeled after Baskerville's work.

abcdefghijklmnop

qrstuvwxyzAB

CDEFGHIJKLM

NOPQRSTUV

WXYZ$1234567

890(.,""''-;:!)?&

72 Point

abcdefghijklmnopq
rstuvwxyzABC
DEFGHIJKLMN
OPQRSTUVW
XYZ$1234567890
(.,""''-,.:!)?&

Baskerville

abcdefghijklmnopqrstuvwxyz
ABCDEFGHIJKLMNOPQRSTUVW
XYZ$1234567890(.,""''-;:!)?&

abcdefghijklmnopqrstuvw
xyzABCDEFGHIJKLMN
OPQRSTUVWXYZ$12
34567890(.,""''-;:!)?&

abcdefghijklmnopqrstuvwxyz
ABCDEFGHIJKLMNOPQRSTU
VWXYZ$1234567890(.,""''-;:!)?&

abcdefghijklmnopqrstuvwxyz
ABCDEFGHIJKLMNOPQRSTUVW
XYZ$1234567890(.,""''-;:!)?&

Baskerville Italic

18 Point

abcdefghijklmnopqrstuvwxyz
ABCDEFGHIJKLMNOPQRSTUVWXYZ
$1234567890(.,’‘“”-;:!)?&

48 Point

abcdefghijklmnopqrstuvw
xyz ABCDEFGHIJKLMNO
PQRSTUVWXYZ$12345
67890(.,’‘“”-;:!)?&

36 Point

abcdefghijklmnopqrstuvwxyz
ABCDEFGHIJKLMNOPQRSTUV
WXYZ$1234567890(.,’‘“”-;:!)?&

30 Point

abcdefghijklmnopqrstuvwxyz
ABCDEFGHIJKLMNOPQRSTUVWXYZ
$1234567890(.,’‘“”-;:!)?&

abcdefghijklmnopqrstuvwxyz
ABCDEFGHIJKLMNOPQRSTUVWXYZ
$1234567890(.,'"-;:!)?&

abcdefghijklmnopqrstuvwxyz
ABCDEFGHIJKLMNOPQRSTUVWXYZ
$1234567890(.,'"-;:!)?&

abcdefghijklmnopqrstuvwxyz
ABCDEFGHIJKLMNOPQRSTUVWXYZ
$1234567890(.,'"-;:!)?&

abcdefghijklmnopqrstuvwxyz
ABCDEFGHIJKLMNOPQRSTUVWXYZ
$1234567890(.,'"-;:!)?&

Baskerville

The whole duty of Typography, as of Calligraphy, is to communicate to the imagination, without loss by the way, the thought or image intended to be communicated by the Author. And the whole duty of beautiful typography is not to substitute for the beauty or interest of the thing thought and intended to be conveyed by the symbol, a beauty or interest of its own, but, on the one hand, to win access for that communication by the clearness and beauty of the vehicle, and on the other hand, to take advantage of every pause or stage in that communication to interpose some characteristic & restful beauty in its own art. We thus have a reason for the clearness and beauty of the text as a whole, for the especial beauty of the first or introductory page and of the title, and for the especial beauty of the headings of chapters, capital or initial letters, and so on, and an opening for the illustrator as we shall see by and by. Further, in the case of Poetry, verse, in my opinion, appeals by its form to the eye, as well as to *the ear, and should be placed on the page so that its structure may be*
8/9

The whole duty of Typography, as of Calligraphy, is to communicate to the imagination, without loss by the way, the thought or image intended to be communicated by the Author. And the whole duty of beautiful typography is not to substitute for the beauty or interest of the thing thought and intended to be conveyed by the symbol, a beauty or interest of its own, but, on the one hand, to win access for that communication by the clearness and beauty of the vehicle, and on the other hand, to take advantage of every pause or stage in that communication to interpose some characteristic & restful beauty in its own art. We thus have a reason for the clearness and beauty of the text as a whole, for the especial beauty of the first or introductory page and of the title, and for the especial beauty of the headings of chapters, capital or initial letters, and so on, and an opening for the illustrator as we shall see by and by. Further, in the case of Poetry, *verse, in my opinion, appeals by its form to the eye, as well as to the ear,*
8/10

The whole duty of Typography, as of Calligraphy, is to communicate to the imagination, without loss by the way, the thought or image intended to be communicated by the Author. And the whole duty of beautiful typography is not to substitute for the beauty or interest of the thing thought and intended to be conveyed by the symbol, a beauty or interest of its own, but, on the one hand, to win access for that communication by the clearness and beauty of the vehicle, and on the other hand, to take advantage of every pause or stage in that communication to interpose some characteristic & restful beauty in its own art. We thus have a reason for the clearness and beauty of the text as a whole, for the especial beauty of the first or introductory page and of the title, and for the especial beauty of the headings of chapters, *capital or initial letters, and so on, and an opening for the illustrator as*
8/11

The whole duty of Typography, as of Calligraphy, is to communicate to the imagination, without loss by the way, the thought or image intended to be communicated by the Author. And the whole duty of beautiful typography is not to substitute for the beauty or interest of the thing thought and intended to be conveyed by the symbol, a beauty or interest of its own, but, on the one hand, to win access for that communication by the clearness and beauty of the vehicle, and on the other hand, to take advantage of every pause or stage in that communication to interpose some characteristic & restful beauty in its own art. We thus have a reason for the clearness and beauty of the text as a whole, for the especial beauty of the first or introductory page and of the title, and for the especial *ters, and so on, and an opening for the illustrator as we shall*
9/10

The whole duty of Typography, as of Calligraphy, is to communicate to the imagination, without loss by the way, the thought or image intended to be communicated by the Author. And the whole duty of beautiful typography is not to substitute for the beauty or interest of the thing thought and intended to be conveyed by the symbol, a beauty or interest of its own, but, on the one hand, to win access for that communication by the clearness and beauty of the vehicle, and on the other hand, to take advantage of every pause or stage in that communication to interpose some characteristic & restful beauty in its own art. We thus have a reason for the clearness and beauty of the text as a whole, for the especial beauty of the first or introductory *page and of the title, and for the especial beauty of*
9/11

The whole duty of Typography, as of Calligraphy, is to communicate to the imagination, without loss by the way, the thought or image intended to be communicated by the Author. And the whole duty of beautiful typography is not to substitute for the beauty or interest of the thing thought and intended to be conveyed by the symbol, a beauty or interest of its own, but, on the one hand, to win access for that communication by the clearness and beauty of the vehicle, and on the other hand, to take advantage of every pause or stage in that communication to interpose some characteristic & restful beauty in its own art. We thus have a reason for the clearness and beauty of the *text as a whole, for the especial beauty of the first or introductory*
9/12

abcdefghijklmnopqrstuvwxyz
ABCDEFGHIJKLMNOPQRSTUVWXYZ
$1234567890(.,'"-;:!)?&

abcdefghijklmnopqrstuvwxyz
ABCDEFGHIJKLMNOPQRSTUVWXYZ
$1234567890(.,'"-;:!)?&

abcdefghijklmnopqrstuvwxyz
ABCDEFGHIJKLMNOPQRSTUVWXYZ
$1234567890(.,'"-;:!)?&

abcdefghijklmnopqrstuvwxyz
ABCDEFGHIJKLMNOPQRSTUVWXYZ
$1234567890(.,'"-;:!)?&

The whole duty of Typography, as of Calligraphy, is to communicate to the imagination, without loss by the way, the thought or image intended to be communicated by the Author. And the whole duty of beautiful typography is not to substitute for the beauty or interest of the thing thought and intended to be conveyed by the symbol, a beauty or interest of its own, but, on the one hand, to win access for that communication by the clearness and beauty of the vehicle, and on the other hand, to take advantage of every pause or stage in that communication to interpose some characteristic & restful beauty in its own art. We thus have a reason for *the clearness and beauty of the text as a whole, for the*
10/11

The whole duty of Typography, as of Calligraphy, is to communicate to the imagination, without loss by the way, the thought or image intended to be communicated by the Author. And the whole duty of beautiful typography is not to substitute for the beauty or interest of the thing thought and intended to be conveyed by the symbol, a beauty or interest of its own, but, on the one hand, to win access for that communication by the clearness and beauty of the vehicle, and on the other hand, to take advantage of every pause or stage in that communication to interpose some characteristic & restful *beauty in its own art. We thus have a reason for the*
10/12

The whole duty of Typography, as of Calligraphy, is to communicate to the imagination, without loss by the way, the thought or image intended to be communicated by the Author. And the whole duty of beautiful typography is not to substitute for the beauty or interest of the thing thought and intended to be conveyed by the symbol, a beauty or interest of its own, but, on the one hand, to win access for that communication by the clearness and beauty of the vehicle, and on the other hand, to take advantage of every pause or stage in that communication to interpose some characteristic *& restful*
10/13

The whole duty of Typography, as of Calligraphy, is to communicate to the imagination, without loss by the way, the thought or image intended to be communicated by the Author. And the whole duty of beautiful typography is not to substitute for the beauty or interest of the thing thought and intended to be conveyed by the symbol, a beauty or interest of its own, but, on the one hand, to win access for that communication by the clearness and beauty of the vehicle, and on *the other hand, to take advantage of every pause*
12/13

The whole duty of Typography, as of Calligraphy, is to communicate to the imagination, without loss by the way, the thought or image intended to be communicated by the Author. And the whole duty of beautiful typography is not to substitute for the beauty or interest of the thing thought and intended to be conveyed by the symbol, a beauty or interest of its own, but, on the one hand, to win access for that communication by the *clearness and beauty of the vehicle, and on the*
12/14

The whole duty of Typography, as of Calligraphy, is to communicate to the imagination, without loss by the way, the thought or image intended to be communicated by the Author. And the whole duty of beautiful typography is not to substitute for the beauty or interest of the thing thought and intended to be conveyed by the symbol, a beauty or interest of its own, but, on the one hand, to *win access for that communication by the clear*
12/15

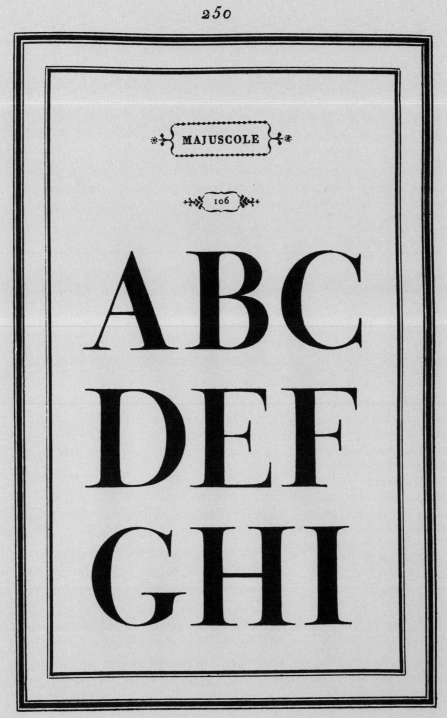

MAJUSCOLE

106

ABC
DEF
GHI

Modern

Bodoni

445.

Page 250 from the *Manuale Tipographico,* 1818.

The word *modern* is a relative term. Often, we use it interchangeably with the term *contemporary;* sometimes it is used to identify movements or periods in the arts representing a radical break with tradition. In typographic design, Modern identifies typefaces of the late 1700s with flat, unbracketed serifs, extreme contrast between thick-and-thin strokes, and geometric construction. The influence of writing and calligraphy was replaced by mathematical measurement and the use of mechanical instruments to construct letterforms.

After the death of type designer and printer, Giambattista Bodoni, his widow and foreman published the *Manuale Tipographico,* displaying specimens of the approximately three hundred type

fonts designed by Bodoni. The page reproduced here in its actual size shows the dazzling contrasts and vigorous proportions of modern-style typography (Fig. 445). The thick-and-thin scotch rules (see Figure 226) echo and complement the thick-and-thin stroke weights.

Modern-style typefaces dominated nineteenth century book typography and have enjoyed continued acceptance during the twentieth century. Numerous variations—from extreme hairline versions to ultrabolds; from narrow, condensed fonts to wide, expanded forms—have been designed. Many contemporary fonts bear the names of eighteenth-century designers: Bodoni, Didot, and Walbaum.

abcdefghijklmnopq
rstuvwxyzABCDEFG
HIJKLMNOPQRST
UVWXYZ$12345678
90(.,""""-;:!)?&

abcdefghijklmnopq
rstuvvwwxyzABCDE
FGHIJKLMNOPQ
RSTUVWXYZ$123
4567890(.,""''-;:!)?&

Bodoni

18 Point

abcdefghijklmnopqrstuvwxyz
ABCDEFGHIJKLMNOPQRSTUVWXYZ
$1234567890 (.,’‘“”-;:!)?&

48 Point

abcdefghijklmnopqrstuvwxyz
ABCDEFGHIJKLMNOPQRSTU
VWXYZ$1234567890 (.,’‘“”-;:!)?&

36 Point

abcdefghijklmnopqrstuvwxyz
ABCDEFGHIJKLMNOPQRSTUVWXYZ
$1234567890 (.,’‘“”-;:!)?&

30 Point

abcdefghijklmnopqrstuvwxyz
ABCDEFGHIJKLMNOPQRSTUVWXYZ
$1234567890 (.,’‘“”-;:!)?&

Bodoni Italic

abcdefghijklmnopqrstuvvwxyz
ABCDEFGHIJKLMNOPQRSTUVWXYZ
$1234567890 (.,""''-;:!)?&

abcdefghijklmnopqrstuvvwxyz
ABCDEFGHIJKLMNOPQRSTU
VWXYZ$1234567890 (.,""''-;:!)?&

abcdefghijklmnopqrstuvvwxyz
ABCDEFGHIJKLMNOPQRSTUVWXYZ
$1234567890 (.,""''-;:!)?&

abcdefghijklmnopqrstuvvwxyz
ABCDEFGHIJKLMNOPQRSTUVWXYZ
$1234567890 (.,""''-;:!)?&

abcdefghijklmnopqrstuvwxyz
ABCDEFGHIJKLMNOPQRSTUVWXYZ
$1234567890(.,"";:!)?&

abcdefghijklmnopqrstuvwxyz
ABCDEFGHIJKLMNOPQRSTUVWXYZ
$1234567890(.,"";:!)?&

abcdefghijklmnopqrstuvwxyz
ABCDEFGHIJKLMNOPQRSTUVWXYZ
$1234567890(.,"";:!)?&

abcdefghijklmnopqrstuvwxyz
ABCDEFGHIJKLMNOPQRSTUVWXYZ
$1234567890(.,"";:!)?&

Bodoni

The whole duty of Typography, as of Calligraphy, is to communicate to the imagination, without loss by the way, the thought or image intended to be communicated by the Author. And the whole duty of beautiful typography is not to substitute for the beauty or interest of the thing thought and intended to be conveyed by the symbol, a beauty or interest of its own, but, on the one hand, to win access for that communication by the clearness and beauty of the vehicle, and on the other hand, to take advantage of every pause or stage in that communication to interpose some characteristic & restful beauty in its own art. We thus have a reason for the clearness and beauty of the text as a whole, for the especial beauty of the first or introductory page and of the title, and for the especial beauty of the headings of chapters, capital or initial letters, and so on, and an opening access for the illustrator as we shall see by and by. Further, in the case of Poetry, verse, in my opinion, appeals by its form to the eye, as well as to the ear, and should be placed on the page so that its structure may be *taken in at a glance and distinctively appreciated, & anything*
8/9

The whole duty of Typography, as of Calligraphy, is to communicate to the imagination, without loss by the way, the thought or image intended to be communicated by the Author. And the whole duty of beautiful typography is not to substitute for the beauty or interest of the thing thought and intended to be conveyed by the symbol, a beauty or interest of its own, but, on the one hand, to win access for that communication by the clearness and beauty of the vehicle, and on the other hand, to take advantage of every pause or stage in that communication to interpose some characteristic & restful beauty in its own art. We thus have a reason for the clearness and beauty of the text as a whole, for the especial beauty of the first or introductory page and of the title, and for the especial beauty of the headings of chapters, capital or initial letters, and so on, and an opening for the *illustrator as we shall see by and by. Further, in the case of Poetry,*
8/10

The whole duty of Typography, as of Calligraphy, is to communicate to the imagination, without loss by the way, the thought or image intended to be communicated by the Author. And the whole duty of beautiful typography is not to substitute for the beauty or interest of the thing thought and intended to be conveyed by the symbol, a beauty or interest of its own, but, on the one hand, to win access for that communication by the clearness and beauty of the vehicle, and on the other hand, to take advantage of every pause or stage in that communication to interpose some characteristic & restful beauty in its own art. We thus have a reason for the clearness and beauty of the text as a whole, for the especial beauty of the first or introductory page and of the title, and for the especial beauty of the headings of chapters, capital or initial letters, and so on, and an opening for the illustrator as we shall see by and by. Further, in the case of Poetry, *ear, and should be placed on the page so that its structure may be*
8/11

The whole duty of Typography, as of Calligraphy, is to communicate to the imagination, without loss by the way, the thought or image intended to be communicated by the Author. And the whole duty of beautiful typography is not to substitute for the beauty or interest of the thing thought and intended to be conveyed by the symbol, a beauty or interest of its own, but, on the one hand, to win access for that communication by the clearness and beauty of the vehicle, and on the other hand, to take advantage of every pause or stage in that communication to interpose some characteristic & restful beauty in its own art. We thus have a reason for the clearness and beauty of the text as a whole, for the especial beauty of the first or introductory page and of the title, and for the especial beauty of the headings of chapters, capital or initial letters, and so on, and an opening *case of Poetry, verse, in my opinion, appeals by its form to the*
9/10

The whole duty of Typography, as of Calligraphy, is to communicate to the imagination, without loss by the way, the thought or image intended to be communicated by the Author. And the whole duty of beautiful typography is not to substitute for the beauty or interest of the thing thought and intended to be conveyed by the symbol, a beauty or interest of its own, but, on the one hand, to win access for that communication by the clearness and beauty of the vehicle, and on the other hand, to take advantage of every pause or stage in that communication to interpose some characteristic & restful beauty in its own art. We thus have a reason for the clearness and beauty of the text as a whole, for the especial beauty of the first or introductory page and of the title, and for the especial beauty of the headings *of chapters, capital or initial letters, and so on, and an opening*
9/11

The whole duty of Typography, as of Calligraphy, is to communicate to the imagination, without loss by the way, the thought or image intended to be communicated by the Author. And the whole duty of beautiful typography is not to substitute for the beauty or interest of the thing thought and intended to be conveyed by the symbol, a beauty or interest of its own, but, on the one hand, to win access for that communication by the clearness and beauty of the vehicle, and on the other hand, to take advantage of every pause or stage in that communication to interpose some characteristic & restful beauty in its own art. We thus have a reason for the clearness and beauty of the text as a whole, for the especial beauty of the first or introductory *for the illustrator as we shall see by and by. Further, in the*
9/12

abcdefghijklmnopqrstuvwxyz
ABCDEFGHIJKLMNOPQRSTUVWXYZ
$1234567890(.,'"-;:!)?&

abcdefghijklmnopqrstuvwxyz
ABCDEFGHIJKLMNOPQRSTUVWXYZ
$1234567890(.,'"-;:!)?&

abcdefghijklmnopqrstuvwxyz
ABCDEFGHIJKLMNOPQRSTUVWXYZ
$1234567890(.,'"-;:!)?&

abcdefghijklmnopqrstuvwxyz
ABCDEFGHIJKLMNOPQRSTUVWXYZ
$1234567890(.,'"-;:!)?&

The whole duty of Typography, as of Calligraphy, is to communicate to the imagination, without loss by the way, the thought or image intended to be communicated by the Author. And the whole duty of beautiful typography is not to substitute for the beauty or interest of the thing thought and intended to be conveyed by the symbol, a beauty or interest of its own, but, on the one hand, to win access for that communication by the clearness and beauty of the vehicle, and on the other hand, to take advantage of every pause or stage in that communication to interpose some characteristic & restful beauty in its own art. We thus have a reason for the clearness and beauty of the text as a whole, for the especial beauty of the first *or introductory page and of the title, and for the especial*
10/11

The whole duty of Typography, as of Calligraphy, is to communicate to the imagination, without loss by the way, the thought or image intended to be communicated by the Author. And the whole duty of beautiful typography is not to substitute for the beauty or interest of the thing thought and intended to be conveyed by the symbol, a beauty or interest of its own, but, on the one hand, to win access for that communication by the clearness and beauty of the vehicle, and on the other hand, to take advantage of every pause or stage in that communication to interpose some characteristic & restful beauty in its own art. We thus have a reason for the clearness and beauty of *the text as a whole, for the especial beauty of the first*
10/12

The whole duty of Typography, as of Calligraphy, is to communicate to the imagination, without loss by the way, the thought or image intended to be communicated by the Author. And the whole duty of beautiful typography is not to substitute for the beauty or interest of the thing thought and intended to be conveyed by the symbol, a beauty or interest of its own, but, on the one hand, to win access for that communication by the clearness and beauty of the vehicle, and on the other hand, to take advantage of every pause or stage in that communication to interpose some characteristic & restful beauty in its own art. *We thus have a reason for the clearness and beauty of*
10/13

The whole duty of Typography, as of Calligraphy, is to communicate to the imagination, without loss by the way, the thought or image intended to be communicated by the Author. And the whole duty of beautiful typography is not to substitute for the beauty or interest of the thing thought and intended to be conveyed by the symbol, a beauty or interest of its own, but, on the one hand, to win access for that communication by the clearness and beauty of the vehicle, and on the other hand, to take ad*vantage of every pause or stage in that com-*
12/13

The whole duty of Typography, as of Calligraphy, is to communicate to the imagination, without loss by the way, the thought or image intended to be communicated by the Author. And the whole duty of beautiful typography is not to substitute for the beauty or interest of the thing thought and intended to be conveyed by the symbol, a beauty or interest of its own, but, on the one hand, to win access for that communication by the clearness and beauty of *the vehicle, and on the other hand, to take ad-*
12/14

The whole duty of Typography, as of Calligraphy, is to communicate to the imagination, without loss by the way, the thought or image intended to be communicated by the Author. And the whole duty of beautiful typography is not to substitute for the beauty or interest of the thing thought and intended to be conveyed by the symbol, a beauty or interest of its own, but, on the one hand, to win access for that *communication by the clearness and beauty of*
12/15

NEW LINE BETWEEN
ALBANY & NEWBURG

LANDING AT

Hamburgh, Marlborough, Milton, Poughkeepsie, Hyde Park, Kingston, Rhinebeck, Barrytown, Redhook, Bristol, Westcamp Catskill, Hudson, Coxsackie, Stuyvesant, Baltimore & Coeymans.

On and after MONDAY, October 15th,

The Superior Low Pressure Steamer

ST. NICHOLAS

CAPTAIN WILSON,

Will run as a Passage and Freight Boat between Newburgh and Albany, leaving Newburgh

MONDAYS, WEDNESDAYS & FRIDAYS

AT SEVEN O'CLOCK A.M.,

And ALBANY on Tuesdays, Thursdays & Saturdays, at half-past 9 o'clock A.M.

Albany, Oct. 9th, 1849.

Egyptian

ITC Lubalin Graph

446.
Broadsheet, 1849. This slab-serif display type has been lightly inked, and the textured grain of the wooden type is clearly visible, as in the words *St. Nicolas*.

Egyptian or slab-serif typefaces first appeared in the early nineteenth century and enjoyed great popularity. Their bold, machinelike qualities offered a dynamic expression of the industrial age. During the Industrial Revolution, letterpress printers delighted in using bold slab-serif display fonts to give their messages graphic impact (Fig. 446). Rectangular serifs, uniform or almost uniform stroke weight, and geometric letterform construction give Egyptian typefaces a bold, abstract design quality. Egyptian styles whose abrupt right-angle joinery is tempered by curved bracketing include the Clarendon, Century, and Cheltenham type families.

ITC Lubalin Graph is a contemporary Egyptian typeface designed by Herb Lubalin. It is available in five weights: light, book, demi, medium, and bold. Typographic historians have speculated that the first sans serif typefaces may have been created by removing the serifs from slab-serif designs. ITC Lubalin Graph was designed by adding serifs to the geometric sans serif type family Avant Garde Gothic.

72 Point

abcdeefghijkl
mnopqrstuvwx
yzABCDEFGHI
JKLMNOPQRST
UVWXYZ$123
4567890(,'""-;,!)?&

72 Point

abcdefghijkl

mnopqrstuv

wxyzABCDEF

GHIJKLMNOP

QRSTUVWX

YZ$123456789

48 Point

abcdeefghijklmnopq
rstuvwxyzABCDEFGHI
JKLMNOPQRSTUVW
XYZ$1234567890(.,""-;:!)?&

30 Point

abcdeefghijklmnopqrstuvwxyz
ABCDEFGHIJKLMNOPQRSTUVWXYZ
$1234567890(.,""-;:!)?&

18 Point

abcdeefghijklmnopqrstuvwxyz
ABCDEFGHIJKLMNOPQRSTUVWXYZ
$1234567890(.,""-;:!)?&

(.," "''"-;:!)?&

---

48 Point

abcdefghijklmnop
qrstuvwxyz ABCDEF
GHIJKLMNOPQRST
UVWXYZ$1234567890

---

30 Point

abcdefghijklmnopqrstuvwxyz
ABCDEFGHIJKLMNOPQRSTUVW
XYZ$1234567890 (.," "''"-;:!)?&

---

18 Point

abcdefghijklmnopqrstuvwxyz
ABCDEFGHIJKLMNOPQRSTUVWXYZ
$1234567890 (.," "''"-;:!)?&

**ITC Lubalin Graph
Book**

The whole duty of Typography, as of Calligraphy, is to communicate to the imagination, without loss by the way, the thought or image intended to be communicated by the Author. And the whole duty of beautiful typography is not to substitute for the beauty or interest of the thing thought and intended to be conveyed by the symbol, a beauty or interest of its own, but, on the one hand, to win access for that communication by the clearness and beauty of the vehicle, and on the other hand, to take advantage of every pause or stage in that communication to interpose some characteristic & restful beauty in its own art. We thus have a reason for the clearness and beauty of the text as a whole, for the especial beauty of the first or introductory page and of the title, and for the especial beauty of the headings of chapters, capital or initial let-
8/9

The whole duty of Typography, as of Calligraphy, is to communicate to the imagination, without loss by the way, the thought or image intended to be communicated by the Author. And the whole duty of beautiful typography is not to substitute for the beauty or interest of the thing thought and intended to be conveyed by the symbol, a beauty or interest of its own, but, on the one hand, to win access for that communication by the clearness and beauty of the vehicle, and on the other hand, to take advantage of every pause or stage in that communication to interpose some characteristic & restful beauty in its own art. We thus have a reason for the clearness and beauty of the text as a whole, page and of the title, and for the especial beauty
8/10

The whole duty of Typography, as of Calligraphy, is to communicate to the imagination, without loss by the way, the thought or image intended to be communicated by the Author. And the whole duty of beautiful typography is not to substitute for the beauty or interest of the thing thought and intended to be conveyed by the symbol, a beauty or interest of its own, but, on the one hand, to win access for that communication by the clearness and beauty of the vehicle, and on the other hand, to take advantage of every pause or stage in that communication to interpose some characteristic & restful beauty in its own art. We thus have a reason for the especial beauty of the first or introductory
8/11

The whole duty of Typography, as of Calligraphy, is to communicate to the imagination, without loss by the way, the thought or image intended to be communicated by the Author. And the whole duty of beautiful typography is not to substitute for the beauty or interest of the thing thought and intended to be conveyed by the symbol, a beauty or interest of its own, but, on the one hand, to win access for that communication by the clearness and beauty of the vehicle, and on the other hand, to take advantage of every pause or stage in that communication to interpose some characteristic & restful beauty in its own art. We beauty of the text as a whole, for the especial
9/10

The whole duty of Typography, as of Calligraphy, is to communicate to the imagination, without loss by the way, the thought or image intended to be communicated by the Author. And the whole duty of beautiful typography is not to substitute for the beauty or interest of the thing thought and intended to be conveyed by the symbol, a beauty or interest of its own, but, on the one hand, to win access for that communication by the clearness and beauty of the vehicle, and on the other hand, to take advantage of every pause or stage in that communication to interpose some characteristic & restful beauty in its own art. We
9/11

The whole duty of Typography, as of Calligraphy, is to communicate to the imagination, without loss by the way, the thought or image intended to be communicated by the Author. And the whole duty of beautiful typography is not to substitute for the beauty or interest of the thing thought and intended to be conveyed by the symbol, a beauty or interest of its own, but, on the one hand, to win access for that communication by the clearness and beauty of the vehicle, and on the other hand, to take advantage of every pause or stage in that communication to interpose some char-
9/12

abcdefghijklmnopqrstuvwxyz
ABCDEFGHIJKLMNOPQRSTUVWXYZ
$1234567890(.,'"-;:!)?&

abcdefghijklmnopqrstuvwxyz
ABCDEFGHIJKLMNOPQRSTUVWXYZ
$1234567890(.,'"-;:!)?&

abcdefghijklmnopqrstuvwxyz
ABCDEFGHIJKLMNOPQRSTUVWXYZ
$1234567890(.,'"-;:!)?&

abcdefghijklmnopqrstuvwxyz
ABCDEFGHIJKLMNOPQRSTUVWXYZ
$1234567890(.,'"-;:!)?&

The whole duty of Typography, as of Calligraphy, is to communicate to the imagination, without loss by the way, the
thought or image intended to be communicated by the Author. And the whole
duty of beautiful typography is not to substitute for the beauty or interest of the
thing thought and intended to be conveyed by the symbol, a beauty or interest
of its own, but, on the one hand, to win
access for that communication by the
clearness and beauty of the vehicle, and
on the other hand, to take advantage of
every pause or stage in that communica-
10/11

The whole duty of Typography, as of Calligraphy, is to communicate to the imagination, without loss by the way, the
thought or image intended to be communicated by the Author. And the whole
duty of beautiful typography is not to substitute for the beauty or interest of the
thing thought and intended to be conveyed by the symbol, a beauty or interest
of its own, but, on the one hand, to win
access for that communication by the
clearness and beauty of the vehicle, and
on the other hand, to take advantage of
10/12

The whole duty of Typography, as of Calligraphy, is to communicate to the imagination, without loss by the way, the
thought or image intended to be communicated by the Author. And the whole
duty of beautiful typography is not to substitute for the beauty or interest of the
thing thought and intended to be conveyed by the symbol, a beauty or interest
of its own, but, on the one hand, to win
access for that communication by the
clearness and beauty of the vehicle, and
10/13

The whole duty of Typography, as
of Calligraphy, is to communicate
to the imagination, without loss
by the way, the thought or image
intended to be communicated by
the Author. And the whole duty of
beautiful typography is not to substitute for the beauty or interest of
the thing thought and intended to
be conveyed by the symbol, a
beauty or interest of its own, but,
on the one hand, to win access for
12/13

The whole duty of Typography, as
of Calligraphy, is to communicate
to the imagination, without loss
by the way, the thought or image
intended to be communicated by
the Author. And the whole duty of
beautiful typography is not to substitute for the beauty or interest of
the thing thought and intended to
be conveyed by the symbol, a
beauty or interest of its own, but,
12/14

The whole duty of Typography, as
of Calligraphy, is to communicate
to the imagination, without loss
by the way, the thought or image
intended to be communicated by
the Author. And the whole duty of
beautiful typography is not to substitute for the beauty or interest of
the thing thought and intended to
be conveyed by the symbol, a
12/15

Avant Garde X-light

abcdefghijklmnopqrstuvwxyz
ABCDEFGHIJKLMNOPQRSTUVWXYZ
$1234567890(.,'""–,.!)?&

Avant Garde Book

abcdefghijklmnopqrstuvwxyz
ABCDEFGHIJKLMNOPQRSTUVWXYZ
$1234567890(.,'""–,.!)?&

Avant Garde Medium

abcdefghijklmnopqrstuvwxyz
ABCDEFGHIJKLMNOPQRSTUVWXYZ
$1234567890(.,""""-,.!)?&

Avant Garde Bold

abcdefghijklmnopqrstuvwxyz
ABCDEFGHIJKLMNOPQRSTUVWX
YZ$1234567890(.,""""–,.!)?&

Bembo

abcdefghijklmnopqrstuvwxyz
ABCDEFGHIJKLMNOPQRSTUVWX
YZ$1234567890(.,'""""-;:!)?&

Bembo Italic

abcdefghijklmnopqrstuvwxyz
ABCDEFGHIJKLMNOPQRSTUVWX
YZ$1234567890(.,'‘‘’’-;:!)?&

Bembo Bold

abcdefghijklmnopqrstuvwxyz
ABCDEFGHIJKLMNOPQRSTU
VWXYZ$1234567890(.,'‘‘’’-;:!)?&

Benguiat Book

abcdefghijklmnopqrstuvwxyz
ABCDEFGHIJKLMMNOPQRSTUVWX
YZ$1234567890(.,'‘‘’’-;:!)?&

Benguiat Italic

abcdefghijklmnopqrstuvwxyz
ABCDEFGHIJKLMMNOPQRSTUVW
XYZ$1234567890(.,'‘‘’’-;:!)?&

Benguiat Bold

abcdefghijklmnopqrstuvwxyz
ABCDEFGHIJKLMMNOPQRSTU
VWXYZ$1234567890(.,'‘‘’’-;:!)?&

Beton Extra Bold

abcdefghijklmnopqrstuvwxyz
ABCDEFGHIJKLMNOPQRSTUV
WXYZ$1234567890(.,'""-;:!)?&

Bookman

abcdefghijklmnopqrstuvwxyz
ABCDEFGHIJKLMNOPQRSTUVW
XYZ $1234567890(.,'""-;:!)?&

Bookman Italic

abcdefghijklmnopqrstuvwxyz
ABCDEFGHIJKLMNOPQRSTUV
WXYZ$1234567890(.,'""-;:!)?&

Caslon 471

abcdefghijklmnopqrstuvwxyz
ABCDEFGHIJKLMNOPQRSTUVWXYZ
$1234567890(.,'""-;:!)?&

Caslon 471 Italic

abcdefghijklmnopqrstuvwxyz
ABCDEFGHIJKLMNOPQRSTUVWXYZ
$1234567890(.,'""-;:!)?&

Caslon Bold

abcdefghijklmnopqrstuvwxyz
ABCDEFGHIJKLMNOPQRSTUV
WXYZ$1234567890 .,'‘’'-;:!?&

Caslon Bold Italic

abcdefghijklmnopqrstuvwxyz
ABCDEFGHIJKLMNOPQRSTUV
WXYZ$1234567890(.,'‘’'-;:!)?&

Century Schoolbook

abcdefghijklmnopqrstuvwxyz
ABCDEFGHIJKLMNOPQRSTUVWX
YZ$1234567890(.,'‘’'-;:!)?&

Century Schoolbook Italic

abcdefghijklmnopqrstuvwxyz
ABCDEFGHIJKLMNOPQRSTUVWX
YZ$1234567890(.,'‘’'-;:!)?&

Century Schoolbook Bold

abcdefghijklmnopqrstuvwxyz
ABCDEFGHIJKLMNOPQRSTUVWX
YZ$1234567890(.,'‘’'-;:!)?&

abcdefghijklmnopqrstuvwxyz
ABCDEFGHIJKLMNOPQRSTUVWXYZ
$1234567890(.,""''-;:!)?&

abcdefghijklmnopqrstuvwxyz
ABCDEFGHIJKLMNOPQRSTUVWXYZ
$1234567890(.,""''-;:!)?&

abcdefghijklmnopqrstuvwxyz
ABCDEFGHIJKLMNOPQRSTUVW
XYZ$1234567890(.,""''-;:!)?&

abcdefghijklmnopqrstuvwxyz
ABCDEFGHIJKLMNOPQRSTUV
WXYZ$1234567890(.,""''-;:!)?&

abcdefghijklmnopqrstuvwxyz
ABCDEFGHIJKLMNOPQRSTUVWXYZ
$1234567890 (.,""''-;:!)?&

Franklin Gothic

abcdefghijklmnopqrstuvwxyz
ABCDEFGHIJKLMNOPQRSTUVWX
YZ $1234567890(.,'""-;:!)?&

Franklin Gothic Condensed

abcdefghijklmnopqrstuvwxyz
ABCDEFGHIJKLMNOPQRSTUVWXYZ
$1234567890(.,'""-;:!)?&

Futura Book

abcdefghijklmnopqrstuvwxyz
ABCDEFGHIJKLMNOPQRSTUVWXYZ
$1234567890(.,'""-;:!)?&

Futura Demi

abcdefghijklmnopqrstuvwxyz
ABCDEFGHIJKLMNOPQRSTUVWXYZ
$1234567890(.,'""-;:!)?&

Futura Bold Condensed

abcdefghijklmnopqrstuvwxyz
ABCDEFGHIJKLMNOPQRSTUVWXYZ
$1234567890(.,'""-;:!)?&

Gill Sans Medium

abcdefghijklmnopqrstuvwxyz
ABCDEFGHIJKLMNOPQRSTUVWXYZ
$1234567890(.,'""-;:!)?&

Goudy Old Style

abcdefghijklmnopqrstuvwxyz
ABCDEFGHIJKLMNOPQRSTUVWX
YZ$1234567890(.,'""-;:!)?&

Goudy Bold

abcdefghijklmnopqrstuvwxyz
ABCDEFGHIJKLMNOPQRSTUVWX
YZ$1234567890(.,'""-;:!)?&

Helvetica Light

abcdefghijklmnopqrstuvwxyz
ABCDEFGHIJKLMNOPQRSTUVWXYZ
$1234567890(.,'""-;:!)?&

Helvetica

abcdefghijklmnopqrstuvwxyz
ABCDEFGHIJKLMNOPQRSTUVWX
YZ$1234567890(.,'""-;:!)?&

Helvetica Medium

abcdefghijklmnopqrstuvwxyz
ABCDEFGHIJKLMNOPQRSTUVW
XYZ$1234567890(.,'""-;:!)?&

Helvetica Bold

abcdefghijklmnopqrstuvwxyz
ABCDEFGHIJKLMNOPQRSTUV
WXYZ$1234567890(.,'""-;:!)?&

Helvetica Extra Bold Condensed

abcdefghijklmnopqrstuvwxyz
ABCDEFGHIJKLMNOPQRSTUVWXYZ
$1234567890(.,'""-;:!)?&

Kabel Medium

abcdefghijklmnopqrstuvwxyz
ABCDEFGHIJKLMNOPQRSTUVWXYZ
$1234567890(.,'""-;:!)?&

Kabel Bold

abcdefghijklmnopqrstuvwxyz
ABCDEFGHIJKLMNOPQRSTUVWXYZ
$1234567890(.,'""-;:!)?&

abcdefghijklmnopqrstuvwxyz
ABCDEFGHIJKLMNOPQRSTUVWX
YZ$1234567890(.,'""!-;:!)?&

abcdefghijklmnopqrstuvwxyz
ABCDEFGHIJKLMNOPQRSTUVWXYZ
$1234567890(.,'""-;:!)?&

abcdefghijklmnopqrstuvwxyz
ABCDEFGHIJKLMNOPQRSTUVWXYZ
$1234567890(.,'""-;:!)?&

abcdefghijklmnopqrstuvwxyz
ABCDEFGHIJKLMNOPQRSTUVW
XYZ$1234567890(.,'""-;:!)?&

abcdefghijklmnopqrstuvwxyz
ABCDEFGHIJKLMNOPQRSTUVWXYZ
$1234567890(.,'`"'=;:!)?&

Sabon Roman

abcdefghijklmnopqrstuvwxyz
ABCDEFGHIJKLMNOPQRSTUVWX
YZ$1234567890(.,'""–;:!)?&

Times Roman

abcdefghijklmnopqrstuvwxyz
ABCDEFGHIJKLMNOPQRSTUVWX
YZ$1234567890(.,'"-;:!)?&

Times Roman Italic

abcdefghijklmnopqrstuvwxyz
ABCDEFGHIJKLMNOPQRSTUVWX
YZ$1234567890(.,'""–;:!)?&

Times Roman Bold

abcdefghijklmnopqrstuvwxyz
ABCDEFGHIJKLMNOPQRSTUVW
XYZ$1234567890(.,'""–;:!)?&

Trump Mediaeval

abcdefghijklmnopqrstuvwxyz
ABCDEFGHIJKLMNOPQRSTUVWXYZ
$1234567890(.,'""–;:!)?&

Text column specimens

The text settings shown are presented for comparative analysis of typeface texture, tone, and legibility. They can be photostated or photocopied for use in layouts. Different column structures with varying line length, paragraph indications, and justification are shown. These factors influence the visual appearance and readability of the specimens.

Of all the achievements of the human mind, the birth of the alphabet is the most momentous. "Letters, like men, have now an ancestry, and the ancestry of words, as of men, is often a very noble possession, making them capable of great things": indeed, it has been said that the invention of writing is more important than all the victories ever won or constitutions devised by man. The history of writing is, in a way, the history of the human race, since in it are bound up, severally and together, the development of thought, of expression, of art, of intercommunication, and of mechanical invention.

When and to whom in the dim past the idea came that man's speech could be better represented by fewer symbols (to denote certain unvarying sounds) selected from the confused mass of picture ideographs, phonograms, and their like, which constituted the first methods of representing human speech, we have no certain means of knowing. But whatever the source, the development did come; and we must deal with it. To present briefly the early history of the alphabet requires that much collateral matter must be disregarded and a great deal that is omitted here must necessarily be taken for granted; the writer desires, however, to present what seems to him to be a logical and probable story of the alphabet's beginnings.

Although it has not yet been proved conclusively, it is quite possible, and altogether probable, that the traders of Phoenicia and the Aegean adopted both the use of papyrus and Egyptian hieratic writing, from which developed the Phoenician alphabet. Whether all the earliest writing systems of different countries sprang from one common stock of picture writing, we shall, perhaps, never surely know; we do know that the picture writing of Egypt exercised a very great influence, and it seems quite safe for us to assume that crude attempts by those ancient Nile-dwellers to express thought visible or to record facts by a series of pictures – or by diagrams sufficiently pictorial, at least, to connect them with well-known objects (disregarding the earlier mnemonic stage or use of memory aids like the quipu or knotted cord, of which the rosary is a modern example) – constitute the origin of the abstract and arbitrary signs or symbols which we call "letters."

Let us assume, as logically we may, that picture writing in which a drawing depicting or suggesting the object itself came first; next must have come the ideograph, the sign suggesting the name of the object represented instead of representing the thing itself; & next the phonogram, or sign that suggests a sound only.

In the first class just named belong the wedge-

10/12 ITC Garamond Book

Of all the achievements of the human mind, the birth of the alphabet is the most momentous. "Letters, like men, have now an ancestry, and the ancestry of words, as of men, is often a very noble possession, making them capable of great things": indeed, it has been said that the invention of writing is more important than all the victories ever won or constitutions devised by man. The history of writing is, in a way, the history of the human race, since in it are bound up, severally and together, the development of thought, of expression, of art, of intercommunication, and of mechanical invention.

When and to whom in the dim past the idea came that man's speech could be better represented by fewer symbols (to denote certain unvarying sounds) selected from the confused mass of picture ideographs, phonograms, and their like, which constituted the first methods of representing human speech, we have no certain means of knowing. But whatever the source, the development did come; and we must deal with it. To present briefly the early history of the alphabet requires that much collateral matter must be disregarded and a great deal that is omitted here must necessarily be taken for granted; the writer desires, however, to present what seems to him to be a logical and probable story of the alphabet's beginnings.

Although it has not yet been proved conclusively, it is quite possible, and altogether probable, that the traders of Phoenicia and the Aegean adopted both the use of papyrus and Egyptian hieratic writing, from which developed the Phoenician alphabet. Whether all the earliest writing systems of different countries sprang from one common stock of picture writing, we shall, perhaps, never surely know; we do know that the picture writing of Egypt exercised a very great influence, and it seems quite safe for us to assume that crude attempts by those ancient Nile-dwellers to express thought visible or to record facts by a series of pictures — or by diagrams sufficiently pictorial, at least, to connect them with well-known objects (disregarding the earlier mnemonic stage or use of memory aids like the quipu or knotted cord, of which the rosary is a modern example) — constitute the origin of the abstract and arbitrary signs or symbols which we call "letters."

Let us assume, as logically we may, that picture writing in which a drawing depicting or suggesting the object itself came first; next must have come the ideograph, the sign suggesting the name of the object represented instead of representing the thing itself; & next the phonogram, or sign that suggests a sound only.

In the first class just named belong the wedge-shaped, or cuneiform, characters inscribed in the clay tablets, cylinders, and monuments of Assyria, Babylonia, &

10/12 Futura Medium

Of all the achievements of the human mind, the birth of the alphabet is the most momentous. "Letters, like men, have now an ancestry, and the ancestry of words, as of men, is often a very noble possession, making them capable of great things": indeed, it has been said that the invention of writing is more important than all the victories ever won or constitutions devised by man. The history of writing is, in a way, the history of the human race, since in it are bound up, severally and together, the development of thought, of expression, of art, of intercommunication, and of mechanical invention.

When and to whom in the dim past the idea came that man's speech could be better represented by fewer symbols (to denote certain unvarying sounds) selected from the confused mass of picture ideographs, phonograms, and their like, which constituted the first methods of representing human speech, we have no certain means of knowing. But whatever the source, the development did come; and we must deal with it. To present briefly the early history of the alphabet requires that much collateral matter must be disregarded and a great deal that is omitted here must necessarily be taken for granted; the writer desires, however, to present what seems to him to be a logical and probable story of the alphabet's beginnings.

Although it has not yet been proved conclusively, it is quite possible, and altogether probable, that the traders of Phoenicia and the Aegean adopted both the use of papyrus and Egyptian hieratic writing, from which developed the Phoenician alphabet. Whether all the earliest writing systems of different countries sprang from one common stock of picture writing, we shall, perhaps, never surely know; we do know that the picture writing of Egypt exercised a very great influence, and it seems quite safe for us to assume that crude attempts by those ancient Nile-dwellers to express thought visible or to record facts by a series of pictures—or by diagrams sufficiently pictorial, at least, to connect them with well-known objects (disregarding the earlier mnemonic stage or use of memory aids like the quipu or knotted cord, of which the rosary is a modern example)—constitute the origin of the abstract and arbitrary signs or symbols which we call "letters."

Let us assume, as logically we may, that picture writing in which a drawing depicting or suggesting the object itself came first; next must have come the ideograph, the sign suggesting the name of the object represented instead of representing the thing itself; & next the phonogram, or sign that suggests a sound only.

In the first class just named belong the wedge-shaped, or cuneiform, characters inscribed in the clay tablets, cylinders, and monuments of Assyria, Babylonia, & other Near Eastern countries—characters the very existence of which was overlooked or forgotten for some sixteen hundred years. They were almost purely pictorial—were drawings only, really not writing at all, and, as far as we now know, have little direct bearing on the derivation of our present alphabet.

To this first class also belong the hieroglyphs of Egypt, highly elaborated types of picture writing which changed so little over a long period that "it is like a language which has never forgotten the derivation of its words, or corrupted their etymological forms, however much it may have altered its meaning." Developed at least five thousand years B.C., the purely pictorial character was preserved by its Egyptian users until the end. Sir Edw. Maunde Thompson asserts that "we may without exaggeration...carry back the invention of Egyptian writing to six or seven thousand years B.C." Most of the material available goes back not farther than the First Dynasty (3300 B.C.).

Possibly the earliest method of recording the payment of taxes indicates, too, the earliest stage in the process of learning to write. The

Of all the achievements of the human mind, the birth of the alphabet is the most momentous. "Letters, like men, have now an ancestry, and the ancestry of words, as of men, is often a very noble possession, making them capable of great things": indeed, it has been said that the invention of writing is more important than all the victories ever won or constitutions devised by man. The history of writing is, in a way, the history of the human race, since in it are bound up, severally and together, the development of thought, of expression, of art, of intercommunication, and of mechanical invention.

When and to whom in the dim past the idea came that man's speech could be better represented by fewer symbols (to denote certain unvarying sounds) selected from the confused mass of picture ideographs, phonograms, and their like, which constituted the first methods of representing human speech, we have no certain means of knowing. But whatever the source, the development did come; and we must deal with it. To present briefly the early history of the alphabet requires that much collateral matter must be disregarded and a great deal that is omitted here must necessarily be taken for granted; the writer desires, however, to present what seems to him to be a logical and probable story of the alphabet's beginnings.

Although it has not yet been proved conclusively, it is quite possible, and altogether probable, that the traders of Phoenicia and the Aegean adopted both the use of papyrus and Egyptian hieratic writing, from which developed the Phoenician alphabet. Whether all the earliest writing systems of different countries sprang from one common stock of picture writing, we shall, perhaps, never surely know; we do know that the picture writing of Egypt exercised a very great influence, and it seems quite safe for us to assume that crude attempts by those ancient Nile-dwellers to express thought visible or to record facts by a series of pictures – or by diagrams sufficiently pictorial, at least, to connect them with well-known objects (disregarding the earlier mnemonic stage or use of memory aids like the quipu or knotted cord, of which the rosary is a modern example) – constitute the origin of the abstract and arbitrary signs or symbols which we call "letters."

Let us assume, as logically we may, that picture writing in which a drawing depict-

Of all the achievements of the human mind, the birth of the alphabet is the most momentous. "Letters, like men, have now an ancestry, and the ancestry of words, as of men, is often a very noble possession, making them capable of great things": indeed, it has been said that the invention of writing is more important than all the victories ever won or constitutions devised by man. The history of writing is, in a way, the history of the human race, since in it are bound up, severally and together, the development of thought, of expression, of art, of intercommunication, and of mechanical invention.

When and to whom in the dim past the idea came that man's speech could be better represented by fewer symbols (to denote certain unvarying sounds) selected from the confused mass of picture ideographs, phonograms, and their like, which constituted the first methods of representing human speech, we have no certain means of knowing. But whatever the source, the development did come; and we must deal with it. To present briefly the early history of the alphabet requires that much collateral matter must be disregarded and a great deal that is omitted here must necessarily be taken for granted; the writer desires, however, to present what seems to him to be a logical and probable story of the alphabet's beginnings.

Although it has not yet been proved conclusively, it is quite possible, and altogether probable, that the traders of Phoenicia and the Aegean adopted both the use of papyrus and Egyptian hieratic writing, from which developed the Phoenician alphabet. Whether all the earliest writing systems of different countries sprang from one common stock of picture writing, we shall, perhaps, never surely know; we do know that the picture writing of Egypt exercised a very great influence, and it seems quite safe for us to assume that crude attempts by those ancient Nile-dwellers to express thought visible or to record facts by a series of pictures—or by diagrams sufficiently pictorial, at least, to connect them with well-known objects (disregarding the earlier mnemonic stage or use of memory aids like the quipu or knotted cord, of which the rosary is a modern example)—constitute the origin of the abstract and arbitrary signs or symbols which we call "letters."

Let us assume, as logically we may, that picture writing in which a drawing depicting or suggesting the object itself came first; next must have come the ideograph, the sign suggesting the name of the object represented instead of representing the thing itself; & next the phonogram, or

10/12 Helvetica

Of all the achievements of the human mind, the birth of the alphabet is the most momentous. "Letters, like men, have now an ancestry, and the ancestry of words, as of men, is often a very noble possession, making them capable of great things": indeed, it has been said that the invention of writing is more important than all the victories ever won or constitutions devised by man. The history of writing is, in a way, the history of the human race, since in it are bound up, severally and together, the development of thought, of expression, of art, of intercommunication, and of mechanical invention.

When and to whom in the dim past the idea came that man's speech could be better represented by fewer symbols (to denote certain unvarying sounds) selected from the confused mass of picture ideographs, phonograms, and their like, which constituted the first methods of representing human speech, we have no certain means of knowing. But whatever the source, the development did come; and we must deal with it. To present briefly the early history of the alphabet requires that much collateral matter must be disregarded and a great deal that is omitted here must necessarily be taken for granted; the writer desires, however, to present what seems to him to be a logical and probable story of the alphabet's beginnings.

Although it has not yet been proved conclusively, it is quite possible, and altogether probable, that the traders of Phoenicia and the Aegean adopted both the use of papyrus and Egyptian hieratic writing, from which developed the Phoenician alphabet. Whether all the earliest writing systems of different countries sprang from one common stock of picture writing, we shall, perhaps, never surely know; we do know that the picture writing of Egypt exercised a very great influence, and it seems quite safe for us to assume that crude attempts by those ancient Nile-dwellers to express thought visible or to record facts by a series of pictures — or by diagrams sufficiently pictorial, at least, to connect them with well-known objects (disregarding the earlier mnemonic stage or use of memory aids like the quipu or knotted cord,

10/12 Univers 55

Of all the achievements of the human mind, the birth of the alphabet is the most momentous. "Letters, like men, have now an ancestry, and the ancestry of words, as of men, is often a very noble possession, making them capable of great things": indeed, it has been said that the invention of writing is more important than all the victories ever won or constitutions devised by man. The history of writing is, in a way, the history of the human race, since in it are bound up, severally and together, the development of thought, of expression, of art, of intercommunication, and of mechanical invention.

When and to whom in the dim past the idea came that man's speech could be better represented by fewer symbols (to denote certain unvarying sounds) selected from the confused mass of picture ideographs, phonograms, and their like, which constituted the first methods of representing human speech, we have no certain means of knowing. But whatever the source, the development did come; and we must deal with it. To present briefly the early history of the alphabet requires that much collateral matter must be disregarded and a great deal that is omitted here must necessarily be taken for granted; the writer desires, however, to present what seems to him to be a logical and probable story of the alphabet's beginnings.

Although it has not yet been proved conclusively, it is quite possible, and altogether probable, that the traders of Phoenicia and the Aegean adopted both the use of papyrus and Egyptian hieratic writing, from which developed the Phoenician alphabet. Whether all the earliest writing systems of different countries sprang from one common stock of picture writing, we shall, perhaps, never surely know; we do know that the picture writing of Egypt exercised a very great influence, and it seems quite safe for us to assume that crude attempts by those ancient Nile-dwellers to express thought visible or to record facts by a series of pictures — or by diagrams sufficiently pictorial, at least, to connect them with well-known objects (disregarding the earlier mnemonic stage or use of memory aids like the quipu or knotted cord, of which the rosary is a modern example) — constitute the origin of the abstract and arbitrary signs or symbols which we call "letters."

Let us assume, as logically we may, that picture writing in which a drawing depicting or suggesting the object itself came first; next must have come the ideograph, the sign suggesting the name of the object represented instead of representing the thing itself; & next the phonogram, or sign that suggests a sound only.

In the first class just named belong the wedge-shaped, or cuneiform, characters inscribed in the clay tablets, cylinders, and monuments of Assyria, Babylonia, & other Near Eastern countries — characters the very existence of which was overlooked or forgotten for some sixteen hundred years. They were almost purely pictorial — were drawings only, really not writing at all, and, as far as we now know, have little direct bearing on the derivation of our present alphabet.

To this first class also belong the hieroglyphs of Egypt, highly elaborated types of picture writing which changed so little over a long period that "it is like a language which has never forgotten the derivation of its words, or corrupted their etymological forms, however much it may have altered its meaning." Developed at least five thousand years B.C., the purely pictorial

Of all the achievements of the human mind, the birth of the alphabet is the most momentous. "Letters, like men, have now an ancestry, and the ancestry of words, as of men, is often a very noble possession, making them capable of great things": indeed, it has been said that the invention of writing is more important than all the victories ever won or constitutions devised by man. The history of writing is, in a way, the history of the human race, since in it are bound up, severally and together, the development of thought, of expression, of art, of intercommunication, and of mechanical invention.

When and to whom in the dim past the idea came that man's speech could be better represented by fewer symbols (to denote certain unvarying sounds) selected from the confused mass of picture ideographs, phonograms, and their like, which constituted the first methods of representing human speech, we have no certain means of knowing. But whatever the source, the development did come; and we must deal with it. To present briefly the early history of the alphabet requires that much collateral matter must be disregarded and a great deal that is omitted here must necessarily be taken for granted; the writer desires, however, to present what seems to him to be a logical and probable story of the alphabet's beginnings.

Although it has not yet been proved conclusively, it is quite possible, and altogether probable, that the traders of Phoenicia and the Aegean adopted both the use of papyrus and Egyptian hieratic writing, from which developed the Phoenician alphabet. Whether all the earliest writing systems of different countries sprang from one common stock of picture writing, we shall, perhaps, never surely know; we do know that the picture writing of Egypt exercised a very great influence, and it seems quite safe for us to assume that crude attempts by those ancient Nile-dwellers to express thought visible or to record facts by a series of pictures — or by diagrams sufficiently pictorial, at least, to connect them with well-known objects (disregarding the earlier mnemonic stage or use of memory aids like the quipu or knotted cord, of which the

10/12 Baskerville

10/12 ITC Lubalin Graph Book

A. A. Abbreviation for *Author's Alteration,* used to flag a mistake or correction by the author.

ABA form. Design principle of form interrelationships, involving repetition and contrast.

Accents. Small marks over, under, or through a letterform, indicating specific pronunciation or changes in stress.

Agate. Vertical unit used to measure space in newspaper columns, originally five-and-one-half-point type. Fourteen agate lines equal approximately one inch.

Alignment. Precise arrangement of letterforms upon an imaginary horizontal or vertical line.

Alphabet length. Horizontal measure of the lowercase alphabet in a type font, used to approximate the horizontal measure of type set in that font.

Ampersand. Typographic character (&) representing the word *and.*

Area composition. The organization of typographic and other graphic elements into their final positions by electronic means (keyboard, graphics tablets and electronic pens, etc.), eliminating the need for hand assembly or paste-up.

Ascender. Stroke on a lowercase letter that rises above the meanline.

ASCII code. Abbreviation for American Standard Code of Information Interchange. The numbers 0 through 127 represent the alphanumeric characters and functions on the keyboard.

Backslant. Letterforms having a diagonal slant to the left.

Baseline. An imaginary horizontal line upon which the base of each capital letter rests.

Binary code. Number system using only two digits: zero and one.

Bit. Smallest unit of information in a computer, consisting of only one digit, zero or one.

Body size. Depth of a piece of metal type, usually measured in points.

Body type. Text material, usually set in sizes from six to twelve point. Also called text type.

Boldface. Type with thicker, heavier strokes than the regular font. Indicated as *BF* in type specifications.

Byte. Unit of computer information. A byte consists of eight or more bits.

C. and l.c. Used in marking copy, to instruct the typesetter to use capitals and lowercase.

C. and s.c. Used in marking copy, to instruct the typesetter to use capitals and small capitals.

Cap height. Height of the capital letters, measured from the baseline to the capline.

Capitals. Letters larger than — and often differing from — the corresponding lowercase letters. Also called uppercase.

Capline. Imaginary horizontal line defined by the height of the capital letters.

Caps. See *Capitals.*

Caption. Title, explanation, or description accompanying an illustration or photograph.

Casting off. Determining the length of manuscript copy, enabling a calculation of the area that type will occupy when set in a given size and style.

Cathode-ray tube (CRT). An electronic tube with a phosphorescent surface that produces a glowing image when activated by an electronic beam.

Central processing unit (CPU). Computer component that controls all other parts, performs logical operations, and stores information.

Character. Symbol, sign, or mark in a language system.

Character count. Calculation of the total number of characters in manuscript copy that is to be typeset.

Chase. Heavy metal frame into which metal type is locked for proofing or printing.

Cicero. European typographic unit of measure, approximately equal to the American pica.

Cold type. Type which is set by means other than casting molten metal. A term most frequently used to indicate strike-on composition rather than photo or digital typesetting.

Colophon. Inscription, frequently placed at the end of a book, that contains facts about its production.

Command. Code that is keyboarded and entered into a computer's memory, that will instruct a typesetter, editing terminal, or other peripheral as to the specific typographic functions to be performed.

Comp. See *Comprehensive layout.*

Compensation. In visual organization, the counterbalancing of elements.

Composing stick. Adjustable hand-held metal tray, used to hold handset type as it is being composed.

Composition. Alternate term for typesetting.

Compositor. Person who sets type.

Comprehensive layout. An accurate representation of typography and other graphic elements to be printed. Also called comp.

Computer. Electronic device that performs predefined (programmed) high-speed mathematical or logical calculations.

Condensed. Letterforms whose horizontal width has been compressed.

Consonance. In design, harmonious interaction between elements.

Copyfitting. Calculating the area that will be occupied by a given manuscript when set in a specified size and style of type.

Counter. Space enclosed by the strokes of a letterform.

Counterform. "Negative" spatial areas defined and shaped by letterforms, including both interior counters and spaces between characters.

CPI. Characters per inch.

CPU. See *Central processing unit.*

CRT. See *Cathode-ray tube.*

Cursive. Typestyles that imitate handwriting, often with letters that do not connect.

Cutoff rules. Rules used to separate pages into various units, such as advertisements or news stories.

Daisy wheel. Strike-on printing wheel containing relief characters on spokes, radiating from a central disk. As the wheel spins, a hammer impacts the characters against an inked ribbon.

Data. Information, particularly information upon which a computer program is based.

Data bank. Mass storage of large quantities of information, indexed for rapid retrieval.

Data processing. The storing and handling of information by a computer.

Data transmission. Rapid electronic transfer of coded data via telephone or other communication links.

Dazzle. Visual effect caused by extreme contrast in the strokes of letterforms.

Descender. Stroke on a lowercase letterform that falls below the baseline.

Digital computer. A device that translates data into a discrete number system to facilitate electronic processing.

Disk. Thin, flat, circular plate with a magnetic surface upon which data may be stored. Also, a circular grid containing the master font in some typesetting systems.

Display type. Type sizes fourteen point and above, used primarily for headlines and titles.

Dissonance. In design, visual tension and contrast between typographic elements.

Drop initial. Display letterform set into the text.

E. A. Abbreviation for *Editor's Alteration,* used to flag errors or corrections made by the editor.

Editing terminal. Workstation consisting of a keyboard and visual display device, used to input and edit copy prior to typesetting.

Egyptian. Typefaces characterized by slablike serifs similar in weight to the main strokes.

Elite. Size of typewriter type approximately equal to ten-point typography.

Ellipses. Three dots used to indicate an omission in quoted material.

Em. The square of the body size of any type, used as a unit of measure. In some expanded or condensed faces, the em is also expanded or condensed from the square proportion.

Em dash. A dash one em long. Also called a long dash.

Em leader. Horizontal dots or dashes with one em between their centers.

Em space. A space equal to the width of an em quad.

En. One-half of an em (see *Em*).

En dash. A dash one en long. Also called a short dash.

En leader. Horizontal dots or dashes with one en between their centers.

En space. Space equal to the width of an en quad.

Expanded. Letterforms whose horizontal width has been extended.

Face. The part of metal type that is inked for printing. Also, another word for typeface.

Family. See *Type family.*

Firmware. Software in hardware form.

Fit. Refers to the spatial relationships between letters after they are set into words and lines.

Flush left (or right). The even vertical alignment of lines at the left (or right) edge of a column.

Folio. Page number.

Font. Character set of a given size and style including upper and lowercase letters, numerals, and punctuation marks.

Format. The overall typographic and spatial schema established for a publication or any other application.

Formatting. In digital typesetting and photo-typesetting, the process of issuing specific commands that establish the typographic format.

Foundry type. Metal type used in hand composition.

Furniture. Rectangular pieces of wood, metal, or plastic used to fill in excess space when locking up a form for letterpress printing.

Galley. A three-sided, shallow metal tray used to hold metal type forms before printing.

Galley proof. Originally, a type proof pulled from metal type assembled in a galley. Frequently used today to indicate any first proof, regardless of the type system.

"Golf" ball. An interchangeable metal ball approximately one inch in diameter with raised characters on its surface, used as the printing element in some typewriters.

Grid. Underlying structure composed of a linear framework used by designers to organize typographic and pictorial elements. Also, a film or glass master font, containing characters in a predetermined configuration and used in phototypesetting.

Grotesque. Name for sans serif typefaces.

Gutter. The interval separating two facing pages in a publication.

Gutter margin. Inner margin of a page in a publication.

Hairline. Thinnest strokes on a typeface having strokes of varying weight.

Hand composition. Method of setting type by placing individual pieces of metal type from a type case into a composing stick.

Hanging indent. In composition, a column format in which the first line of type is set to a full measure while all additional lines are indented.

Hanging punctuation. Punctuation set outside the column measure to achieve an optical alignment.

Hard copy. Computer output printed on paper.

Hardware. The physical equipment of a computer system, such as the CPU, input/output devices, and peripherals.

Heading. Copy that is given emphasis over the body of text, through changes in size, weight, or spatial interval.

Headline. The most significant type in the visual hierarchy of a printed communication.

Hot type. Type produced by casting molten metal.

Hyphenation. The syllabic division of words, when they must be broken at the end of a line. In electronic textsetting, hyphenation can be determined by the operator, or automatically by the computer.

Imposition. The arrangement of pages in a printed signature to achieve the proper sequencing after the sheets are folded and trimmed.

Incunabula. European printing during the first half-century of typography, from Gutenberg's invention of movable type until the year 1500.

Indent. An interval of space at the beginning of a line to indicate a new paragraph.

Inferior characters. Small characters, usually slightly smaller than the x-height, positioned on or below the baseline and used for footnotes or fractions.

Initial. A large letter used at the beginning of a column; for example, at the beginning of a chapter.

Input. Raw data, text, or commands entered into a computer memory from a peripheral device, such as a keyboard.

Interletter spacing. The spatial interval between letters, also called letterspacing.

Interline spacing. The spatial interval between lines, also called leading.

Interword spacing. The spatial interval between words, also called wordspacing.

Italic. Letterforms having a pronounced diagonal slant to the right.

Justified setting. A column of type with even vertical edges on both the left and the right, achieved by adjusting interword spacing. Also called flush left, flush right.

K. Computer term for one thousand bytes of memory.

Kerning. Optical adjustment of interletter spacing that reduces space between characters to produce a better fit.

Keyboard. A device having keys or buttons used to enter data into typesetting and computer systems.

Laser. A concentrated light source that can be optically manipulated. Coined from "Light Amplification by Stimulated Emission of Radiation."

Latin. Typestyles characterized by triangular, pointed serifs.

Leader. Typographic dots or periods that are repeated to connect other elements.

Lead-in. Introductory copy set in a contrasting typeface.

Leading. See *Interline spacing.*

Letterpress. The process of printing from a raised, inked surface.

Letterspacing. See *Interletter spacing.*

Ligature. A typographic character produced by combining two or more letters.

Line breaks. The relationships of line endings in a ragged-right or ragged-left setting. Rhythmic line breaks are achieved by adjusting the length of individual lines of type.

Line length. The measure of the length of a line of type, usually expressed in picas.

Lining figures. Numerals identical in size to the capitals and aligned on the baseline: 1 2 3 4 5 6 7 8 9 10.

Linotype. A machine that casts an entire line of raised type on a single metal slug.

Logotype. Two or more type characters that are combined as a sign or trademark.

Lowercase. The alphabet set of small letters, as opposed to capitals.

LPM. Lines per minute, a unit of measure expressing the speed of a typesetting system.

Ludlow. A typecasting machine that produces individual letters from hand-assembled matrices.

Machine composition. General term for the mechanical casting of metal type.

Makeup. The assembly of typographic matter into a page, or a sequence of pages, ready for printing.

Margin. The unprinted space surrounding type matter on a page.

Mark up. The marking of typesetting specifications upon manuscript copy.

Masthead. The visual identification of a magazine or newspaper, usually a logotype.

Matrix. In typesetting, the master image from which type is produced. The matrix is a brass mold in linecasting and a glass plate bearing the font negative in phototypesetting.

Meanline. An imaginary line marking the tops of lowercase letters, not including the ascenders.

Measure. See *Line length.*

Minuscules. An early term for small, or lowercase, letters.

Minus spacing. A reduction of interline spacing, resulting in a baseline-to-baseline measurement that is smaller than the point size of the type.

Mixing. The alignment of more than one typestyle or typeface on a single baseline.

Modern. Term used to describe typefaces designed at the end of the eighteenth century. Characteristics include vertical stress, hairline serifs, and pronounced contrasts between thick and thin strokes.

Monotype. A trade name for a keyboard-operated typesetting machine that casts individual letters from matrices.

Negative. The reversal of a positive photographic image.

Oblique. A slanted roman character. Unlike many italics, oblique characters do not have cursive design properties.

Offset lithography. A printing method using flat photo-mechanical plates, in which the inked image is transferred or offset from the printing plate onto a rubber blanket, then onto the paper.

Old Style. Typeface styles derived from fifteenth- to eighteenth-century designs, and characterized by moderate thick-and-thin contrasts, bracketed serifs, and a handwriting influence.

Old Style figures. Numerals that exhibit a variation in size, including characters aligning with the lowercase x-height, and others with ascenders or descenders: 1234567890.

Optical adjustment. The precise visual alignment and spacing of typographic elements. In interletter spacing, the adjustment of individual characters to achieve consistent spacing.

Outline type. Letterforms described by a contour line that encloses the entire character on all sides. The interior usually remains open.

Output. The product of a computer operation. In computerized typesetting, output is reproduction proofs of composition.

Pagination. The sequential numbering of pages.

Paragraph mark. Typographic elements that signal the beginning of a paragraph. For example, ¶.

Parallel construction. In typography, the use of similar typographic elements or arrangements to create a visual unity or to convey a relationship in content.

P.E. Abbreviation for *Printer's Error,* used to flag a mistake made by the compositor rather than by the author.

Photocomposition. The process of setting type by projecting light onto a light-sensitive film or paper.

Photodisplay typesetting. The process of setting headline type on film or paper by photographic means.

Phototype. Type matter set on film or paper by photographic projection of type characters.

Photounit. Output component of a photocomposition system, which sets the type and exposes it to light-sensitive film or paper.

Pica. Typographic unit of measurement: 12 points equal 1 pica. 6 picas equal approximately one inch. Line lengths and column widths are measured in picas.

Point. The smallest unit of measure in typography: 12 points equal 1 pica. 1 point equals approximately 1/72 of an inch. Type body size and interline spacing are measured in points.

Processor. In a computer system, the general term for any device capable of carrying out operations upon data. In phototypography, the unit that automatically develops the light-sensitive paper or film.

Program. A sequence of instructions that directs the operations of a computer to execute a given task.

Quad. In metal type, pieces of type metal shorter than type-high, which are used as spacing matter to separate elements and fill out lines.

Quoins. Wedges used to lock up metal type in the chase. These devices are tightened and loosened by a quoin key.

Ragged. See *Unjustified type.*

Raster scan. The generation of an image upon a cathode-ray tube made by refreshing the display area line by line.

Recto. In publication design, the right-hand page. Page one (and all odd-numbered pages) always appears on a recto. The left-hand page is called the verso.

Reverse. Type or image that is dropped out of a printed area, revealing the paper surface.

Reverse leading. A reduction in the amount of interline space, making it less than normal for the point size. For example, twelve-point type set on an eleven-point body size becomes reverse leading of one point.

River. In text type, a series of interword spaces that accidentally align vertically or diagonally, creating an objectionable flow of white space within the column.

Roman. Upright letterforms, as distinguished from italics. More specifically, letters in an alphabet style based on the upright, serifed letterforms of Roman inscriptions.

Rule. In handset metal type, a strip of metal that prints as a line. Generally, any line used as an element in typographic design, whether handset, photographic, digital, or hand-drawn.

Run-around. Type that is set with a shortened line measure to fit around a photograph, drawing, or other visual element inserted into the running text.

Run in. To set type without a paragraph indentation or other break. Also, to insert additional matter into the running text as part of an existing paragraph.

Running head. Type at the head of sequential pages, providing a title or publication name.

Sans serif. Typefaces without serifs.

Script. Typefaces based on handwriting, usually having connecting strokes between the letters.

Semantics. The science of meaning in linguistics; the study of the relationships between signs and symbols, and what they represent.

Serifs. Small elements added to the ends of the main strokes of a letterform in serifed typestyles.

Set width. In metal type, the width of the body upon which a letter is cast. In phototype and digital type, the horizontal width of a letterform measured in units, including the normal space before and after the character. This interletter space can be increased or decreased to control the tightness or looseness of the fit.

Shoulder. In metal type, the flat top of the type body that surrounds the raised printing surface of the letterform.

Side head. A title or other heading material placed to the side of a type column.

Slab serifs. Square or rectangular serifs that align horizontally and vertically to the baseline and are usually the same (or heavier) weight as the main strokes of the letterform.

Slug. A line of metal type cast on a linecasting machine, such as the Linotype. Also, strips of metal spacing material in thicknesses of six points or more.

Small capitals. A set of capital letters having the same height as the lowercase x-height, frequently used for cross reference and abbreviations. Also called small caps, and often abbreviated s.c.

Software. Components of a computer system consisting of the programs or instructions that control the behavior of the computer hardware.

Solid. Lines of type that are set without additional interline space. Also called set solid.

Sorts. In metal type, material that is not part of

a regular font, such as symbols, piece fractions, and spaces. Also, individual characters used to replace worn-out type in a font.

Stand-alone typesetting system. A typesetting system that is completely self-contained, including editing terminal, memory, and character generation.

Stet. A proofreader's mark meaning that copy marked for correction should not be changed; rather, it should be left as originally set.

Storage. In computer typesetting, a device (such as a disk, drum, or tape) that can receive information and retain it for future use.

Straight matter. Text material set in continuous columns with limited deviation from the basic typographic specifications.

Subscript. A small character beneath (or adjacent to and slightly below) another character.

Superscript. A small character above (or adjacent to and slightly above) another character.

Swash letters. Letters ornamented with flourishes or flowing tails.

Syntax. In grammar, the way in which words or phrases are put together to form sentences. In design, the connecting or ordering of typographic elements into a visual unity.

System. A related group of interdependent design elements forming a whole. In computer science, a complete computing operation including software and hardware (Central Processing Unit, memory, input/output devices, and peripherals or devices required for the intended functions).

Terminal. See *Visual display terminal.*

Text. The main body of written or printed material, as opposed to display matter, footnotes, appendices, etc.

Text type. See *Body type.*

Transitional. Classification of typestyles combining aspects of both Old Style and Modern typefaces; for example, Baskerville.

Typeface. The design of alphabetical and numerical characters unified by consistent visual properties.

Type family. The complete range of variations of a typeface design, including roman, italic, bold, expanded, condensed, and other versions.

Type-high. The standard foot-to-face height of metal types; 0.9186 inches in English-speaking countries.

Typescript. Typewritten manuscript material used as copy for typesetting.

Typesetting. The composing of type by any method or process, also called composition.

Type specimen. A typeset sample produced to show the visual properties of a typeface.

Typo. See *Typographical error.*

Typographer. A firm specializing in typesetting. Sometimes used to denote a compositor or typesetter.

Typographical error. A mistake in typesetting, typing, or writing.

Typography. Originally the composition of printed matter from movable type. Now the art and process of typesetting by any system or method.

U. and l.c. Abbreviation for uppercase and lowercase, used to specify typesetting that combines capitals with lowercase letters.

Unit. A subdivision of the em, used in measuring and counting characters in photo- and digital typesetting systems.

Unitization. The process of designing a typeface so that the individual character widths conform to a typesetter's unit system.

Unitized font. A font with character widths conforming to a typesetter's unit system.

Unit system. A counting system first developed for Monotype, used by most typesetting machines. The width of characters and spaces are measured in units. This data is used to control line breaks, justification, and interword and interletter spacing.

Unit value. The established width, in units, of a typographic character.

Unjustified type. Lines of type set with equal interword spacing, resulting in irregular line lengths. Also called ragged.

Uppercase. See *Capitals.*

Verso. In publication design, the left-hand page. Page two (and all even-numbered pages) always appears on a verso. The right-hand page is called the recto.

Visual display terminal. A computer input/output device utilizing a cathode-ray tube to display data on a screen. Information from memory, storage, or a keyboard can be displayed.

Weight. The lightness or heaviness of a typeface, which is determined by ratio of the stroke thickness to character height.

White space. The "negative" area surrounding a letterform. See *Counter* and *Counterform.*

White space reduction. A decrease in the amount of interletter space, achieved in typesetting by reducing the unit value of typeset characters.

Widow. A very short line that appears at the end of a paragraph, column, or page, or at the top of a column or page. These awkward typographic configurations should be corrected editorially.

Woodtype. Hand-set types cut from wood by a mechanical router. Formerly used for large display sizes that were not practical for metal casting, woodtype has been virtually eliminated by display photographic typesetting.

Word. In computer systems, a logical unit of information, composed of a predetermined number of bits.

Wordspace. See *Interword spacing.*

Wordspacing. In typesetting, adding space between words to extend each line to achieve a justified setting.

x-height. The height of lowercase letters, excluding ascenders and descenders. This is most easily measured on the lowercase *x.*

Copyfitting

Copyfitting is the process of converting a type-written manuscript into text type that will accurately fit a typographic layout. Throughout this process, a designer should carefully consider legibility factors, visual characteristics, and spatial requirements. Understanding copyfitting enables the designer to control the details of typesetting, which can contribute to a typographic design of clarity and distinction. A suggested method for proper copyfitting follows.

1. Count all the characters in the typewritten manuscript.

This manuscript should be as clean and orderly as possible to increase accuracy while keeping costs to a minimum. Copy should be double-spaced in a single column. Although the size of typewriter type varies with different machines, there are generally two sizes: elite, with twelve characters to an inch, and pica, with ten characters to an inch. To begin, determine the number of characters in an average line length of the typewritten manuscript by counting the number of characters in four typical lines (including all spaces and punctuation), adding the number of characters in these lines, and dividing this total by four. Then, multiply this average by the number of lines in the whole manuscript to get the total number of characters.

2. Fit the copy to the layout.

After choosing a specific typeface and size, refer to the layout, and measure the line length in picas. Determine how many characters of the chosen typeface will fit on a line. This can easily be determined by referring to a characters-per-pica or characters-per-line table (Appendix B) often found in specimen books or provided by typographers. If a characters-per-pica figure is given, multiply the number of characters per pica by the number of picas in a line. If a characters-per-line table is provided, simply find the line length which indicates the number of characters in the average typeset line. Divide the number of characters per line into the total number of characters in the typewritten manuscript to determine the total number of typeset lines. Compare the vertical column depth of this number of typeset lines to the vertical column depth on the layout. (Remember to consider the effect of paragraph indication, particularly

if you are using additional interline space between paragraphs.) Will the depth of the typeset lines correspond to the depth of the area allowed on the layout? If the typesetting will run too long, or if it will be too short to fill the space, adjustments can be made. These adjustments might include changing the type size, interline spacing, or typeface.

3. Mark the manuscript.

After fitting the copy to the layout, it is important to clearly mark specifications for the typographer on the manuscript. Specifications should always include: type size and interline spacing in points; complete name of the typeface, including weight and width (Garamond Bold Condensed); line length in picas; line alignment (justified, flush left/ragged right, or centered); paragraph indication (indent one pica, or one line space between paragraphs); variations and special instructions (italics, underlining, changes in size, weight, or typeface).

Line length in picas

Character count table for text type specimens

	1	10	12	14	16	18	20	22	24	26	28	30
8 point Baskerville	3.25	33	39	46	52	59	65	72	78	85	91	98
9 point Baskerville	2.90	29	35	41	46	52	58	64	70	75	81	87
10 point Baskerville	2.60	26	31	36	42	47	52	57	62	68	73	78
12 point Baskerville	2.30	23	28	32	37	41	46	51	55	60	64	69
8 point Bodoni	3.40	34	41	48	54	61	68	75	82	88	95	102
9 point Bodoni	3.10	31	37	43	50	56	62	68	74	81	87	93
10 point Bodoni	2.80	28	34	39	45	50	56	62	67	73	78	84
12 point Bodoni	2.40	24	29	34	38	43	48	53	58	62	67	72
10 point Helvetica	2.40	24	29	34	38	43	48	53	58	62	67	72
8 point ITC Garamond Light	3.35	34	40	47	54	60	67	74	80	87	94	101
9 point ITC Garamond Light	3.05	31	37	43	49	55	61	67	73	79	85	92
10 point ITC Garamond Light	2.75	28	33	39	44	50	55	61	66	72	77	83
12 point ITC Garamond Light	2.35	24	28	33	38	42	47	52	56	61	66	71
8 point ITC Garamond Book	3.25	33	39	46	52	59	65	72	78	85	91	98
9 point ITC Garamond Book	2.95	30	35	41	47	53	59	65	71	77	83	89
10 point ITC Garamond Book	2.65	27	32	37	42	48	53	58	64	69	74	80
12 point ITC Garamond Book	2.25	23	27	32	36	41	45	50	54	59	63	68
8 point ITC Garamond Bold	3.00	30	36	42	48	54	60	66	72	78	84	90
9 point ITC Garamond Bold	2.65	27	32	37	42	48	53	58	64	69	74	80
10 point ITC Garamond Bold	2.40	24	29	34	38	43	48	53	58	62	67	72
12 point ITC Garamond Bold	2.05	21	25	29	33	37	41	45	49	53	57	62
8 point Lubalin Graph Med.	2.80	28	34	39	45	50	56	62	67	73	78	84
9 point Lubalin Graph Med.	2.45	25	29	34	39	44	49	54	59	64	69	74
10 point Lubalin Graph Med.	2.30	23	28	32	37	41	46	51	55	60	64	69
12 point Lubalin Graph Med.	1.95	20	23	27	31	35	39	43	47	51	55	59
8 point Univers 45	3.20	32	38	45	51	58	64	70	77	83	90	96
9 point Univers 45	2.90	29	35	41	46	52	58	64	70	75	81	87
10 point Univers 45	2.60	26	31	36	42	47	52	57	62	68	73	78
12 point Univers 45	2.25	23	27	32	36	41	45	50	54	59	63	68
8 point Univers 55	2.90	29	35	41	46	52	58	64	70	75	81	87
9 point Univers 55	2.60	26	31	36	42	47	52	57	62	68	73	78
10 point Univers 55	2.40	24	29	34	38	43	48	53	58	62	67	72
12 point Univers 55	2.10	21	25	29	34	38	42	46	50	55	59	63
8 point Univers 65	2.60	26	31	36	42	47	52	57	62	68	73	78
9 point Univers 65	2.40	24	29	34	38	43	48	53	58	62	67	72
10 point Univers 65	2.20	22	26	31	35	40	44	48	53	57	62	66
12 point Univers 65	1.90	19	23	27	30	34	38	42	46	49	53	57

**Suggested
working methods
in typographic
design**

Display typography

1. Carefully examine the copy. Consider its meaning and its relationship to other elements on the page. Study the visual aspects of display copy: word lengths, number of words, word structure (presence and location of ascenders and descenders), and interletter relationships (see Fig. 217).

2. Select typefaces for exploration, considering their relationship to content, legibility factors, and typesetting and printing methods.

3. Begin a series of small preliminary sketches, exploring alternative design possibilities. Consider type size and weight, division of the copy into lines, line arrangements (justified, unjustified, centered), and overall spatial organization. If a grid is being used, each sketch should reflect its structure.

4. Evaluate the sketches, and select one or more for further development. Criteria should be based on an overview of visual syntax, message, and legibility.

5. Prepare actual-size rough sketches of the page, working freely. Once again, select a sketch or sketches for further development.

6. Study type specimens to select the exact style, size, and weight to be used. Often, designers make tracings of the specimens to explore subtle visual characteristics of the type and to determine the desired interletter, interword, and interline spacing.

7. After these design decisions are made, the final layout can be prepared. It becomes the basis for type specification, client approval, and preparation of reproduction art. The degree of refinement may vary from a rough sketch to a tight comprehensive with set type, depending on the nature of the project.

Text typography

1. In the small preliminary sketches, text areas should be treated as rectangles or other simple shapes.

2. An initial character count of the typewritten manuscript (see Appendices A and B) should be made to determine its length.

3. Select a typestyle, considering its appropriateness to content and its relationship to the display type. Carefully study the type specimens to evaluate legibility, texture, and tone.

4. Working on tracing paper or at a computer terminal, plan a specific format, establishing line length, vertical column depth, and margins.

5. Select the desired type size and interline spacing. Then, copyfitting, as described in Appendix A, should be used to determine the specific area occupied by the text type.

6. Adjustments are now made in the format or the type specifications if the copyfitting procedure indicates that the type will not fit the allocated space.

7. Attention should be given to details: paragraph indication, interletter and interword spacing, and treatment of headings, folios, captions, and other supporting text material.

8. The designer can now prepare final layouts and mark specifications on the manuscript with assurance that the set type will conform to this plan.

Reviewing type proofs

After proofs are received from the typesetter, the designer should carefully examine them while the proofreader is checking for editorial accuracy.

1. Compare the set type with the layouts for proper fit. Determine what, if any, adjustments are necessary.

2. Check the type proofs to ensure that specifications were followed. Font selection, line lengths, and interline spacing should conform to the instructions.

3. Make sure that details were handled correctly. For example, did the typesetters overlook words set in italic or bold?

4. Use a T-square and triangle to check the horizontal and vertical alignment of columns.

5. Examine the interline and interword intervals, particularly in display type, to make sure that they conform to the specifications. Often, designers make subtle optical adjustments by cutting apart the proofs.

6. Look for awkward text settings, such as rivers, widows, and undesirable line breaks in unjustified typography. The editor or writer may be able to make small editorial changes to correct these problems.

7. Inspect proof quality. Common problems include rounded terminals due to inaccurate exposure, poor image sharpness, uneven or gray tone from incorrect processing, "dancing" characters that don't align properly on the baseline, poor kerning between misfit letters, and inconsistent proof tone within a long text.

8. Standard proofreaders' marks, listed in Appendix D, should be used to specify corrections.

Instruction	Notation in margin	Notation in type	Corrected type
Delete	ℐ	the ~~type~~ font	the font
Insert	type	the font	the type font
Let it stand	stet	the type font	the type font
Reset in capitals	(cap)	the type font	THE TYPE FONT
Reset in lowercase	(lc)	THE TYPE FONT	the type font
Reset in italics	(ital)	the type font	the *type* font
Reset in small capitals	(SC)	See type font.	See TYPE FONT.
Reset in roman	(rom)	the (type) font	the type font
Reset in boldface	(bf)	the type font	**the type font**
Reset in lightface	(lf)	the type (font)	the type font
Transpose	(tr)	the font type	the type font
Close up space	⌒	the ty pe	the type
Delete and close space	ℐ	the type fognt	the type font
Move left	⌐	⌐ the type font	the type font
Move right	⌐	the type font	the type font
Run in	(run in)	The type font is Univers. It is not Garamond.	The type font is Univers. It is not Garamond.
Align	‖	‖ the type font the type font the type font	the type font the type font the type font
Spell out	(sp)	③ type fonts	Three type fonts
Insert space	#	the type font	the type font
Insert period	⊙	The type font	The type font.
Insert comma	⸴	One two, three	One, two, three
Insert hyphen	⌒=⌒	Ten point type	Ten-point type
Insert colon	⊙	Old Style types	Old Style types:
Insert semicolon	⋏	Select the font spec the type.	Select the font; spec the type.
Insert apostrophe	⌄	Baskervilles type	Baskerville's type
Insert quotation marks	⌄ / ⌄	the word type	the word "type"
Insert parenthesis	(/)	The word type is in parenthesis.	The word (type) is in parenthesis.
Insert en dash	⟨N⟩	Flush left	Flush–left
Insert em dash	⟨M⟩ / ⟨M⟩	Garamond an Old Style face is used today.	Garamond—an Old Style face—is used today.
Start paragraph	¶	The type font is Univers 55.	The type font is Univers 55.
No paragraph indent	no ¶	⌐ The type font is Univers 55.	The type font is Univers 55.

A chronology of typeface designs

c. 1450: First Textur style type, Johann Gutenberg

1467: First roman style type, Sweynheym and Pannartz

1470: Jenson, Nicolas Jenson

1495: Bembo, Francesco Griffo

1499: Poliphilus, Francesco Griffo

1501: First italic type, Francesco Griffo

1514: Fraktur, Hans Schoensperger

1532: Garamond, Claude Garamond

1557: *Civilité*, Robert Granjon

c. 1570: Plantin, Anonymous

c. 1570: Canon d'Espagne, The Plantin Office

c. 1582: Flemish bold roman, The Plantin Office

1616: Typi Academiae, Jean Jannon

c. 1670: Fell Roman, Peter Walpergen

1690: Janson, Nicholas Kis

1702: Romain du Roi, Philippe Grandjean

1722: Caslon Old Style, William Caslon

c. 1743: Early transitional types, Pierre Simon Fournier le Jeune

c. 1746: Fournier decorated letters, Pierre Simon Fournier le Jeune

1757: Baskerville, John Baskerville

c. 1764: Italique Moderne and Ancienne, Pierre Simon Fournier le Jeune

1768: Fry's Baskerville, Isaac Moore

1780s: Bodoni, Giambattista Bodoni

1784: Didot, Firmin Didot

1790s: Bulmer, William Martin

1796: Fry's Ornamented, Richard Austin

c. 1800: Walbaum, J. E. Walbaum

c. 1810: Scotch Roman, Richard Austin

1815: Two Lines Pica, Antique (first Egyptian style), Vincent Figgins

1815: Five Lines Pica, In Shade (first perspective font), Vincent Figgins

1816: Two-line English Egyptian (first sans serif), William Caslon IV

1820: Lettres Ornees, Fonds de Gille

1828: Roman, Darius Wells

1830: Two-line great primer sans serif, Vincent Figgins

1832: Grotesque, William Thorowgood

1838: Sans surryphs ornamented, Blake and Stephenson

1844: Ionic, Henry Caslon

1845: Clarendon, Robert Besley and Company

1845: Rustic, V. and J. Figgins

1845: Zig-Zag, V. and J. Figgins

1850: Scroll, Henry Caslon

1856: National, Philadelphia Type Foundry

1859: Antique Tuscan Outlined, William Page

c. 1860s: P. T. Barnum, Barnhart Brothers and Spindle

c. 1865: French Antique (later called Playbill), Miller and Richard

c. 1865: Old Style Antique (called Bookman in the U.S.), Miller and Richard

c. 1869: Runic, Reed and Fox

c. 1870: Figgins Condensed No. 2, Stevens Shanks

1870s: Bank Gothic, Barnhart Brothers and Spindler

1878: Circlet, Barnhart Brothers and Spindler

1878: Glyphic, MacKellar, Smiths and Jordan

c. 1885: Geometric, Central Type Foundry

c. 1890: Ringlet, Marr Typefounding

c. 1890: Gothic Outline No. 61, American Type Founders

c. 1890: Rubens, Marr Typefounding

c. 1890: Karnac, Marr Typefounding

1890: Century, L. B. Benton

1890: Golden, William Morris

1892: Troy, William Morris

1893: Chaucer, William Morris

1894: Bradley, Will Bradley

1895: Merrymount Type, Bertram Goodhue

1895: Century Roman, Theodore Low DeVinne and L. B. Benton

1896: Cheltenham, Bertram Goodhue

1896: Vale Type, Charles Ricketts

1898: Grasset, Eugène Grasset

c. 1898: Paris Metro Lettering, Hector Guimard

1898–1906: Akzidenz Grotesque (Standard), Berthold Foundry

1900: Eckmann-Schrift, Otto Eckmann

1900: Century Expanded, Morris F. Benton

1900: Doves Roman, T. J. Cobden-Sanderson and Emery Walker

1901: Endeavor, Charles R. Ashbee

1901: Copperplate Gothic, Frederic W. Goudy

1901–04: Auriol, Georges Auriol

1902: Behrens-Schrift, Peter Behrens

1902: Subiaco, C. H. St. John Hornby

1903: Brook Type, Lucien Pissarro

1904: Korinna, H. Berthold

1904: Franklin Gothic, Morris F. Benton

1907: Behrens-Kursiv, Peter Behrens

1907: Clearface Bold, Morris F. Benton

1907–13: Venus, Bauer Foundry

1908: Behrens-Antiqua, Peter Behrens

1908: News Gothic, Morris F. Benton

1909: Aurora, Wagner and Schmidt Foundry

1910: Kochschrift, Rudolf Koch

1910–15: Hobo, Morris F. Benton

1911: Kennerly Old Style, Frederic W. Goudy

1912: Nicolas Cochin, G. Peignot

1914: Souvenir, Morris F. Benton

1914: Cloister Old Style, Morris F. Benton

1915: Century Schoolbook, Morris F. Benton

1915–16: Goudy Old Style, Frederic W. Goudy

1916: Centaur, Bruce Rogers

1919–24: Cooper Old Style, Oswald Cooper

1921: Cooper Black, Oswald Cooper

1923: Windsor, Stephenson Blake Foundry

1923: Neuland, Rudolf Koch

1926: Weiss Roman, E. R. Weiss

1927–29: Futura, Paul Renner

1927–29: Kabel, Rudolf Koch

1928: Ultra Bodoni, American Type Founders

1928–30: Gill Sans, Eric Gill

1928: Modernique, Morris F. Benton

1929: Zeppelin, Rudolf Koch

1929: Golden Cockerel, Eric Gill

1929: Bernhard Fashion, Lucien Bernhard

1929: Bifur, A. M. Cassandre

1929: Broadway, Morris F. Benton

1929: Novel Gothic, H. Becker

1929: Lux, J. Erbar

1929–30: Metro, William A. Dwiggins

1929–30: Perpetua, Eric Gill

1929–34: Corvinus, Imre Reiner

1930: Joanna, Eric Gill

1930: Dynamo, Ludwig and Mayer Foundry

1931: Prisma, Rudolf Koch

1931: Times New Roman, Stanley Morison

1931: Stymie, Morris F. Benton

1931–36: Beton, Heinrich Jost

1932–40: Albertus, Berthold Wolpe

1933: Agency Gothic, Morris F. Benton

1933: Atlas, K. H. Schaefer

1935: Huxley Vertical, Walter Huxley
1936: Acier Noir, A. M. Cassandre
1937: Peignot, A. M. Cassandre
1937: Onyx, Gerry Powell
1938: Caledonia, William A. Dwiggins
1938: Libra, S. H. De Roos
1938: Lydian, Warren Chappell
1938: Empire, American Typefounders
1939: Chisel, Stephenson Blake Foundry
1940: Trajanus, Warren Chappell
1945: Stradivarius, Imre Reiner
1946: Profil, Eugen and Max Lenz
1948: Trade Gothic, Mergenthaler Linotype
c. 1950: Brush, Harold Brodersen
1950: Michelangelo, Hermann Zapf
1950: Palatino, Hermann Zapf
1951: Sistina, Hermann Zapf
1952: Horizon, K. F. Bauer and Walter Baum
1952: Melior, Hermann Zapf
1952: Microgramma, A. Butti
1953: Mistral, Roger Excoffon
1954: Trump Mediaeval, Georg Trump
1955: Columna, Max Caflisch
1955–56: Egyptienne, Adrian Frutiger
1956: Craw Clarendon, Freeman Craw
1956: Murry Hill, E. J. Klumpp
1957: Meridien, Adrian Frutiger
1957: Univers, Adrian Frutiger
c. 1957: Helvetica, Max Miedinger
1962: Eurostile, Aldo Novarese
1962–66: Antique Olive, Roger Excoffon
1964: Sabon, Jan Tschichold
1965: Friz Quadrata, Ernest Friz
1967: Serifa, Adrian Frutiger
1967: Americana, Richard Isbell
1967: Cartier, Carl Dair
1967: Avant Garde Gothic, Herb Lubalin
1970: ITC Souvenir, Edward Benguiat
1974: Tiffany, Edward Benguiat
1974: Newtext, Ray Baker
1974: ITC Korinna, Ed Benguiat and Vic Caruso
1974: Serif Gothic, Herb Lubalin and Tony DiSpigna
1974: ITC Lubalin Graph, Herb Lubalin, Tony DiSpigna,
        and Joe Sundwall
1975: ITC Bauhaus, based on Bayer's universal alphabet
1976: Snell Roundhand, Matthew Carter
1976: Zapf Book, Hermann Zapf
1976: Eras, Albert Hollenstein and Albert Boton
1976: Zapf International, Hermann Zapf
1977: ITC Quorum, Ray Baker
1977: Korinna Kursiv, Edward Benguiat
1977: Italia, Colin Brignall
1977: Benguiat, Edward Benguiat
1977: ITC Garamond, Tony Stan
1979: Zapf Chancery, Hermann Zapf
1979: Benguiat Gothic, Edward Benguiat
1980: ITC Novarese, Aldo Novarese
1980: Icone, Adrian Frutiger
1980: Marconi, Hermann Zapf
1980: Edison, Hermann Zapf
1980: Isbell, Dick Isbell and Jerry Campbell
1983: ITC Weidemann, Kurt Weidemann and Kurt Strecker
1984: ITC Usherwood, Les Usherwood

Bibliography

Allen, Wallace, and Carroll, Michael. *A Design for News.* Minneapolis, MN: The Minneapolis Star and Tribune Company, 1981.

Anderson, Donald M. *A Renaissance Alphabet.* Madison, WI: University of Wisconsin Press, 1971.

_____ *The Art of Written Forms.* New York: Holt, Rinehart and Winston, 1969.

Arnheim, Rudolf. *The Power of the Center: A Study of Composition in the Visual Arts.* Berkeley, CA: University of California Press, 1982.

Bojko, Szymon. *New Graphic Design in Revolutionary Russia.* New York: Praeger, 1972.

Burns, Aaron. *Typography.* New York: Van Nostrand Reinhold, 1961.

Chang, Amos I. *The Tao of Architecture.* Princeton, NJ: Princeton University Press, 1981.

Dair, Carl. *Design with Type.* Toronto: University of Toronto Press, 1967.

Damase, Jacques. *Revolution Typographique.* Geneva: Galerie Mott, 1966.

Doczi, György. *The Power of Limits. Proportional Harmonies in Nature, Art and Architecture.* Boulder, CO: Shambhala Publications, 1981.

Drogin, Marc. *Medieval Calligraphy: Its History and Technique.* Montclair, NJ: Allanheld and Schram, 1980.

Friedman, Mildred, ed. *De Stijl: 1917–1931, Visions of Utopia.* New York: Abbeville Press, 1982.

Gardner, William. *Alphabet at Work.* New York: St. Martin's Press, 1982.

Gerstner, Karl. *Compendium for Literates: A System of Writing.* Translated by Dennis Q. Stephenson. Cambridge, MA: The MIT Press, 1974.

Goines, David Lance. *A Constructed Roman Alphabet.* Boston: David R. Godine, 1981.

Goudy, Frederic W. *The Alphabet and Elements of Lettering.* New York: Dover, 1963.

_____ *Typologia: Studies in Type Design and Type-making.* Berkeley, CA: University of California, 1940.

Gray, Nicolete. *Nineteenth-Century Ornamented Type Faces.* Berkeley, CA: University of California Press, 1976.

Haley, Allan. *Phototypography: A Guide for in-House Typesetting.* New York: Charles Scribner's Sons, 1980.

Harlan, Calvin. *Vision and Invention: A Course in Art Fundamentals.* New York: Prentice-Hall, 1969.

Hofmann, Armin. *Graphic Design Manual: Principles and Practice.* New York: Van Nostrand Reinhold, 1965.

Hurlburt, Allen. *The Grid System.* New York: Van Nostrand Reinhold, 1978.

_____ *Layout: The Design of the Printed Page.* New York: Watson-Guptill, 1977.

_____ *Publication Design.* New York: Van Nostrand Reinhold, 1976.

Jensen, Robert, and Conway, Patricia. *Ornamentalism: The New Decorativeness in Architecture and Design.* New York: Clarkson N. Potter, 1982.

Kelly, Rob Roy. *American Wood Type 1828–1900: Notes on the Evolution of Decorated and Large Type and Comments on Related Trades of the Period.* New York: Van Nostrand Reinhold, 1969.

Kepes, Gyorgy. *Sign, Image, Symbol.* New York: George Braziller, 1966.

Knobler, Nathan. *The Visual Dialogue.* New York: Holt, Rinehart and Winston, 1967.

Lobell, Frank. *Between Silence and Light: Spirit in the Architecture of Louis I. Kahn.* Boulder, CO: Shambhala Publications, 1979.

Machlis, Joseph. *The Enjoyment of Music: An Introduction to Perceptive Listening.* New York: W. W. Norton, 1977.

McLean, Ruari. *Jan Tschichold: Typographer.* Boston: David R. Godine, 1975.

_____ *The Thames and Hudson Manual of Typography.* London: Thames and Hudson, 1980.

Meggs, Philip B. *A History of Graphic Design.* New York: Van Nostrand Reinhold, 1983.

Morison, Stanley. *First Principles of Typography.* Cambridge: Cambridge University Press, 1936.

_____, and Day, Kenneth. *The Typographic Book, 1450–1935.* Chicago: The University of Chicago Press, 1964.

Müller-Brockmann, Josef. *Grid Systems in Graphic Design: A Visual Communications Manual.* Niederteufen, Switzerland: Arthur Niggli Ltd., 1981.

Rehe, Rolf F. *Typography: How to Make it Most Legible.* Carmel, CA: Design Research Publications, 1974.

Roberts, Raymond. *Typographic Design: Handbooks to Printing.* London: Ernest Benn Limited, 1966.

Rogers, Bruce. *Paragraphs on Printing.* New York: Dover, 1979.

Rondthaler, Edward. *Life with Letters — As They Turned Photogenic.* New York: Hastings House, 1981.

Rosen, Ben. *Type and Typography.* New York: Van Nostrand Reinhold, 1963.

Ruder, Emil. *Typography: A Manual of Design.* Teufen AR: Arthur Niggli, 1967.

Ruegg, Ruedi. *Basic Typography.* Zurich: ABC Verlag, 1972.

Schmid, Helmut. *Typography Today.* Tokyo: Seibundo Shinkosha, 1980.

Scott, Robert Gillam. *Design Fundamentals.* New York: McGraw-Hill, 1951.

Solt, Mary Ellen, ed. *Concrete Poetry.* Bloomington, IN: Indiana University Press, 1970.

Spencer, Herbert. *Pioneers of Modern Typography.* London: Lund Humphries, 1969.

_____ *The Visible Word.* New York: Hastings House, 1969.

Sutnar, Ladislav. *Visual Design in Action — Principles, Purposes.* New York: Hastings House, 1961.

Swann, Cal. *Techniques of Typography.* New York: Watson-Guptill, 1969.

Updike, Daniel Berkeley. *Printing Types: Their History, Forms and Use.* Cambridge, MA: Harvard University Press, 1937.

98. From *The Specimen Book of Types cast at the Austin Foundry by Wood & Sharwoods;* London, c. 1841.

99. From *A General Specimen of Printing Types.* Published by W. Thorowgood and Company; London, 1848.

100. Photograph; Library of Congress Rare Book and Special Collections Division, Washington, DC.

101. Photograph; Library of Congress Rare Book and Special Collections Division, Washington, DC.

102. From the wood type specimen book of William H. Page & Company; Greenville, Connecticut, 1859.

103. Private collection.

104. Honoré Daumier; French 1808–79. *The Third-Class Carriage.* Oil on canvas, 65.4 × 90.2m (25¾ × 35½ in.). Metropolitan Museum of Art, New York. Bequest of Mrs. H.O. Havemeyer, 1929. The H.O. Havemeyer Collection.

105. Private collection.

106. Private collection.

107. Courtesy of the New York Convention and Visitors Bureau.

108. Private collection.

109. Private collection.

110. Wood engraving from *The Inland Printer;* Chicago, December 1889.

112. Courtesy of the French Government Tourist Office.

113. Photograph; courtesy of the Archives: The Coca-Cola Company.

114. Paul Gauguin; French 1848–1903. *Fatata Te Miti (By the Sea),* 1892. Canvas, 0.679 × 0.915m (26¾ × 36 in.). National Gallery of Art, Washington, DC. Chester Dale Collection, 1962.

117. William Morris. *News from Nowhere.* Published by Kelmscott Press; London, 1892.

118. Title page from *Van nu en Straks.* Designed by Henri van de Velde, 1893.

119. Title page from *Limbes de Lumieres* by Gustave Kahn; Brussels, 1897.

120. From *The Inland Printer;* Chicago, June 1900.

121. Title page from *A Lady of Quality* by Francis Hodgson Burnett. Published by Charles Scribner's Sons; New York, 1897.

122. Cover for Vienna Secession Catalog No. 5; Vienna, 1899.

123. Photograph; courtesy of the French Government Tourist Office.

124. Dedication page from *Feste des Lebens und der Kunst: Ein Betrachtung des Theaters als hochsten Kultursymbols (Celebrations of Life and Art: A Consideration of the Theater as the Highest Cultural Symbol)* by Peter Behrens; Darmstadt, 1900.

125. Filippo Marinetti, Futurist poem, S.T.F., 1914.

126. Cover, *Delikatessen Haus Erich Fromm, Haupt-List 2;* Cologne, c. 1910.

127. Wassily Kandinsky. *Improvisation 31 (Sea Battle),* 1913. National Gallery of Art, Washington, DC. Ailsa Mellon Bruce Fund.

128. War Bond Fund Drive poster for the British government by Bert Thomas, c. 1916.

129. Advertisement for the *Kleine Grosz Mappe (Small Grosz Portfolio)* from *Die Neue Jugend.* Designed by John Heartfield. Published by Der Malik-Verlag, Berlin, June 1917.

130. First cover for *De Stijl,* the journal of the de Stijl movement. Designed by Vilmos Huszar. Published/Edited by Theo van Doesburg, The Netherlands; October 1917.

131. Raoul Hausmann. *Poeme Phonetique,* 1919.

132. Piet Mondrian; Dutch 1872–1944. *Diamond Painting in Red, Yellow, and Blue.* Oil on canvas, 40 × 40 in. National Gallery of Art, Washington, DC. Gift of Herbert and Nannette Rothschild, 1971.

133. Poster announcing availability of books, by Alexander Rodchenko; Moscow, c. 1923. Private collection.

134. Illustration by Mike Fanizza.

135. Title page from *Die Kunstismen* by El Lissitzky and Hans Arp. Published by Eugen Rentsch Verlag; Zurich, 1925.

136. Proposed universal alphabet. Designed by Herbert Bayer as a student at the Bauhaus.

137. Constantin Brancusi; Rumanian 1876–1957. *Bird in Space.* Marble, stone, and wood, hgt. 3.446m (136½ in.). National Gallery of Art, Washington, DC. Gift of Eugene and Agnes Meyer, 1967.

138. Title page for special insert, "Elementare Typographie" from *Typographische Mitteilungen;* Leipzig, October 1925.

139–40. Advertisements by Piet Zwart; courtesy of N.V. Nederlandsche Kabelfabriek, Delft.

141. Trial setting using Futura. Designed by Paul Renner. Published by Bauersche Giesserei; Frankfurt am Main, 1930.

142. Photograph; courtesy of New York Convention and Visitors Bureau.

143. Max Bill. Poster for an exhibition of African Art at the Kunstgewerbemuseum, Zurich.

144. Alexey Brodovitch. Poster for an industrial design exhibition at the Philadelphia Museum of Art.

145. Walker Evans. Photograph, "Fields family, sharecroppers," Hale County, Alabama. Library of Congress, Washington, DC.

146. Jean Carlu. Advertisement for Container Corporation of America, December 21, 1942.

147. Max Bill. Poster for an exhibition of Art Concrete at the Kunsthalle, Basel.

148. Paul Rand. Title page for *On My Way* by Hans Arp. Published by Wittenborn, Schultz, Inc; New York, 1948.

149. Willem de Kooning. *Painting,* 1948. Enamel and oil on canvas, 42⅝ × 56⅛ in. Collection; Museum of Modern Art, New York. Purchase.

150. Ladislav Sutnar. Cover for *Catalog Design Progress* by K. Lonberg-Holm and Ladislav Sutnar. Published by Sweet's Catalog Service; New York, 1950.

151. Illustration by Stephen Chovanec.

152. Henri Matisse; French 1869–1954. *Woman with Amphora and Pomegranates.* Paper on canvas (collage), 2.436 × 0.963m (96 × 37⅞ in.). National Gallery of Art, Washington, DC. Ailsa Mellon Bruce Fund, 1973.

153. Josef Muller-Brockmann. Poster for a musical concert; Zurich, Switzerland, January 1955.

154. Saul Bass. Advertisement from the Great Ideas of Western Man series, Container Corporation of America.

155. Willem Sandberg. Back and front covers for *Experimenta Typographica.* Published by Verlag Galerie der Spiegel; Cologne, 1956.

156. Saul Bass. Film title for *Anatomy of a Murder.* Produced and directed by Otto Preminger, 1959.

157. Photograph; courtesy of the New York Convention and Visitors Bureau.

158. Carlo L. Vivarelli. Cover for *Neue Grafik.* Published by Verlag Otto Walter AG; Olten, Switzerland, 1959.

159. Henry Wolf. Cover for *Harper's Bazaar* magazine, December 1959.

160. Gerald Holton. Symbol for the Campaign for Nuclear Disarmament; Great Britain, c. 1959.

161. Otto Storch. Typography from *McCall's* magazine; July 1959.

162. Karl Gerstner. Poster for the newspaper *National Zeitung;* Zurich, 1960.

163. Herb Lubalin. Advertisement for Sudler and Hennessey Advertising, Inc.; New York.

164. George Lois. Advertisement for A.H. Robins Company, Incorporated.

165. Photograph; courtesy of the Virginia State Travel Service.

166. Seymour Chwast and Milton Glaser, Push Pin Studios, Inc. Poster for the Lincoln Center for the Performing Arts, New York.

167. George Lois. Cover for *Esquire* magazine, October 1966.

168. Seymour Chwast and Milton Glaser, Push Pin Studios, Inc. Poster for Filmsenco, New York.

169. Photograph; courtesy of the Public Relations Department, City of Montreal, Canada.

170. Designer not known. Symbol widely used in the environmental movement.

171. Photograph; courtesy of the National Aeronautics and Space Administration.

172. Wolfgang Weingart. Experimental interpretation of a poem by Elsbeth Bornoz; Basel, Switzerland.

173. Herb Lubalin. Volume 1, Number 1, of *U&lc.* Published by the International Typeface Corporation, New York.

174. Cook and Shanosky, commissioned by the American Institute of Graphic Arts under contract to the U.S. Department of Transportation. From *Symbol Signs,* a series of thirty-four passenger-oriented symbols for use in transportation facilities.

175. Bruce Blackburn, then of Chermayeff and Geismar Associates. Symbol for the U.S. Bicentennial Commission and stamp for the U.S. Postal Service, first released in 1971.

176. Photograph; courtesy of the French Government Tourist Office.

177. Trademark reproduced by permission of Frederic Ryder Company; Chicago.

178. Willi Kunz. Poster for an exhibition of photographs by Fredrich Cantor, FOTO Gallery, New York.

179. Title film for *All That Jazz,* Twentieth Century-Fox. Director/

Designer: Richard Greenberg, R/Greenberg Associates, Inc., New York.

180. Tim Priddy. Announcement for Best Products Company, Inc. Richmond.

181. Photograph; courtesy of the Office of the Mayor, Portland, Oregon.

209. Philip Meggs. Experimental typography.

212, 215, 230, and 248. Frank Armstrong. Armstrong Design Consultants; New Canaan, CT.

213. Willi Kunz. Poster; 14 × 16½ in.

253. Ben Day. From *Handel & Haydn* magazine.

254. Frank Armstrong. Armstrong Design Consultants; New Canaan, CT. Photograph by Sally Anderson-Bruce.

256. Designer: Philip Meggs.

259. Designer: Ben Day.

268. Ben Day. Exhibition catalog cover.

275 and 403–12. Courtesy of the National Aeronautics and Space Administration.

278. Eugen Gomringer. "ping pong," from *Concrete Poetry: A World View.* Edited by Mary Ellen Solt, Indiana University Press, 1970.

292. Courtesy of *Reader's Digest.*

297. Photograph; courtesy of Olivetti.

302. Gerrit Rietveld. Red/blue chair, 1918. Collection Stedelijk Museum, Amsterdam.

303 and 422–28. Reprinted with permission of *Minneapolis Star and Tribune.*

306. Rob Carter. Courtesy of Best Products Co., Inc.

308. Photograph; courtesy of Daniel Friedman.

309. Photograph; courtesy of Best Products Co., Inc.

310. Eugene Gaillard. French marquetry cabinet, late nineteenth century. Carved mahogany. Collection of Sydney and Frances Lewis.

317. Photograph; courtesy of the Department of Dance, Virginia Commonwealth University.

330, 336, and 343. Photographs; courtesy of Mergenthaler Linotype Company.

340. Photograph; courtesy of Visual Graphics Corporation.

342. Courtesy of Visual Graphics Corporation.

344. Courtesy of Autologic, Inc.; Newbury Park, CA.

348. Courtesy of Serif & Sans, Inc.; Boston, MA.

349. Microphotographs courtesy of Mike Cody, Virginia Commonwealth University.

442. Photograph; The Rare Book and Special Collections Division, The Library of Congress, Washington, DC.

446. From *American Advertising Posters of the Nineteenth Century* by Mary Black; courtesy of Dover Publications, Inc.

Sources for specimen quotations

Pages 166–171, 198–203, 210–211, 218–219, and 226–227. From *The Book Beautiful* by Thomas James Cobden-Sanderson. Hammersmith: Hammersmith Publishing Society, 1902.

Pages 238–241. From *The Alphabet and Elements of Lettering* by Frederic W. Goudy, courtesy of Dover Publications, Inc.

Index

Printing: Halliday Lithograph, West Hanover, Massachusetts

Binding: Halliday Lithograph, Plympton, Massachusetts

Typography: Riddick Advertising Art, Richmond, Virginia
9/11 Univers 55, with 7/11 Univers 55 captions and 9/11
Univers 65 headings set by the Alphatype CRS Digital
Phototypesetter, with Phototypositor display specimens

Design: Rob Carter, Stephen Chovanec, Ben Day, and Philip Meggs

Design Assistance: Tina Brubaker Chovanec, Justin Deister, John Demao,
Akira Ouchi, Tim Priddy, Anne Riker, Joel Sadagursky
and Jennifer Mugford Wieland

Photography: George Nan

The authors wish to thank the following people for their
contributions to this book. Margaret Bates, Tina Brubaker
Chovanec, Martina D'Alton, Wendy Lochner, and Linda
Venator provided editorial support. Jack Flynn, Cathy
Stone, Kate Bridgman and Eileen Kirby of Riddick
Advertising Art contributed immeasurably to the type-
setting process. Jerry Bates of Virginia Commonwealth
University, Lynn Painter of Mobility Printing, and
Charles Dietz of Dietz Press provided invaluable graphic
arts assistance. Murry N. DePillars offered encourage-
ment and support.